HOT SPOT

SUB-SAHARAN AFRICA

Recent Titles in Hot Spot Histories

Latin America
David W. Dent

Asia and Oceania
Edited by Clinton Fernandes

North America and Europe
Joseph R. Rudolph Jr.

HOT
SPOT

SUB-SAHARAN
AFRICA

Toyin Falola
and Adebayo O. Oyebade

Hot Spot Histories

 GREENWOOD

AN IMPRINT OF ABC-CLIO, LLC
Santa Barbara, California • Denver, Colorado • Oxford, England

Library of Congress Cataloging-in-Publication Data

Falola, Toyin.
    Hot spot : Sub-Saharan Africa / Toyin Falola and Adebayo O. Oyebade.
       p. cm. — (Hot spot histories)
    Includes bibliographical references and index.
    ISBN 978-0-313-35971-2 (hard copy : acid-free paper) — ISBN 978-0-313-
35972-9 (ebook) 1. Africa, Sub-Saharan—Politics and government. 2. Ethnic
conflict—Africa, Sub-Saharan. 3. Political violence—Africa, Sub-Saharan.
4. Political violence—Africa, Sub-Saharan. 5. Political stability—Africa,
Sub-Saharan. I. Oyebade, Adebayo. II. Title.
    DT352.8.F355   2010
    967.03′2—dc22   2010009400

ISBN: 978-0-313-35971-2
E-ISBN: 978-0-313-35972-9

14 13 12 11 10   1 2 3 4 5

This book is also available on the World Wide Web as an eBook.
Visit www.abc-clio.com for details.

Greenwood
An Imprint of ABC-CLIO, LLC

ABC-CLIO, LLC
130 Cremona Drive, P.O. Box 1911
Santa Barbara, California 93116-1911

This book is printed on acid-free paper (∞)

Manufactured in the United States of America

Contents

Preface

Most parts of Africa are peaceful. For most of its history, peoples and communities have lived in peace and harmony. Kinships, organized into villages, towns, and cities, sustained themselves on the deliberate strategy of building cohesion, resolving conflicts in a peaceful and amicable way, and preventing long-term hostility that can damage the social fabric.

However, the continent also manifests serious contradictions. To start with, the past is full of accounts of wars and violence. The process of building states, kingdoms, and empires required the use of the military. Once created, the states were successful in maintaining peace and political stability over a wider region. Kings and chiefs must protect their citizens to claim legitimacy and relevance.

The most traumatic moment began with the encounters with the outside world. Whether it was trade across the Sahara, the Atlantic, or the Indian Ocean, all involved the traffic in human beings. Slaves were produced by violence—raiding expeditions and wars resulted in war captives who lost their citizenship and were transported to distant lands. African wars in the age of slavery undermined their humanity, care, and concern for one another. With firearms supplied from Europe, they became more bloody and ruthless than ever before.

The ending of the trans-Atlantic slave trade saw the transition to the European colonization of Africa after 1885. Wars of conquest and wars of resistance were many. Modern Africa was a product of violence and wars. To regain its sovereignty, another moment of crisis ensued after World War II. Anti-colonial nationalism led to the violent Mau Mau uprisings in Kenya and the Algerian War of Independence, both in the 1950s; the prolonged wars in all the Portuguese-speaking colonies in the 1960s, 1970s, and 1980s; and the bitter and costly anti-apartheid struggles in South Africa that ended in the 1990s.

As we enter the contemporary period, a number of places became "hot spots" as captured in this book. The themes explored in this book reflect a number of issues:

1. the inability to resolve past historical conflicts (e.g., Sudan);
2. the inability to resolve the management of plural ethnic societies (e.g., civil wars in Nigeria, Niger, Sierra Leone, and Liberia);
3. the inability to manage the crises of racial identity (Darfur, Mauritania);
4. the inability to integrate a dual ethnic society (Rwanda where the Hutu and Tutsi have a weak integrative political order);
5. conditions that promote secessionist movements (Ethiopia and Eritrea, Biafra and Nigeria, Katanga in the Congo, etc.);
6. contested ideologies and nationalism, expressed as ethnic and religious fundamentalism (Sudan, Nigeria, Uganda, Burundi, Ethiopia, Sierra Leone);
7. armed struggles by oppositional forces (insurrections in the Democratic Republic of the Congo, Sudan, Uganda);
8. Foreign intervention (removal or assassination of political leaders);
9. the Cold War;
10. resource curse, a situation where abundance of strategic materials such as oil, diamonds, and gold promote instability (Sierra Leone, Angola, Congo); and
11. underdevelopment and struggles over limited resources (e.g., Liberia).

"Hot spots" will not stay "hot" forever. The search for peace is inevitable. The narrative of peace is unavoidable. The narrative of peace has to replace the narrative of war. We would like to offer our humble suggestions to promote peace. Sustainable development represents the starting point. Poverty is one of the key roots of the problem. Those in power manifest an uncontrollable degree of greed that complicates the ability to manage resources to take care of the majority of the population. Those who have tasted power and have seen the rewards and privileges of it want to stay in power. Those who are out of power see the need to get it, not necessarily because they want to serve the public with honesty and dedication but because they want to loot. Violence is justified in pursuit of the dream. Democracy, if it is genuine, can promote peace.

Where there is oil, diamonds, and gold, foreign companies will always set their eyes on them. Without internal mechanisms to protect a country, it will fall prey into the hands of ruthless merchants who form an alliance with corrupt local politicians. The solution to this serious problem is transparency in collecting revenues and accountability in spending them.

Governments at regional and international levels have a responsibility to protect the lives of innocent people, to prevent wars, and to create conditions to promote peace. Regional integration of the continent into powerful blocs and subsequently a continental one will put an end to bloodshed. Responsible governments must be committed to peace at all levels. Corrupt and authoritarian governments provoke conflicts and opposition. Effective democracy, which allows representatives from ethnic and religious groups to participate in decision making, will reduce conflicts.

It remains for us to thank a few people who made this book a reality. Ms. Carrie Lett, editorial assistant at Greenwood, commissioned the project. For Adebayo Oyebade, this is his second book with Greenwood. For Toyin Falola, this is his eighth book. We remain permanently grateful and appreciative of their efforts to promote African scholarship. Greenwood's Culture and Customs of Africa Series, for which Falola acts as its editor, is pretty well established. Next, we have to thank our supportive wives (Bisi and Sade) and children, the pillars of support. In our various universities, valuable friends and colleagues have encouraged and inspired us. Toyin Falola is grateful to the friendship and support of Professor Niyi Afolabi of the Department of Spanish and Portuguese Studies, the University of Texas at Austin. Adebayo Oyebade would like to acknowledge the encouragement of his friends and colleagues: Dr. Moses Ochonu of Vanderbilt University, and Dr. Erik Schmeller, Dr. Sheri Brown, Dr. Gashawbeza Bekele, Dr. Daniel Gibran, and Dr. Michael Bertrand of Tennessee State University.

Toyin Falola and Adebayo Oyebade
December 2009

Abbreviations

ACRI	African Crisis Response Initiative
ADFLC	Alliance of Democratic Forces for the Liberation of Congo-Zaire
AFL	Armed Forces of Liberia
AFRC	Armed Forces Ruling Council (of Sierra Leone)
AFRICOM	Africa Command
AG	Action Group
AMIS	African Union Mission in Sudan
ANC	African National Congress
ANP	Afrikaner National Party
BIAGEN	Biafran Committee for Prevention of Genocide
DRC	Democratic Republic Congo
ECOMOG	ECOWAS Monitoring Group
ECOWAS	Economic Community of West African States
EDU	Ethiopian Democratic Union
ELF	Eritrean Liberation Front
EO	Executive Outcomes
EPLF	Eritrean Peoples Liberation Front
EPRDF	Ethiopian People's Revolutionary Democratic Front
EPRP	Ethiopian People's Revolutionary Party
FDLR	Democratic Forces for the Liberation of Rwanda
FLEC	Front for the Liberation of the Enclave of Cabinda
FLS	Frontline States
FN	*Forces Nouvelles de Côte d'Ivoire* (New Forces)
FNLA	*Frente Nacional de Libertação de Angola* (National Front for the Liberation of Angola)
FRELIMO	*Frente de Libertação de Moçambique* (Front for the Liberation of Mozambique)

HSM	Holy Spirit Movement
ICTR	International Criminal Tribunal for Rwanda
ICU	Islamic Courts Union
IGADD	Intergovernmental Authority on Drought and Development
IMF	International Monetary Fund
INPFL	Independent National Patriotic Front of Liberia
IRC	International Rescue Committee
JEM	Justice and Equality Movement
LDF	Lofa Defense Force
LPC	Liberia Peace Council
LRA	Lord's Resistance Army
LURD	Liberians United for Reconciliation and Democracy
MEND	Movement for the Emancipation of the Niger Delta
MFDC	Movement of Democratic Forces in the Casamance
MJP	*Mouvement pour la Justice et la Paix* (Movement for Justice and Peace)
MODEL	Movement for Democracy in Liberia
MOSOP	Movement for the Survival of the Ogoni People
MPIGO	*Mouvement Populaire Ivoirien du Grand Ouest* (Ivorian Popular Movement of the Great West)
MPLA	*Movimento Popular de Libertação de Angola* (Popular Movement for the Liberation of Angola
MRU	Mano River Union
NADECO	National Democratic Coalition
NCNC	National Council of Nigerian Citizens
NDPVF	Niger Delta People's Volunteer Force
NGOs	Non-Governmental Organizations
NLC	Nigeria Labor Congress
NMOG	Neutral Military Observer Group
NNDP	Nigerian National Democratic Party
NPC	Northern People's Congress
NPFL	National Patriotic Front of Liberia
NPFL-CRC	National Patriotic Front of Liberia-Central Revolutionary Council
NRM	National Resistance Movement
OAU	Organization of African Unity
ONUMOZ	United Nations Operation in Mozambique
OPC	Oodua People's Congress
OPEC	Organization of Petroleum Exporting Countries
OPO	Ovamboland People's Organization
PAC	Pan Africanist Congress
PLAN	People's Liberation Army of Namibia

PLUA	*Partido da Luta Unida dos Africanos de Angola* (Party of the United Struggle for Africans in Angola)
RCD	Rally for Congolese Democracy
RENAMO	*Resistência Nacional Moçambicana* (Mozambican National Resistance)
RPF	Rwandan Patriotic Front
RUF	Revolutionary United Front
SADC	Southern African Development Community
SADF	South African Defense
SANNC	South African Native National Congress
SAP	Structural Adjustment Program
SASM	South African Students' Movement
SASO	South African Students' Organization
SCNC	Southern Cameroons National Council
SLM	Sudan Liberation Movement
SPLA	Sudan People's Liberation Army
SPLM	Sudan People's Liberation Movement
SPM	Somali Patriotic Movement
SWANU	South West Africa National Union
SWAPO	South West Africa People's Organization
TPLF	Tigray People's Liberation Front
UANC	United African National Council
ULIMO	United Liberation Movement of Liberia for Democracy
UN	United Nations
UNAMID	African Union-United Nations Mission in Darfur
UNAMIR	United Nations Assistance Mission for Rwanda
UNAMSIL	United Nations Mission in Sierra Leone
UNITA	*União Nacional para a Independência Total de Angola* (National Union for the Total Independence of Angola)
UNLA	Uganda National Liberation Army
UNMEE	United Nations Mission in Ethiopia and Eritrea
UNMIL	United Nations Mission in Liberia
UNOMIL	United Nations Observer Mission in Liberia
UNOMSIL	United Nations Observer Mission in Sierra Leone
UNOMUR	United Nations Observer Mission Uganda-Rwanda
UPC	Uganda People's Congress
ZANU	Zimbabwe African National Union
ZAPU	Zimbabwe African People's Union
ZIPRA	Zimbabwe People's Revolutionary Army

Timeline of Selected Conflicts

1054	The *al-Murabethin* (or Almoravid), an Islamic movement of the Sanhaja Berbers, launches a jihad against the ancient empire of Ghana. The invasion leads to the demise of the empire.
1235	Sundiata Keita, a Mandinka prince, defeats the oppressive ruler of the Sosso Kingdom, Sumanguru Kanté, at the Battle of Kirina. This defeat marks the beginning of the rise of the Mali Empire.
1450s	The European slave trade in Africa across the Atlantic begins. The procurement of slaves in West and Southwest Africa causes intercommunal violence.
1591	The empire of Songhai is defeated by the better-equipped army of the sultan of Morocco. At the Battle of Tondibi, the noted Western Sudanese center of scholarship and trade, Timbuktu, is captured and looted.
1630s	The woman ruler of Ndongo Kingdom, Nzinga Mbande, leads resistance struggle against Portugal's imperial design.
1650s	Expansion of Dutch and other European settlers in the Cape region of Southern Africa leads to systematic destruction of the Khoisan.
1720s	Islamist revivalist movements in Western Sudan lead to the establishment of the imamates of Futa Jallon, Bondu, and Futa Toro.

1723	In South Africa, the Boers engage the Xhosa in a series of frontier wars.
1748	The powerful Yoruba cavalry state of Oyo invades and subdues Dahomey Kingdom.
1804–1809	Fulani revolutionary leader, Uthman dan Fodio, leads a jihad in Hausaland against the non-Muslim Hausa rulers. The jihadists triumph at the Battle of Alkalawa in 1808, and an Islamic empire, the Sokoto Caliphate, is created in present-day northern Nigeria.
1807	The British Parliament outlaws the Atlantic slave trade. A year later, the United States ends the trade. However, illegal trafficking of slaves across the Atlantic continues.
1810	Muslim cleric Seku Ahmadu Lobbo leads an Islamic revolution against the non-Muslim state of Macina. The jihad results in the establishment of a theocratic state in present-day Mali.
1820s	Southern Africa witnesses disturbances called *Mfecane* (or *difaqane*) as a result of a number of factors including Zulu militarism, regional power struggles, and competition over scarce resources.
1830–1893	Yorubaland is plagued by intergroup civil wars. The British intervention in the Kiriji/Ekitiparapo War in 1886 brings the conflicts to an end. However, communal tensions continue well into the end of the nineteenth century when the entire region came under British imperial control.
1837	Fulani jihadists invade the Yoruba kingdom of Oyo, sacking its capital, Oyo-Ile.
1850–1861	An Islamic revolution, the Tijaniyya Jihad, led by al-Hajj Umar against the Bambara states of Segu and Kaarta, leads to the establishment of an Islamic empire striding parts of present-day Mali and Burkina Faso.
1861	The piecemeal but violent process of the British occupation of Nigeria commences with the establishment of a consulate in Lagos.
1879	The bloody Anglo-Zulu War ends the independence of the Zulu nation. The state is incorporated into the British Empire.
1881	The Mahdist revolt in Sudan begins, aimed at liberating Sudan from Turkish, Egyptian, and

	eventually British control. Anglo-Egyptian forces nip the Islamic insurgence in the bud by 1898.
1885	The Belgian monarch, King Leopold II, claims the Congo Free State as his personal fiefdom. Repressive rule over the territory begins.
1892	France conquers Dahomey and establishes its control over that area of West Africa.
1896	The Italian army is defeated by the Ethiopians at the Battle of Adwa (Adowa) in the first Italo-Ethiopian War.
1897	In the so-called "Punitive Expedition," British forces invade Benin, capital of the great empire of Benin. The city is looted and much of its rich art, including its famous bronze work, is destroyed or carted away by the invading forces.
1898	Samori ibn Touré's resistance against the French imperial interest collapses. His Mandinka state in present-day Republic of Guinea becomes a part of the budding French empire in West Africa.
1899–1902	The bloody Second Anglo-Boer War brings the Boer republics of Transvaal and the Orange Free State under British control. Earlier effort in the First Anglo-Boer War of 1880–1881 had failed to achieve this.
1905–1907	In the Maji Maji Rebellion in Tanganyika (now Tanzania), Africans violently resist colonial German policies.
1929	Women of Aba in southeastern Nigeria stage an anti-tax revolt against the colonial government.
1935	Fascist Italy invades Ethiopia, the only African nation in the League of Nations, sparking the Second Italo-Ethiopian War, which led to Italian military occupation of Ethiopia for five years.
1941	Ethiopia is liberated by British troops, ending Italian occupation.
1948–1994	South Africa is ruled by white minority regimes under the virulently racist and oppressive apartheid system. The African population reacts by a long but successful anti-apartheid struggle.
1951–1956	A violent uprising in Kenya by the Mau Mau (land and freedom army) forces the British authority to initiate reforms to the colonial system.

1955–1972   The first phase of the long and devastating Sudanese Civil War occurs.

1960   Anti-apartheid campaign in South Africa in the 1960s becomes more militant. On March 21, South African police murdered 69 unarmed anti-pass laws protesters in the township of Sharpeville. The Sharpeville Massacre is one of the most violent acts perpetrated by the apartheid government against blacks.

1960–1965   The first major post-independence conflict in Africa, the Congo Crisis, occurs. The Congolese prime minister, Patrice Lumumba, is murdered. The crisis is escalated by extra-African intervention driven by Cold War ideological consideration.

1960–1966   Nigeria's first republic is engulfed in a political crisis, leading to the first military intervention in national politics.

1961   In South Africa, the African National Congress (ANC) forms an armed wing, *Umkhonto we Sizwe*, in June. The force commences armed resistance in December.

1961–1974   Bloody war of national liberation occurs in the Portuguese colony of Angola, culminating in independence on November 11, 1975.

1961–1991   Eritrean separatists fight a war for independence against the Ethiopian government. Eritrea is granted independence on May 24, 1993.

1963–1973   National liberation war against Portuguese colonialism is fought in Guinea-Bissau. Independence is granted on September 10, 1974.

1963   The Organization of African Unity (OAU) is established in Addis Ababa, under the chairmanship of Emperor Haile Selassie. A Commission of Mediation, Conciliation, and Arbitration is enshrined within the organization in 1964 to help resolve interstate conflicts.

1964   Border skirmishes occur between Somalia and Ethiopia, on one hand, and between Somali and Kenya, on the other hand.

1964–1974   Mozambique fights a bloody guerrilla war of national liberation against Portuguese colonialism. Mozambique is granted independence on June 25, 1975.

1966	Mass killing of the Igbo occurs in northern Nigeria. The pogroms are directly related to the subsequent outbreak of the Nigerian Civil War.
1966–1980	Black Zimbabweans employ armed struggle to end racist white minority rule. Independence under black majority rule is attained on April 18, 1980.
1966–1990	Namibia fights a war of national liberation to end apartheid South Africa's control. Independence is achieved on March 21, 1990.
1967–1970	A bloody civil war in Nigeria ends the secession of the southeastern part of the country, which had declared itself the Republic of Biafra.
1971–1979	President Idi Amin, perhaps the most brutal of all Africa's dictators, rules Uganda with an iron hand. During his reign of terror, several thousand Ugandans are reportedly murdered.
1972	Selective genocide occurs in Burundi in which the Hutu intelligentsia is marked for destruction by government forces. The massacre claims about 150,000 lives.
1974–1991	The Derg Revolution occurs in Ethiopia, virtually turning the state into a totalitarian one, characterized by bloody repression of opponents of the ruling military elite. During the Red Terror of 1977–1987, the revolution exterminates thousands of dissenters. Ethiopia also experiences civil war between 1974 and 1991.
1975–1992	Angola is embroiled in a devastating civil war mainly between the government controlled by the Popular Movement for the Liberation of Angola (*Movimento Popular de Libertação de Angola*; MPLA) and the rebel National Union for the Total Independence of Angola (*União Nacional para a Independência Total de Angola*; UNITA).
1976	On June 16, the racist police in apartheid South Africa kill over six hundred black secondary school students in Soweto protesting the Bantu Education Act that compelled blacks to receive instruction in Afrikaans. The brutality of the Soweto riots brings the anti-apartheid struggle to international attention.
1977–1992	A destructive civil war ravages Mozambique as the rebel *Resistência Nacional Moçambicana*

	(RENAMO, or as sometimes referred to, the Mozambican National Resistance, MNR), fights the government controlled by the Front for the Liberation of Mozambique (*Frente de Libertação de Moçambique*; FRELIMO).
1977–1978	Somali forces invade the Ogaden region of Ethiopia in the pursuit of its irredentist policy. The Somalis are defeated in the Ogaden War.
1978–1979	War occurs between Tanzania and Uganda following incursion into Tanzania by President Idi Amin's army. Tanzania's subsequent invasion of Uganda leads to the overthrow of the brutal Amin regime that has killed about 300,000 people.
1980	Several days of Maitatsine rioting, a violent Islamic uprising in Nigeria's northern city of Kano, ends in the deaths of thousands of people.
1980s	Violence escalates in the black townships of South Africa, causing the government to declare a state of emergency.
1983–2005	The Sudanese Civil War continues in a second phase.
1986	By the order of President Ronald Reagan, the U.S. Air Force bombs military targets in Libya in order to destroy alleged terrorist centers in the country and reduce the ability of Muammar Gaddafi, the Libyan leader, to sponsor terror acts.
1987–	Joseph Kony, a self-professed spirit medium, leads an armed group, the Lord's Resistance Army (LRA), in a devastating war in northern Uganda. The ongoing war has spilled into neighboring Sudan, the Democratic Republic of Congo (DRC), and Central African Republic (CAR).
1988	Hutu/Tutsi violence in Burundi continues, claiming thousands of lives on both sides.
1989–1996	Civil War in Liberia wrecks its economy, decimates infrastructure, and kills about 150,000 people, representing over 5 percent of its population.
1990	The West African intervention force, the ECOWAS Monitoring Group (ECOMOG), is established, originally as a peace-monitoring instrument. Dominated by Nigeria, the force has increasingly taken on combat operations, intervening in the civil wars in Liberia and Sierra Leone.

1990s	Somalia enters into a persistent period of collapse. A civil war soon ensues, lasting till present. Somalia remains virtually a collapsed state.
1990s–	A new level of violence commences in the Niger Delta of Nigeria. Local communities aggressively demand from the Nigerian federal government a fair share of their region's riches. They also oppose the environmental destruction of their lands as a result of oil drilling by multinational corporations.
1991–2002	Civil war occurs in Sierra Leone as the Revolutionary United Front (RUF) engages the government in a brutal conflict. RUF campaigns are marked by brutal attacks on the civil population, resulting in mass amputations of victims' limbs, the deaths of about 50,000 people, and displacement of over a million people.
1992	The United States president, George H. W. Bush, orders American forces into Somalia in a humanitarian intervention operation code named "Operation Restore Hope." In the attempt to capture the Somali warlord, Mohammed Aideed, a unit of American troops is ambushed by Somali militia men, which leads to the shooting down of two American Blackhawk helicopters and the killing of 18 American soldiers.
1992–2002	After a lull, the Angolan civil war resumes following the refusal of the rebel leader Jonas Savimbi to accept the result of the 1992 elections, which he lost. The killing of Savimbi in combat by government forces on February 22, 2002, finally brings the war to an end.
1993	Interethnic killings break out in Burundi after the assassination of President Melchoir Ndadaye. About 50,000 are killed.
1994	A month-long genocide in Rwanda results in the massacre of about 800,000 ethnic Tutsi and moderate Hutus by Hutu extremists.
1996–1997	Warlord Laurent Kabila leads an uprising against President Mobutu in Zaire. Mobutu is overthrown, and Kabila assumes power and changes the name of the country to the Democratic Republic of Congo (DRC). Kabila himself is assassinated in

	2002. The DRC has since been immersed in a brutal civil war in which a lot of atrocities have been committed, including mass rape of women.
1997	May 25, Sierra Leone's president, Tejan Kabbah, is overthrown in a coup d'état. A new military junta, the Armed Forces Revolutionary Council (AFRC), allies itself with the rebel RUF. Nigeria's navy subsequently bombards Freetown in an attempt to dislodge the rebels from the city. ECOWAS approves the use of force to restore deposed President Kabbah.
1998	President Kabbah is restored to power in March following military action against the AFRC by the Nigerian-led ECOMOG intervention force.
1998	In August, terrorists linked to Osama bin Laden's al-Qaeda simultaneously bomb the American embassies in Dar-es-Salam, Tanzania, and Nairobi, Kenya, killing over two hundred Africans and a dozen Americans in both attacks.
1998–2000	A devastating border war between Eritrea and Ethiopia destroys a hitherto cordial relationship between the two states.
1998–2003	The civil war in Liberia is renewed as opposition rebel groups battle the government in an attempt to overthrow President Charles Taylor.
1999	In "Operation No Living Things," deadly and devastating attacks are launched in January by RUF. In the attacks, the rebels killed thousands of people in Freetown.
1999–2000	Several states in northern Nigeria adopt the Islamic legal code, the *Sharia'a*. As a result of this development, religious tension prevalent in the country is heightened. Since then, numerous violent clashes between Christians and Muslims mostly orchestrated by Muslim fundamentalists have caused the deaths of thousands of people in many parts of the country.
2002–2007	Full-scale civil war occurs in Côte d'Ivoire, which began with mutiny in the army.
2003	War erupts in the Darfur region of Sudan.
2003	The United States establishes a military base in Djibouti to coordinate its counterterrorist operations in the Horn of Africa.

2003–2009	The oil-rich Niger Delta of Nigeria is engulfed in deadly conflicts, from intercommunal violence to attacks on oil installations and kidnapping of foreign oil workers by militant groups. State security's crackdown on the recalcitrant militants demanding more control over the region's oil wealth has led to a staggering death toll in the region.
2004	The American secretary of state, Colin Powell, declares the war in Darfur genocide against the people of the region, perpetrated by government forces and local militia, the Janjaweed.
2006	In March, former President Charles Taylor of Liberia is arrested in Nigeria and returned to Sierra Leone to stand trial at the war crimes court. He is accused of masterminding atrocities during Sierra Leone's Civil War.
2007–	Incidents of piracy attacks off the coast of Somalia and the Gulf of Aden increase dramatically. On April 8, 2009, Somali pirates attack an American-flagged commercial vessel, MV *Maersk Alabama*, about 350 miles off the coast of Somalia.

CHAPTER 1

Introduction: Africa and Historical Context of Hot Spots

THE HISTORICAL CONTEXT

Conflicts have forced millions of our people into a drifting life as refugees and internally displaced persons, deprived of their means of livelihood, human dignity and hope.

> "Declaration on the Establishment, within the OAU, of Mechanism for Conflict Prevention, Management and Resolution," AHG/Decl. 3 (XXIX), 29th Ordinary Session, Cairo, Egypt, June 28–30, 1993.

As an economist, I am acutely aware of the devastation to African economies due to armed violence. In my own country, conflict has led to the squandering of rich mineral, agricultural, and human resources that should have benefited Liberia and its people. Although economic recovery has begun, it will take many years to recover from the destruction of infrastructure, the damage to businesses, and the loss of life and livelihood.

> Ellen Johnson-Sirleaf, president of Liberia, forward to Iansa, Oxfam International, and Saferworld, "Africa's Missing Billions: International Arms Flows and the Cost of Conflict," *Briefing Paper* No. 107 (2007), 2. http://www.globalpolicy.org/security/smallarms/2007/10costconflict.pdf

Conflicts have occurred in human society from time immemorial. Indeed, global history has demonstrated that conflict is an essential and integral element of the state and international system. Conflicts across the ages have been of various types, dimensions, intensities, and duration, and have occurred in every region of the world. Conflicts have been caused by a myriad of factors, and their legacies have been wide ranging as well.

Like most parts of the world, Africa has had its own share of conflicts. But what marks out the continent as distinct in the history of contemporary global conflicts is that it has witnessed far more armed conflicts than any other region of the world. According to an October 2007 report compiled by three non-governmental organizations (NGOs)—Oxfam, IANSA, and Saferworld—between 1990 and 2005, 23 African states were involved in conflict.[1] Conflicts in Africa have also tended to be more long-lasting and devastating, and, consequently, of more catastrophic consequences for the states involved, and even for an entire region and the continent. The human, material, and economic costs to Africa of its innumerable conflicts have been staggering. It is an understatement to state that sustainable political, social, and economic development in Africa has been severely retarded by the impacts of its conflicts.

From the foregoing, it becomes obvious that conflict constitutes an important force in the shaping of African history, from pre-colonial times to the present. The preponderance of violent conflicts in Africa, however, does not suggest an alleged primordial tendency and innate savagery on the part of Africans. External influences, from pre-colonial to present period, have been instrumental in generating conflicts or aggravating ongoing ones.

This book is about hot spots in Africa, focusing on conflict areas of the sub-Saharan part of the continent. The discourse provides critical analyses of the major post-independence conflicts, intense enough to pose a threat, or at least appearing so, to national, regional, or international security. In this context, conflict is broadly defined to encompass a whole range of a state of strife with the potential of leading to significant threat to civil order. In this regard, hot spots in Africa are thus not just warfare situations, but also other pervert conditions such as political instability and state failure, ethno-religious tensions, governance and political corruption, economic mismanagement and poverty, cult violence, youth gangsterism, terrorism, and the like, capable of creating a conducive atmosphere for deep conflict.

The book is divided into five chapters: introduction, West Africa, Nigeria, Southern Africa, and East Africa and the Great Lakes region. In this introductory chapter, a conceptual framework is provided. The chapter broadly examines chronological and thematic themes useful in the understanding of the historicity and complexities of African conflicts. Using specific examples, the chapter starts with an overview of the dynamics of conflicts in pre-colonial Africa, and then examines the legacy of colonial rule on post-independence conflicts. Finally, the chapter overviews some salient elements of African conflicts in contemporary times.

Conflicts in Pre-colonial Africa

Conflict has always been a tangible historical reality in every period of the African past. In pre-colonial times, that is, the period before European colonization of the continent, roughly from the late nineteenth century, communal and intergroup conflicts of various degrees of violence and intensity dotted the landscape of virtually every African polity. Conflicts emanated for a myriad of sociopolitical and economic reasons. Conflicts could be entirely a manifestation of exigencies internal to the continent such as struggle for consolidation of group identity, state's expansionist and hegemonic tendency, competition over scarce resources, and rivalry over commerce. Some conflicts, on the other hand, were a product of external influences.

Internal Dynamics

The rise of centralized and powerful states and their desire to maintain political suzerainty in their regions was a major factor for great wars in pre-colonial Africa. In every region of the continent, powerful states sought territorial expansion by waging wars on less powerful neighbors, and even on faraway people. Conquered territories were often incorporated into the political structure of the conquering state as vassals, and kept subservient to the central authority. This was a political arrangement with predisposition for further conflict. Never fully assimilated, the conquered entities were always seeking every opportunity to rebel against the imperial administration and assert their independence.

The great expansive states of pre-colonial Africa achieved enormous power and prestige partly through territorial aggrandizement. For instance, the great medieval kingdoms of the Western Sudan—Ghana, Mali, and Songhai—were conquering states that waged many wars of expansion. One of the greatest conquerors and military generals in pre-colonial Africa was Sonni Ali, emperor of the Songhai Empire, who in the late fifteenth century pursued an expansionist foreign policy that greatly extended the frontiers of the empire. His many military campaigns ensured the incorporation of vast territories in the Western Sudan into the empire. Indeed, under him, Songhai's territorial limits extended considerably, stretching from the southern fringes of the Sahara in the north, to the Mossi country in the south, and from Jenne, on the great bend of the Niger in the West, to western Hausaland in the East. Sonni Ali's military conquests paved the way for the emergence of Songhai, during the time of his successors, as the most extensive and powerful state in the history of West Africa.

In trading societies, the struggle for commercial supremacy often created turmoil among states. Medieval Western Sudan also offers an example of this case. The trans-Saharan trade, a complex, long-distance commercial enterprise between the inhabitants of North Africa and those of West Africa, was one of the most significant phenomena in the history of the region. Existing for hundreds of years, the trade linked Mediterranean Africa, through the Sahara and the Savannah, with West Africa's forest belt through a number of caravan routes. During the heydays of the trading system between the eighth and the sixteenth centuries, the struggle for the control of trading centers and caravan routes by various Western Sudanese interests was an important feature of the history of conflicts in the region. The control of the trade routes offered whoever attained that feat an opportunity to profit from it. States gained by imposing and collecting customs duties and other taxes on import and export commodities such as gold, salt, ivory, copper, kola nuts, and slaves. At various periods, the great Western Sudanese empires competed to attain supremacy over the trade. Contending powers fought wars to control major trading centers such as Gao, Jenne, Walata, and Timbuktu. The case of Timbuktu is particularly noteworthy. Medieval Timbuktu, founded by the Tuareg of the southern Sahara, was perhaps the most important Western Sudanese city. It was a notable center of Islamic scholarship, the home of the impressive university, Sankore, which flourished up till the late sixteenth century. But more important than its scholarly credentials in this context, Timbuktu was a formidable commercial center, located close to the Niger River, and sitting at the crossroads of the trans-Saharan trade routes, especially those linking important producing centers such as the Taghaza salt mine located in the desert, and Bambuk, Bure, and Wangara, gold producing regions in the forest. Thus, given the commercial importance of Timbuktu, its control was of utmost importance to many states. Originally controlled by the Tuareg, at various times in its history, the city came under the authority of the kings of Ghana, Mali, and Songhai empires. In 1591, it was plundered by the Moroccans from North Africa.

Pre-colonial African conflicts could also be attributed to other internal factors. In early nineteenth-century Southern Africa, violent civil disturbances occurred among the groups in the region. The series of warfare that the Zulu called *Mfecane* (also called *difaqane* by the Sotho), has sometimes been credited solely to Zulu militarism and the attempts at state formation and struggle for power consolidation by groups in the region. Indeed, the powerful Zulu Kingdom that emerged under its warlike leader, Shaka, did so in this atmosphere of conflict. Shaka, with his formidable, disciplined army, conquered new territories in the region. Many groups fled in the wake of Shaka's military campaigns and went on to establish themselves somewhere else. Thus out of the violent turmoil of the time emerged other centralized states such as the Kingdoms of Lesotho and Swaziland.

But the *Mfecane* was much more than a product of Zulu expansionism. It was as much in combination with other internal factors. Southern Africa of the period was undergoing ecological calamity in terms of exhaustion of natural resources and intense drought leading to severe famine and hardship. Population increase in the region compounded the dismal condition as parties conflicted over the desire to control scarce resources. Population displacement and migrations followed the violent conflicts.[2]

Ability for successful military adventurism in pre-colonial Africa naturally depended greatly on military might. The great states with expansionist tradition—Songhai, Kongo, Kanem-Bornu, Asante, Oyo, Dahomey, Zulu, and many others—possessed powerful, disciplined military forces with highly skilled soldiers. In most cases, armies were raised in times of war. Some states did, however, boast of standing armies of professional soldiers capable of reasonable rapid mobilization. Armies of powerful states were often very large, with soldiers numbering several thousand. Sonni Ali had a large army with which he was able to defeat contending enemies such as the Mossi, the Tuareg, the Dogon, and the Fulani.

While large armies could be advantageous in winning battles, they did not necessarily guarantee victory over better trained or better equipped forces. The Songhai army that was humiliated by the Moroccans at the Battle of Tondibi in 1591 greatly outnumbered the latter. It was a huge army said to consist of about 9,700 to 30,000 infantry and 12,500 to 18,000 cavalry.[3] But the Moroccan army, an infantry force of less than 5,000 soldiers, was better armed than the large Songhai army.

The importance of weapons systems cannot be overemphasized in a situation of intense conflict. It is a significant dynamic in how a military campaign plays out. As in any other regions and historical periods, in pre-colonial Africa, the type of weapons available to belligerents to a large extent determined the outcome of military conflicts. Initially, African armies fought with offensive weapons such as machetes, swords, bows and arrows, javelins, spears, clubs, axes, knives and daggers, and defensive ones such as shields and helmets. In many parts of the continent, there was firm belief in the employment of supernatural powers in winning battles. Thus, soldiers, such as in Dahomey and Yoruba armies, wore charms as part of their military paraphernalia.

At least by the late sixteenth century, firearms had begun to appear in battlefields in Africa. The Moroccan army that defeated Songhai at Tondibi was equipped with Harquebus, an early type of a portable gun. But that was, perhaps, the first appearance of firearms in the Western Sudan. At any rate, by the late nineteenth century, the use of more sophisticated weapons had become more popular in African battlefields. Availability of firearms to African belligerents was at the courtesy of Europeans traders on the coast trading in guns and gunpowder. Firearms such as muskets, rifles, and other guns capable of rapid firepower were used by African armies.

The military in most parts of Africa consisted of the infantry. In forest areas, armies were made up of largely foot soldiers. In some areas conducive to horse breeding such as savannah and desert regions, armies could be composed mainly of cavalry. The powerful and imperialistic Yoruba kingdom of Oyo located in northern Yorubaland, a grassland region, built a standing force made up of infantry and cavalry at the peak of its power in the late seventeenth and eighteenth centuries. Some states with proximity to water outlets built marine forces. For example, Songhai's military included a navy equipped with fleets of war canoes that operated on the Niger.

Mercenary soldiering was not prevalent in pre-colonial Africa. A noted case, however, was the military of the sultan of Morocco that defeated Songhai in 1591. The Moroccan army, commanded by Judar Pasha, a soldier of Spanish ancestry, included mercenaries, some of whom were prisoners recruited from Portugal and Muslim Spain.

Although there were notable women warriors in pre-colonial Africa, a rare phenomenon in military formation was large-scale employment of women as soldiers, sometimes numbering thousands. In the eighteenth and nineteenth centuries, the militaristic state of Dahomey was well known for using as part of its infantry force a corps of all-women soldiers, the Amazons, as they were popularly known. The Amazons emerged as a corps of bodyguards under King Gezo, who ruled from 1818 to 1858. As warriors, these women received intense training, wore uniforms, and demonstrated a high level of professionalism and discipline. The Amazons, who were sometimes engaged in military campaigns such as against the Egba of the Yorubaland in the mid-nineteenth century, and later against the French, were noted in the region for courage and fierceness.[4]

External Influences

Like other regions of the world, dynamic historical forces and events external to Africa have played a significant role in the shaping of the continent's history. Indeed, in practically all periods of African history to the present, external influences have either introduced new conflicts into the continent, or exacerbated local ones. One of the most defining events of pre-colonial Africa was the advent of Islam on the continent.

A religion of Middle Eastern origin, Islam reached Africa via the northern region of the continent by means of conquest. The Islamic wars of conquest that would lead to the Islamization of North Africa occurred first in Egypt, when in about 642 CE, the country fell to the invading Muslim forces from Arabia. Over the next centuries, the rest of the Maghreb would succumb to Jihadist armies.

Conflict over religion had not always been a widespread practice in African history. The notion of religious conversion, whether by force or peaceful means, is foreign to indigenous African beliefs. African people identified with the family religion, or that of their extended group, into which they were born. The spread of Islam by conquests in North Africa introduced the element of conflict into religious adherence in Africa.

It is true that Islamization was achieved by peaceful means in some parts of Africa. The diffusion of the religion in West Africa in the age of the great medieval states occurred, partly, as a result of a combination of factors. Among the elite class of major cities like Timbuktu and Jenne, the diffusion of Islam was an intellectual exercise. The courts of Muslim rulers like those of Mansa Musa of Mali and Askia Mohammed Touré of Songhai promoted the religion as a political ideology. Commerce was also an important instrument of the spread of the religion. The trans-Saharan trade was at once a commercial enterprise and a religious endeavor. Muslim Arab and Berber traders of North Africa and the famous Wangara traders and others in West Africa helped to propagate the regions. Along the East African Swahili coast, Islam diffused as a result of commercial intercourse with Egypt and across the Indian Ocean with Arabia.

Islam, however, did not become a religion of the masses by peaceful means. Forced conversion was an indispensable element of proselytization. Essentially, Islam drew a sharp line between *dar-al-Islam* (abode of Islam or peace) and *dar-al-harb* (abode of war, constituting infidels). Muslims were at liberty to wage holy war (*jihad*) against unbelievers.

In the Western Sudan, in the eighteenth and nineteenth centuries, Islamic revolutions greatly extended the frontiers of Islam. Fulani Muslim reformers and their invading armies, the *mujahidin*, overran pre-Islamic states, or professed Islamic states where its leaders condoned traditional religion and practices. In some places, at the end of the *jihad*, Muslim theocracies emerged out of such states. The institution of Islamic states occurred in the Senegambian region where Futa Jallon, Bondu, and Futa Toro emerged as imamates in the eighteenth century; the area that would become Northern Nigeria where the Sokoto Caliphate was created in the early nineteenth century, and in the Niger River inland delta region where the state of Masina, and, subsequently, the Segu-Tukulor Empire, were created also in the nineteenth century.

The *jihads* constituted major religious conflict situations in pre-colonial Africa. The wars between the forces of Islam and those elements they considered unbelievers were often long. Resistance to the jihadist reformist impulses by many groups such as the Mossi of the Volta River basin heightened religious conflicts in many places.

Aside from the penetration of Islam, another profound external influence on Africa was the European incursion into the continent from the fifteenth century. One of the main European ventures in Africa before the age of formal colonization was commerce, particularly in human merchandise. The European slave trade across the Atlantic introduced violent conflicts or exacerbated existing ones. The demand for captives by the Europeans promoted communal conflicts. Wars, raids, brigandage, banditry, plundering, and pillaging became avenues for procuring slaves. The rivalry over the control of the slave trade brought about intense interstate conflicts. The mid-nineteenth century Yoruba civil wars to a considerable extent fuelled the Atlantic slave trade.

New forms of major conflicts occurred as European imperial design began to be manifested through territorial acquisitions. In virtually every place in Africa, after the Berlin West African Conference of 1884–1885, European colonial powers embarked on military invasions to conquer lands. Almost everywhere in the continent, Africans violently resisted European military incursions. While the forces of the imperialists easily overran some places, in others they met stiff and prolonged resistance. The latter occurred in Western Igboland in present-day Eastern Nigeria, where the Ekumeku, a well-organized movement of Igbo youth sometimes described as a secret society, engaged the British in a long-drawn series of guerrilla wars from the late nineteenth to the early twentieth century.[5]

By the early twentieth century, African resistance to European occupation had been crushed virtually everywhere. African armies, often poorly armed, were no match to the invading forces of the European powers that were equipped with machine guns, artillery, and other modern and sophisticated weapons. However, resistance to imperialism did not end with European conquests. As structures of dominance became institutionalized during the early colonial period, sporadic protests continued. In Tanganyika, a German colony, the Maji Maji War, a violent uprising against imperial rule by Africans in the early twentieth century, demonstrated Africans' persistent opposition to colonial policies.[6] In another example, Igbo women of Aba in Eastern Nigeria revolted in 1929 against the colonial government's policies under the indirect rule system, particularly a plan to impose direct taxation on women. Often described as the Aba Women's War, this mass revolt of peasant women against the colonial system and its African agents, the Warrant Chiefs, saw the destruction of the colonial government's native courts and the burning of government property. The protest was not without fatality, as some 50 women were reportedly killed.[7]

Anti-Colonial Wars

The post–World War II period changed the character of anti-colonial struggle in Africa. In the previous era, nationalist leaders were often contented with asking for reforms to the colonial system to accommodate their own interests. But the post-1945 period saw the emergence of mass-based uncompromising nationalist movements that demanded African self-determination. The postwar period, consequently, was that of decolonization, a process that brought about the dismantlement of colonial empires in many parts of the continent.[8] By 1960, about 17 African states had obtained independence.

Colonial powers such as Britain and France quickly recognized the prevailing postwar political change and managed, in most of their colonies, to avoid major conflicts during the period of decolonization. In colonies like the Gold Coast and Nigeria, political independence thus came on a platter of gold. This is to say that although nationalist struggle was marked with episodic events such as riots, popular protests and agitations, labor unrest, and trade union and working-class strikes, the road to self-government and national sovereignty was largely devoid of conflicts on a violent and prolonged scale. Independence was achieved largely through the path of political negotiations and constitutional reforms.

Violent conflicts could not be avoided where the colonial power adopted a policy of aggressive repression of African nationalism. This happened mostly in settler colonies, that is, colonies with large numbers of Europeans as permanent settlers, most of them farmers. Although a minority of the population, white settlers in Kenya, Algeria, Angola, Mozambique, Southern Rhodesia, and Southwest Africa typically exercised considerable economic and political power. A major character of settler colonies was large-scale land appropriation by the colonial power for settlers' occupation. The Southern Rhodesia 1930 Land Apportionment Act that was designed to restrict African access to land and enhance settler land ownership was typical of other settler colonies. In Algeria by 1945, settlers owned about one-third of the most fertile lands of the country.

Appropriation of lands necessarily turned Africans landless. In Kenya, many displaced people became "squatters" on European lands, working as low-wage laborers. Tax requirements, as in Mozambique, enhanced a system of forced labor introduced by the colonial administration. But not only were Africans deprived of land, colonial regulations, as in Kenya, also often denied them the right to grow cash crops. Added to the dismal economic situation of Africans in settler colonies was the burden of colonial taxation.

European settlers in settler colonies did not only exercise significant economic power, they also constituted a powerful political force. Southern Rhodesia's white supremacist regime provides a good example of settler political power. As African nationalism gained momentum in the early 1960s, white settlers who had always enjoyed a privileged position in the colony under British rule moved to block any possibility of African majority rule. Vehemently racist, Southern Rhodesian whites formed a racist political party, the Rhodesian Front (RF), in March 1962, which promoted the ideology of white supremacy and was determined to reduce Africans to a permanent second-class position. RF thus became an instrument of halting the growing tide of African nationalism and eventuality of independence under black majority rule. As the ruling political party in Southern Rhodesia, a feat made possible by an all-white electorate, RF took a drastic measure on November 11, 1965, aimed at finally ensuring that political power did not get into the hands of Africans. Under its leader, Ian Douglas Smith, RF pronounced the full independence of Southern Rhodesia from Britain under the control of the white minority regime. The so-called Unilateral Declaration of Independence, although widely condemned and attracting some economic sanctions of the white-ruled regime, was a clear-cut demonstration of settler power. In essence, aside from virulent racist colonial policies and economic and political repression, a major element of the nationalist struggle in settler colonies was settler power. Settler intransigence to African nationalism and opposition to reforms compounded colonial repression and inevitably produced armed struggle.

Kenya was one of the earliest colonies to undergo a violent decolonization process. Here, an elite-led mainstream nationalist movement was complemented by a violent uprising in 1952 by a peasant movement among the Kikuyu of Central Kenya, known as Mau Mau. Although land recovery was primacy in the Mau Mau struggle, the uprising led by its "land and freedom army" was also an attempt at achieving a broader nationalistic objective of ridding Kenya of oppressive foreign rule.

Much more complex than the Kenya rebellion were violent decolonization conflicts in colonies like Algeria (1954–1962), Angola (1961–1975), Portuguese Guinea (1962–1974), Mozambique (1964–1975), and Southern Rhodesia (1964–1979). These were full-scale wars directed at attaining independence. Given the recalcitrant attitude of the colonial powers such as Portugal to the question of self-determination, the conflicts were much more protracted and violent. They also attracted greater international attention, partly because of the high level of violence. During the Algerian war, Arab countries, most especially in Africa, supported the Algerians, and international opinion generally favored the nationalists. In the case of Angola and Mozambique, Soviet support for the liberation movement introduced Cold War politics into the conflicts as the United States began to back Portugal. The liberation wars were also more effectively organized by elite nationalist leaders than the peasant-led Mau Mau rebellion. Many of the leaders of the liberation organizations such as Ahmed Ben Bella of Algeria's *Front de Libération Nationale* (Front of National Liberation; FLN), Aghostino Neto of Angola's Popular Movement for the Liberation of Angola (*Movimento Popular de Libertação de Angola*; MPLA), Samora Machel of Mozambique's Front for the Liberation of Mozambique (*Frente de Libertação de Moçambique*; FRELIMO), and Robert Mugabe of Zimbabwe's Zimbabwe African National Union (ZANU), were highly educated ideologues.

Guerrilla warfare was the nature of the armed struggle against recalcitrant colonial powers and the settler community where it proved a stumbling block to independence. Guerrilla war, which entails ambushes and hit-and-run strikes at selected targets, seemed reasonable to be employed where the European powers displayed overwhelmingly superior military force and firepower. Employing guerrilla tactics, Mau Mau fighters in Kenya attacked from the Aberdare Mountains, destroying settler farms, crops, and farm animals. Europeans were also killed, as well as Africans who they considered traitors because of their collaboration with the colonial regime. Initially, Algerian guerrillas operating from rural suburbs targeted military and government installations and facilities, but consequently carried their terrorist campaigns into urban centers, striking at civilians, particularly French citizens.

Colonial retribution against guerrilla fighters was also very brutal everywhere. Counterinsurgency forces numbering close to half a million troops, including French paratroopers, were introduced into the Algerian war in 1956, turning what the French government had hitherto dubbed a "public order operation" into total war. Heavily armed with sophisticated weapons, French forces conducted brutal search-and-destroy operations against the guerrillas aided by aerial bombardments. As part of its repressive measures, the counterinsurgency military command erected a 200-mile-long, electrified barbed-wire fence, the Morice Line, along the border with Tunisia to prevent cross-border activities by Algerian insurgents in Tunisia. The use of land mines was also introduced by the French. In like manner, Portugal responded to the wars in Angola, Mozambique, and Portuguese Guinea with overwhelming military force designed to cripple the guerrilla operations.

Where wars of national liberation occurred, the colonial powers achieved military victory, but were unable to translate this to political victory. Before the end of the bloody and long Algerian War, division in France over the war had indicated that Algerian independence was inevitable. The French had no alternative but to negotiate with the Algerian nationalists, and complete independence was granted in July 1962. Portugal's inability to consolidate military victory during the liberation wars in its colonial empire, especially in Mozambique, caused discontentment at home, most notably within the armed forces. This eventually led to a coup d'état on April 25, 1974, that overthrew the fascist government of Prime Minister Marcelo Caetano and brought about a new government in Lisbon that saw the futility of the continuation of the conflict and was ready to negotiate a political end to it. Peaceful negotiations eventually brought independence to Angola on November 11, 1975, and to Mozambique on June 25, 1975.

As violent decolonization conflict, the human and material costs of liberation wars were always great, not only on the side of Africans fighting for independence, but also on the part of the recalcitrant colonial powers. When the Mau Mau Rebellion was finally put down by the British in 1956, it was at an untold cost to the Kikuyu. The Corfield Report, which published the result of a government-commissioned study of the uprising, gave the number of Mau Mau and other Africans killed during the conflict at almost 13,000. Europeans also sustained heavy casualties. The Corfield Report put the financial cost of the conflict to the government at exceeding £55 million.[9] The costs of the Algerian, Angolan, and Mozambican wars were even more staggering. The estimate of the death toll among the Algerians in the eight years of their brutal war was between 1.5 and 2 million. This war was accompanied by atrocities such as torture, kidnapping, and other forms of brutalization, to which the parties on both sides of the conflict were guilty.

A massive refugee crisis and large-scale displacement of populations also featured in the liberation wars. In Algeria, over a million people, European settlers, in particular, who had vehemently resisted the nationalist movement, and Algerians who were proponents of the existence of an Algeria within the French commonwealth, fled the country after attainment of independence for fear of retribution. In addition to over 50,000 Angolans who had died by 1962, another half a million had fled to what was then Zaire (now Democratic Republic of Congo; DRC) as refugees.[10] Also, the wars caused major infrastructural damage, especially in the cities, and agricultural devastation in the rural areas, problems that the post-colonial state must grapple with.

As to be expected, bitterly fought liberation wars inevitably shaped the nature of post-independence relationships between former colonies and erstwhile colonial masters. While colonies that did not go through liberation wars developed close relationships with their former colonial overlords, states that went through liberation wars did not. The long, violent wars in these states thus discouraged a neo-colonial relationship with the former colonial power.

Unlike in Algeria, Angola, Mozambique, and Portuguese Guinea, where the liberation wars were waged against external colonial powers, those in Southern Rhodesia and Southwest Africa were to end internal colonialism. Nationalists in Southern Rhodesia took to armed struggle to end white minority rule. Black majority rule was achieved in 1980 as the country assumed a new name, Zimbabwe. In Southwest Africa, the liberation war was to assert independence from Apartheid South Africa under a virulently racist white minority regime. Originally a German colony, Southwest Africa came under the control of South Africa when it occupied it during World War I. In 1920, the League of Nations stripped Germany of ownership of the colony and officially labeled it a "mandated territory" of South Africa. In theory, the League's mandate entitled South Africa to hold the colony in trust on its behalf, and move it toward independence. In reality, however, Southwest Africa was a de facto colony of South Africa. The Pretoria regime not only refused to relinquish control of Southwest Africa, indeed, it extended its racist laws to the colony. With no possibility of peaceful process of decolonization, Southwest African nationalists embarked on a guerrilla war against South Africa. Independence was achieved by Southwest Africa, now called Namibia, on March 21, 1990.

In South Africa itself, the struggle by the majority black population to end white supremacist rule and its apartheid policy was a long, bitter, and violent one. The minority regime had since the institution of apartheid, a system of racial segregation, in 1948 systematically denied Africans basic rights. Not only that, it had made virtually every avenue of reform impossible, violently repressing any form of opposition. Hundreds of Black South Africans who opposed apartheid were brutalized by the state's racist security forces. Many activists died from confrontation with the police. Many anti-apartheid leaders were arrested, detained, and imprisoned, and some, like Steve Biko, even murdered in jail. In the face of violent repression, anti-apartheid forces were left with no other alternative than to embark on armed struggle. Internal unrest against apartheid left South Africa virtually in a state of civil war.

Armed struggle, with international pressure on the South African regime, began to yield fruits by the early 1990s. Apartheid laws were repealed; the ban on nationalist organizations like the African National Congress (ANC), which had been operating underground, was lifted; and the most prized political prisoner in South Africa and an icon of black struggle, Nelson Mandela, was released from prison in February 1990, after 27 years of incarceration. South Africa finally achieved a multiracial government in 1994 with Mandela inaugurated as president, and his party, the ANC, having won the first non-racial election in South African history.

Post-Independence Africa

Since 1960, Africa's year of independence when 17 states attained independence, the continent has been bedeviled with conflicts, whether of low intensity, or of violent and destructive proportions. There is hardly any African state that has escaped from one intrastate conflict or the other. Sources of conflicts have been multidimensional, including border disputes, religious antagonism, ethnic (and sometimes, racial) animosities, competition for scarce resources, economic downturn, environmental degradation, elite power struggle, democratization and human rights issues, terrorism, and many others. In many cases, particularly during the Cold War, African conflicts were exacerbated by extra-African meddling. The superpowers and their surrogates provided military backing through arms transfers to warring factions or, sometimes, even outright intervention through dispatch of troops. If it was expected that the end of the Cold War in 1992 would usher in a drastic reduction in conflicts in Africa, that expectation has proven to be illusory. Conflicts have continued to occur in nearly every subregion of the continent.

The Legacy of European Imperialism

One of the most profound and incontestable legacies of European imperialism in Africa is that it sowed the seeds of many intense

Table 1.1 Major Decolonization Wars in Africa, 1954–1990[1]

Country	Liberation Movements	Nationalist Leaders	Years of Liberation War
Algeria	National Liberation Front (FLN)	Ahmed Ben Bela	1954–1962
Angola	Popular Movement for the Liberation of Angola (MPLA);	Agostinho Neto	1961–1975
	Union for the Total Independence of Angola (UNITA)	Jonas Savimbi	
Guinea-Bissau & Cape Verde	African Party for the Independence of Guinea and Cape Verde (PAIGC)	Amilcar Cabral	1963–1974
Mozambique	Front for the Liberation of Mozambique (FRELIMO)	Eduardo Mondlane & Samora Machel	1962–1975
South West Africa (Namibia)	South-West Africa People's Organization (SWAPO)	Sam Nujumo	1966–1988
Zimbabwe	Zimbabwe African National Union (ZANU);	Robert Mugabe	1964–1979
	Zimbabwe African People's Union (ZAPU)	Joshua Nkomo	

[1]Works on liberation wars in Africa abound. A general discourse is provided in Adebayo Oyebade, "Radical Nationalism and Wars of Liberation," in Toyin Falola, ed., *Africa, Vol. 4: The End of Colonial Rule: Nationalism and Decolonization* (Durham, NC: Carolina Academic Press, 2002), 63–87. Specifically on the Mau Mau uprising, see S. M. Shamsul Alam, *Rethinking Mau Mau in Colonial Kenya* (New York: Palgrave Macmillan, 2007); Kinuthia Macharia and Muigai Kanyua, *The Social Context of the Mau Mau Movement in Kenya (1952–1960)*, (Lanham, MD: University Press of America, 2006); David Lovatt Smith, *Kenya, the Kikuyu, and Mau Mau* (Herstmonceux, East Sussex, UK: Mawenzi Books, 2005); Wunyabari O. Maloba, *Mau Mau and Kenya: An Analysis of a Peasant Revolt* (Bloomington: Indiana University Press, 1993); and Cora Ann Presley, *Kikuyu Women, the Mau Mau Rebellion, and Social Change in Kenya* (Boulder, CO: Westview Press, 1992). On the Algerian War, see William R. Polk, *Violent Politics: A History of Insurgency, Terrorism and Guerrilla War, From the American Revolution to Iraq* (New York: Harper, 2007); Jo McCormack, *Collective Memory: France and the Algerian War (1954–1962)*, (Lanham, MD: Lexington Books, 2007); Alistair Horne, *Savage War of Peace: Algeria, 1954–1962* (New York: New York Review Books, 2006); Todd Shepard, *The Invention of Decolonization: The Algerian War and the Remaking of France* (Ithaca, NY: Cornell University Press, 2006); Martin S. Alexander, and J. F. V. Keiger, eds., *France and the Algerian War, 1954–62: Strategy, Operations and Diplomacy* (London: Frank Cass Publishers, 2002); and Martin S. Alexander, Martin Evans, and J. F. V. Keiger, eds., *The Algerian War and the French Army: Experiences, Images, Testimonies* (New York: Palgrave Macmillan, 2002). For Angola, see. Adebayo Oyebade, *Culture and Customs of Angola* (Westport, CT: Greenwood Publishers, 2006).

post-colonial conflicts. The scramble for Africa by European imperialist nations in the last two decades of the nineteenth century brought about the Berlin Conference. This was an international meeting of imperialist powers convened by the first German chancellor, Otto Von Bismarck, to set the modus operandi for territorial acquisition in Africa. By the Berlin Act of 1885, European powers interested in African territories concurred on the imperative of avoiding conflicting claims, and in amicable sharing out of African territories among themselves. The Berlin Conference thus formalized the European process of creating colonial borders in Africa. This process, often referred to as the "partition of the Africa," abolished the existing boundaries in Africa and established a new political map of Africa, which has generally survived till today.[11]

The European map-making enterprise necessarily created artificial nations in Africa. The new frontiers were drawn exclusively to cater to European interests, and without due consideration for ethnolinguistic makeup. The new political map of Africa thus, in large measure, separated into different states peoples who had lived together as one in the pre-colonial period. Likewise, people who had never lived together historically as one were lumped together within the same borders. This is true of practically all African states, with few exceptions, such as Somalia. Nigeria, for example, has more than 250 different ethnic groups, with each group having a number of subgroups. Most post-independence African states, consequently, are a mere "geographical expression," as Nigeria was once described by one of its famous politicians, Obafemi Awolowo.[12]

It is inevitable that one of the immediate challenges faced by some African states after independence was how to deal with inherited artificial boundaries. In some instances, attempts were made to redress disputed colonial frontiers. This occurred as a result of irredentist claims or nationalistic desire. These have led to violent conflicts in some places.

Border Conflicts and Irredentism

At its inception in 1963, the newly established pan-African body, the Organization of African Unity (OAU), adopted as one of its cardinal principles the doctrine of the inviolability of frontiers inherited from the colonial powers.[13] The importance of this declaration was further reaffirmed when the resolution of the organization's summit conference held the following year in Cairo, Egypt, endorsed it.[14]

In the early years of African independence in the 1960s, African leaders of the era fully understood, as expressed in the 1964 OAU resolution, that border problems constituted a "grave and permanent factor of dissension" in the continent.[15] Even though African leaders were well aware that these inherited borders were irrationally and haphazardly drawn, they chose to accept them, realizing that any attempt to remedy them would generate more problems than it would solve. However, it soon became evident that the multi-ethnic, -linguistic, and -religious constitution of most independent African states made border crises unavoidable.

Irredentist policy pursued by states like Morocco, Mauritania, and Somali was a direct affront on inherited colonial frontiers. Irredentism is the claim by a given state of ownership of a part of a neighboring state and the desire to annex the claimed territory. The basis for such a policy is the assertion that the claimed territory under another polity historically belonged to the state pursuing the irredentist policy, or that there is close ethnic affinity between its inhabitants and those of the claimed territory across the border.

The earliest case of irredentist territorial claim occurred in Northwest Africa in the early 1960s where Morocco claimed "Greater Mauritania," a territory comprising southwest Algeria, the Spanish territory of Western Sahara, and the French colony of Mauritania. As far back as the decolonization period, a number of Moroccan nationalists had envisioned an independent Moroccan state coterminous to its pre-colonial status in territorial terms. However, at independence in 1956, the frontiers bequeathed by the colonial master, France, fell short of the dream of the nationalists. After independence, Morocco pursued an irredentist policy to re-establish its pre-colonial historical form. Its relentless policy of territorial claims resulted in constant border disputes with Algeria and Mauritania.

Morocco's annexation of Western Sahara in 1976, following Spain's departure, brought it into armed conflict with the Polisario Front, Western Sahara's nationalist organization that aimed at the complete independence of the territory. Constant confrontation also occurred between Morocco and Algeria as a result of the latter's military backing of the Polisario. Meanwhile, Mauritania, which had achieved independence in 1960, also laid claim to Western Sahara, bringing it into violent conflict with the Polisario.

Apart from the complicated border crisis in Northwest Africa, irredentism also manifested in the Horn of Africa, that is, the northeast corner of the continent comprising the states of Ethiopia, Somalia, Eritrea, and Djibouti. In the region, Somalia pursued irredentist policy against its neighbors. Colonial boundaries had separated the Somali people into different imperial empires, namely British, French, and Italian. Immediately after independence in 1960, British Somaliland, now bearing the Republic of Somalia, proclaimed a policy aimed at incorporating into the Somali state ethnic Somalis in Djibouti (former French Somaliland), Kenya, and the Ogaden province of Ethiopia. In order to realize its pan-Somali goal, Somalia promoted and supported secessionist insurgence in these countries.

States like Morocco and Somalia that pursued irredentist policy were not merely in conflict with their neighbors, they were at odds with the rest of Africa. Irredentism, as a policy, ran contrary to one of the most fundamental principles of the pan-African organization, the OAU— that of the inviolability of colonial frontiers. Only Somalia and Morocco refused to sign the OAU Cairo Accord of July 1964, which enjoined member states to respect the boundaries inherited from the colonial powers. Thus, these two states were often isolated by OAU member states. Morocco's irredentist policy, in particular, caused a long-lasting rift between it and the organization.

Border Conflicts and Secession

One of the longest border-related civil wars in Africa occurred in Ethiopia, where its fourteenth province, Eritrea, waged a 30-year war of self-determination against it. Eritrea, originally a UN trust territory after World War II, was federated with Ethiopia in 1952, and then annexed by Ethiopia 10 years later. Eritrean resistance against Ethiopia's annexation began immediately and led to the long, violent, and destructive war of independence. Peaceful negotiations under the auspices of the UN, however, brought the war to an end and paved the way for Eritrean independence in 1993.

The need to redress colonial boundaries also led to a major crisis in the Congo, from 1960 to 1965. Congo, a former Belgian colony, erupted into violence soon after obtaining independence on June 30, 1960. The origins of the crisis lie deep in the legacies of Congo's colonial history. The colonial power never resolved the fundamental dilemma of ethnic differences. Throughout the colonial period, it also never developed an adequate educated class capable of manning political power after independence. It was no surprise, then, that the new post-independence political elite proved utterly incapable of managing the challenges of a newly independent state—hence, the state of anarchy arising from political, military, ethnic, and racial tension that gripped the country within days of its independence. The prevailing turmoil was further compounded by international meddling and superpower Cold War interests.

Wars of secession necessarily exacerbated the Congo Crisis and threatened to disintegrate the state. Even before its independence, the Congo had been confronted with separatist movements, for instance, in the Baluba-dominated south-central region of Kasai. Shortly before Congolese independence was declared, the Kasai province had proclaimed its own autonomy. However, the immediate crisis of secession faced by post-independence Congo was the secession of Katanga. Katanga (later renamed Shaba) was the important, mineral-rich southeast province of the Congo under the control of one of the principal players in the Congo Crisis, Moise Tshombe. Backed by Belgian military and business interests, Katanga declared secession on July 11, 1960, proclaiming itself an independent state. Within six months, the newly established sovereign state itself had to grapple with a secessionist attempt when the Baluba of its northern region declared their own independence. Katanga was unable to wholly control the Baluba throughout its existence as an independent state.

Tshombe's resistance to UN pressures to end secession, and the state's use of military power to bring this about, made the Katangan secession a devastating brutal civil war. In the end, however, the state of Katanga proved to be short lived. UN military operations in December 1962 led to the capture of its capital, Élisabethville (later renamed Lumumbashi). The secessionist regime collapsed on January 15, 1963, when Tshombe surrendered, and the region was subsequently reintegrated back into the Congolese state.

Meanwhile, during the civil war, Congo also faced the Kasai secession when, on August 8, 1960, its leader, Albert Kalonji, declared the equally mineral-rich region, the State of South Kasai. This secessionist attempt also led the Congolese state into a bloody war with the secessionist state, although shorter in duration than that with its southeastern neighbor, Katanga. Congo's military forces crushed the Kasai rebellion in less than six months, ending its secessionist bid. By December 1961, the former South Kasai state had come under the effective control of the Congolese state.

Congo's multidimensional crisis, of which the secessionist attempt played a large role, nearly led to the disintegration of the Congolese state. The Congo experience clearly demonstrated to African states that secession was not to be tolerated. It was not only a destabilizing factor, but a conduit for foreign intervention in internal African affairs as well. Indeed, when the OAU was established in 1963, one of its cardinal principles, respect for the sovereignty and territorial integrity of states,[16] was a condemnation of secession. After Congo, secession became, more that ever before, an anathema. Consequently, when the Nigerian Civil War broke out in 1967 on the account of the secession of Biafra, OAU's stand was unequivocally clear: the secessionist attempt must not be allowed to succeed in Nigeria so as to prevent its occurrence elsewhere in Africa. It should be remembered that colonial

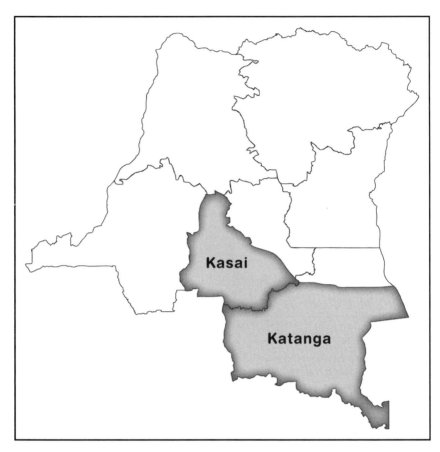

Secessionist Regions of the Congo: Kasai and Katanga. (Courtesy of Sam Saverance.)

frontiers had created in practically all African states potential Katangas or Biafras.

Like the crisis in the Congo, the Nigerian Civil War of 1967–1970 (sometimes referred to as the Biafran War) had some of its roots in colonial history.[17] After Nigeria's independence in 1960, ethnic animosity, which colonialism had failed to resolve, came to the fore. There was the general notion of political domination of the federation by the Hausa-Fulani of the north. Consequently, many groups perceived themselves oppressed. To the Igbo of Eastern Nigeria, the pogroms of 1967 in the north in which hundreds of their kinsmen had been slaughtered, were seen as a confirmation of the futility of their continued existence within the Nigerian federation. In consequence, under the leadership of Eastern Region's governor, Emeka Odumegwu Ojukwu, the Igbo proclaimed the secession of the region from Nigeria on May 30, 1967. This was the immediate cause of the Nigerian Civil War.

Initial peace talks to resolve the Nigerian crisis between the federal government and the secessionist state, the Republic of Biafra, failed. On July 6, 1967, Nigeria declared a total war on Biafra, thus commencing one of the most devastating civil wars in early post-independence Africa.

External intervention, though not on the scale of the Congo Crisis, also dogged the destructive war in Nigeria. The OAU intervention, initially discouraged by Nigeria, provided a platform for the two sides to negotiate a peaceful end to the fratricidal warfare. OAU efforts, in the final analysis, were futile. Uncompromisingly opposed to secession, the organization could not be an impartial mediator. The terms of reference under which it was mandated to mediate the conflict did not allow it any other alternative than to preserve the territorial integrity of Nigeria.[18] In the final analysis, after 30 months of bitter fighting, on January 13, 1970, the Nigerian Civil War ended on the battlefield with Biafra's surrender.

The Secessionist State of Biafra. (Courtesy of Sam Saverance.)

It should be noted that Biafra was not the first thought of secession in Nigeria. During the early 1960s' political crises, a number of regional leaders threatened to pull their regions out of the federation. The northern politicians, in particular, for a while promoted the secession of the Northern Region in a campaign tagged ARABA. A more visible case of attempt at secession was that of the Niger Delta, where in early 1966, Isaac Jasper Adaka Boro led a rebellion aimed at carving out an independent state in the region. This was an abortive attempt that was brutally put down by federal government forces.

Some ethnic-based self-determination organizations in Nigeria have since the 1990s advocated greater autonomy for their respective groups. A few have gone further to call for secession. This was true of Oodua People's Congress (OPC), a militant, nationalist Yoruba organization that in the late 1990s advocated an independent Yoruba state in Southwestern Nigeria, to be achieved, if necessary, by the use of force. Among the Igbo, a neo-Biafran agenda resurfaced when the Movement for the Actualization of the Sovereign State of Biafra (MASSOB) was established in 1999.

Currency of Border-Related Conflicts

Border conflict has continued to plague Africa. Nigeria and Cameroon have had decades-long recurring border clashes over a disputed region, the oil-rich Bakassi Peninsula. Sometimes violent, the dispute only ended in June 2006, when both countries signed an agreement by which Nigeria agreed to withdraw from the region. In 1998, border war erupted between Ethiopia and Eritrea, and lasted till 2000. But tensions have continued to run high between the two countries, sometimes portending a resumption of the conflict. In late 2007, the United Nations warned of another likely war after both countries had for months concentrated troops along their common border. Also in April 2008, UN Secretary-General Ban Ki-moon warned that in the event of the complete withdrawal of the UN peacekeeping mission from the region, the conflict could re-emerge.

Apart from the historic unsuccessful secession attempts of Katanga and Biafra, and the successful breakaway of Eritrea, separatist groups have not ceased to articulate secessionist aspirations in the contemporary period. Since the 1970s, there have been threats of secession in a number of countries. In Angola, for instance, a secessionist movement called Front for the Liberation of the Enclave of Cabinda (FLEC) began to advocate for the breakaway of Cabinda, an oil-rich enclave in the northwestern part of the country. The full-fledged, armed confrontation embarked upon by this movement against the Angolan government only ended in 2006 when FLEC signed an uncertain cease-fire agreement with the government. In Senegal, a secessionist rebellion began in 1983 in the Casamance region in the south of the country, located between Gambia and Guinea Bissau. For over two decades, guerillas of the separatist movement, the Movement of Democratic Forces in the Casamance (MFDC), waged a very bloody war against Senegalese forces.

The new international world order brought about by the end of the Cold War, characterized by demands for democratization and respect for human rights, seemed to have encouraged separatist movements around the world. In Africa, ethnic groups, especially minority ones, which had always felt marginalized and their existence threatened within their state borders, began to agitate for separate existence. Movements seeking self-determination for their groups have been active in a number of states. Claiming marginalization, separatists of the Anglophone regions of Cameroon have since 1993 campaigned for secession. This has caused a series of clashes between the state and the Southern Cameroons National Council (SCNC), the organization championing self-determination. In the Comoros, the Island of Anjouan declared its independence from the Comoros Union in 1997. Its sovereignty lasted until 2002 when it reunited with Comoros. However, another secession bid by the island in July 2007 was militarily crushed by Comoros the following year. Namibia, in 1999, experienced a violent conflict when the Caprivi Strip, its narrow northeast region sandwiched between Angola and Zambia to the north, and Botswana to the south, attempted to secede from the state. In April 2005, in the Democratic Republic of Congo (former Congo, later called Zaire), an alleged secession attempt in Katanga, reportedly involving André Tshombe, the son of the mastermind of the 1960 secession, Moise Tshombe, led to the arrest of some 30 people.[19]

Border-related conflicts have generally been devastating to African states. In some cases, they have led to brutal civil wars as occurred in Nigeria between 1967 and 1970. These conflicts have often adversely affected cross-border populations causing population displacement, large-scale migrations, and massive refugee problems. Apart from the enormous loss of lives and general insecurity of life and property, the conflicts have also caused the destabilization of states and truncated their economic growth.

COLD WAR AND CONFLICTS

The emergence of the Cold War in the immediate post–World War II period coincided with the decolonization era in Africa when colonial states began to gain independence. In the late 1950s and early 1960s, a large number of sovereign African states entered the international arena now increasingly defined by the ideological rivalry between the United States and the Soviet Union. For the next three decades, superpower policies in Africa were to be formulated within the framework of Cold War considerations. The overriding superpower consideration in Africa, then, was to promote their political, economic, strategic, and ideological interests in the continent. In this context, newly independent African states, many of them politically unstable, economically weak, and relatively inexperienced in the global system, easily became prey to Cold War manipulations.[20]

Soviet-American competition in Africa introduced, or at least exacerbated, conflicts on the continent. African conflicts, particularly in Southern and Central Africa, became proxy for superpower antagonism. The United States and the Soviet Union and their respective allies used African conflicts through covert, and sometimes direct, military intervention to promote their Cold War ideological, political, and economic interests in Africa.

Superpower Cold War confrontation in Africa first manifested in the Congo Crisis of 1960–1965. As the crisis spiraled out of control, and with the apparent failure of the United Nations to deal effectively with the conflict, Prime Minister Patrice Lumumba sought the help of the Soviet Union. The United States viewed the invitation of the Soviets into the Congo purely from the prism of the Cold War. It would provide the Kremlin an opportunity to make an inroad into the strategic, mineral-rich state. The possible reality of a Lumumba-led Congolese government backed by the Soviet Union was perceived by the United States as a direct threat to its economic and strategic interests in the region. Washington's Congo policy was thus to contain Soviet influence.

In line with the American policy, the United States sought to remove Lumumba, who was perceived in the West as a staunch communist stooge of the Kremlin, and a likely Soviet instrument in promoting its interest in the Congo. Styled "another Castro" in Washington, Lumumba was eventually assassinated in mysterious circumstances in January 1961, an event that many observers believed was not unconnected to the United States Central Intelligence Agency's (CIA) covert operations in the Congo designed to eliminate the Soviet presence.[21]

Meanwhile, the United States backed another important player in the Congolese crisis, the pro-West army chief Colonel Joseph Mobutu. Through America's support, Mobutu (who later became known as Mobutu Sese Seko) later emerged as the post-Lumumba Congolese leader. With Mobutu in power, budding Soviet influence in Central

Africa disappeared. Uncompromisingly pro-West, Mobutu protected and promoted Western interests in the Congo, now renamed Zaire. Mobutu soon became noted for one of the worst human rights records and a level of corruption unprecedented in Africa. However, as a reliable Western ally and a trusted bulwark against Soviet penetration of Central Africa, his repressive regime continued to receive massive American military and financial aid.

Similar Cold War consideration also defined superpower roles in conflicts in Southern Africa. During the post-independence civil wars in Mozambique and Angola, both the United States and the Soviet Union supported warring groups in the conflicts. In Mozambique, the Soviet Union and a number of its satellite states in Eastern Europe provided military and financial support for its Marxist government under FRELIMO battling rebel forces. Superpower proxy war was more glaring in the Angolan Civil War. The Soviet Union and some of its allies, including Cuba, provided military and economic backing to the left-leaning MPLA, which had formed the post-independence government and declared Angola a Marxist state. The United States, on the other hand, provided similar support for the rebel groups fighting the government, the National Front for the Liberation of Angola (*Frente Nacional de Libertação de Angola*; FNLA) and National Union for the Total Independence of Angola (*União Nacional para a Independência Total de Angola*; UNITA). By pitching its camp behind FNLA and UNITA against the MPLA government, the United States policy was consistent with its desire not to see a Soviet-backed Marxist regime in the important region of Southern Africa.

In South Africa, despite America's anti-apartheid rhetoric, Washington's policy of eliminating a Soviet presence in Southern Africa prevented it from matching its rhetoric with action. Before the political liberalization in South Africa, which began in the late 1980s, the United States considered the ANC, the most prominent black anti-apartheid movement, as communist oriented. America thus covertly opposed the organization, fearful of the threat it could pose to its huge financial investment in South Africa if it succeeded in wresting power from the white minority regime. The United States' consistent refusal to support United Nations sanctions against the racist South African government was part of its strategy of opposition to the ANC.

Also, during the Cold War, African conflicts became the avenue through which foreign powers infused massive amounts of weapons and other military hardware into the continent. The period witnessed a dramatic increase in arms transfers from the United States and other Western powers to Africa. Indeed, the United States became the leading arms supplier to Africa, with clients including Zaire, Somalia, Chad,

Sudan, and Liberia. The Soviet Union and other Soviet-bloc states, in the same vain, also transferred substantial amount of arms to Africa, their major recipients including pro-communist client states such as Ethiopia, Angola, and Mozambique. A number of African states such as Somalia manipulated the Cold War competition between the super-powers by receiving aid from both.

The militarization of Africa went beyond arming contending parties in African conflicts. Aside from arms transfer, external powers have provided financial aid for the training of state armies or rebel militias. In other instances, covert direct military training programs have been accorded these armies. Foreign forces have often fought in African wars, as in the case of Angola during its civil war when the state utilized Cuban combat troops against the rebels. Also, the use of mer-cenaries in African conflicts, sponsored by foreign governments or in-dependent institutions, became prevalent during the Cold War. Mercenaries were featured in the Nigerian civil wars, on the Biafran side, on both sides of the war in Angola and Mozambique, and more recently in Liberia and Sierra Leone. A classic case of the infusion of foreign fighters into African conflicts was Katanga's extensive use of Belgian-recruited European mercenaries during the Congo Crisis of the early 1960s.

Cold War power play in Africa significantly impacted conflicts on the continent. External intervention intensified and helped to prolong some of the conflicts. For example, the Soviet-American role in Angola and Mozambique in arming the belligerents was partly responsible for the prolonged and destructive civil wars. Foreign intervention in African conflicts has also resulted in the destabilization of states and even entire regions.

Table 1.2 Post–Cold War U.S. Arms Transfers to Governments Involved in the Congo War, 1989–1998 (in constant 1998 dollars)

Country	Foreign Military Sales	Commercial Sales	Total
Angola	0	31,000	31,000
Burundi	74,000	312,000	386,000
Chad	21,767,000	24,677,000	46,444,000
DRC	15,151,000	218,000	15,369,000
Namibia	2,311,000	1,934,000	4,245,000
Rwanda	324,000	0	324,000
Sudan	30,258,000	1,815,000	32,073,000
Uganda	1,517,000	9,903,000	11,420,000
Zimbabwe	567,000	828,000	1,395,000
Total	71,969,000	39,718,000	111,687,000

Table 1.3 Post–Cold War International Military Education and Training (IMET) to Countries Involved in the Congo War, 1989–1998 (constant 1998 dollars)

Country	IMET $ Value	No. of Students
Angola	177,000	5
Burundi	1,324,000	53
Chad	1,968,000	115
Congo	1,229,000	50
Namibia	1,589,000	111
Rwanda	1,425,000	66
Sudan	154,000	0
Uganda	3,856,000	154
Zimbabwe	2,661,000	176
TOTAL	14,383,000	730

Source: Department of Defense, Foreign Military Sales, Foreign Military Construction Sales and Military Assistance Facts, *Foreign Military Sales, Construction, and Assistance Facts as of September 1998* (Washington, DC: U.S. Department of Defense, 1999).

The transfer of arms, especially small and light weapons, from the developed world to Africa did not cease with the end of the Cold War. Infusion of weapons has continued especially to hotspots on the continent, thereby significantly exacerbating African conflicts. This is most glaring in the Great Lakes region of Central Africa, an area of post–Cold War intense and devastating conflict. The United States has been a major player in arms sales to the countries involved in the Great Lakes crisis, often referred to as "Africa's World War." Apart from arming the parties in the conflict, the United States has also provided military training to some of them under the International Military Education and Training (IMET) program.

DICTATORSHIP, CORRUPTION, STATE FAILURE, AND CONFLICTS

Staunch superpower support for some of the most corrupt and repressive regimes in Africa was part of the Cold War dynamics in Africa. The best case in point was the United States' steady military and financial support for Mobutu's Zaire for nearly 30 years until the post–Cold War new power configuration removed the dictator's relevance to Western interests. Driven purely by ideological consideration rather than its cherished ideals of good and responsible governance, the

United States helped to sustain Mobutu's long, brutal, and excessively corrupt regime.

The Soviet Union pursued the same ideological game in Africa, supporting dictatorships as long as they were pro-communist. The Soviet support for the leftist regime of Mengistu Haile Mariam of Ethiopia, from the early 1970s to the late 1980s, is a case study. During the period, Mengistu, who was later convicted in absentia by an Ethiopian court of a campaign of genocide, led one of the most repressive dictatorships in Africa. As a Soviet client state, Mengistu's Ethiopia received generous arms flow, which sustained the dictator's brutal regime and its "Red Terror" campaign.

The phenomenon of failed states, prevalent in post–Cold War Africa, has multifaceted and complex causes. However, prolonged conflicts, exacerbated by external manipulations, bear direct relevance to this condition of state dysfunction. Nowhere is this more glaring than in Somalia. Indeed, the case of Somalia borders on State Collapse. It is an example of where Cold War–stimulated proliferation of light arms enhanced warlordism when the state collapsed as a viable political entity in 1991. Somalia has never regained viability, ranking number one in the failed states index for 2008.[22]

CONFLICT RESOLUTION

After the disastrous American intervention in Somalia in 1992, the West became wary of dabbling in intractable African conflicts. This was evident in the reluctance by the United States and other Western powers to intervene in the Rwandan genocide of 1994. However, Western reluctance to intervene in African conflicts has compelled Africans themselves to take responsibility for continental problems. Through existing institutions and conflict resolution mechanisms both at the continental and subregional levels, African states have endeavored to manage their own conflicts.

The imperative to seek African solutions to African conflicts led to a growing trend whereby African organizations not specifically established to take on conflict resolution duties increasingly assumed that responsibility. The Southern African Development Community (SADC) is an example. Originally created as an economic community, SADC, in 1994, "approved the formulation of a sector on politics, diplomacy, international relations, defense, and security" and began to move "toward a common security regime along the lines of the 52-member OSCE (formally the Conference on Security and Cooperation in Europe)."[23] The Intergovernmental Authority on Drought and

Development (IGADD) is another example of a nonmilitary subregional organization that has taken on conflict resolution responsibility. Although it was unsuccessful, the organization played a prominent role in mediating the Somali and the Sudanese conflicts.

The Economic Community of West African States (ECOWAS), the West African regional economic integration organization, is perhaps the best example of the increasing role of nonmilitary subregional organizations in conflict resolutions. When it was set up in 1975, ECOWAS was intended primarily to promote regional economic cooperation and integration.[24] However, since the beginning of the 1990s, the organization had increasingly taken on security matters to the neglect of issues related to economic integration and cooperation within the subregion.

African Initiatives

For much of the lifespan of the OAU before its transformation to the African Union (AU), the organization was not often successful at efforts to resolve African conflicts. Nevertheless, the organization realized the reality of the post–Cold War era in which African states were compelled, more than ever before, to find solutions to their own conflicts. Consequently, in the 1990s, OAU found itself more proactive in responding to crisis situations. It mediated in a number of conflicts and instituted small-scale missions in such places as Rwanda, Burundi, Comoros, DRC, and Ethiopia/Eritrea. Also, one of its most important initiatives was the establishment of the Mechanism for Conflict Prevention, Management, and Resolution in 1993 to enhance its capability to effectively address African conflicts.

As one of its most important priorities, the AU has continued to champion the task of conflict resolution and management in Africa. The organization is imbued with the important power of intervention in states' internal affairs "in respect of grave circumstances, namely: war crimes, genocide and crimes against humanity."[25] One of the major weaknesses of the OAU was its denial of the power to interfere in conflicts considered "internal affairs" of member states. Its principle of "noninterference" thus, on occasions such as the Nigerian Civil War, rendered the organization incapable of playing an active role in conflict resolution.[26]

The Peace and Security Council (PSC) of the AU is an important initiative at promoting peace and pacific resolution of conflicts. The organization has, indeed, been involved in a number of African conflicts principally through peacekeeping troops. Its peacekeeping forces had served in conflict areas such as Burundi, Sudan, and Somalia.

At the subregional level, ECOWAS' intervention in a number of crises in West Africa was an indication of African states' resolve to internally address continental conflicts. The organization began to take responsibility for subregional security in the 1990s with the sudden upsurge in conflicts in the region. It established the ECOWAS Monitoring Group (ECOMOG), a multilateral peacekeeping force that, in some instances, engaged in combat operations. ECOMOG was first deployed to Liberia in 1990 when it became apparent that no extra-African power was readily willing to take up the responsibility of dealing with the bloody war that had erupted in the country.[27] Since the ECOMOG intervention in Liberia's war, the peacekeeping force has played an important role in keeping the peace elsewhere in West Africa including Sierra Leone in 1997, Guinea-Bissau in 1998, Côte d'Ivoire in late 2002, Liberia (again) in August 2003, and Benin Republic in 2004. Despite drawbacks, ECOWAS' intervention in subregional conflicts was a demonstration of the willingness of Africans to take responsibility for solving continental conflicts.

Security Cooperation Initiatives

The role of external powers such as the United States and institutions such as the European Union (EU) and the Group of Eight Industrialized Nations (G8) in the resolution of African conflicts has primarily been limited to supporting the AU and other African initiatives. For instance, since Bill Clinton's presidency, the United States has preferred to respond to African conflicts through regional and subregional organizations. Thus, Washington began to collaborate actively with the OAU (and its successor, the AU), to "develop a credible capability to plan, coordinate, and supervise efforts in conflict resolution."[28] This collaborative strategy has entailed Washington's provision of financial and technical support to African security organizations to enhance their peacekeeping missions. American financial assistance has specifically been directed at assisting the security organizations in the provision of equipment, communication facilities, and in training for observer and peacekeeping missions.

Unwilling to assume the risk involved in a peacekeeping operation, the United States has continued its strategy of collaborating with Africa to enhance its own initiatives. After the Rwandan genocide, the Clinton administration's collaborative strategy put emphasis on improving early warning capability in Africa. Through this preventive diplomacy, the United States envisioned a continent capable of responding to warning signals of conflicts before escalating into a major conflagration.

During the Clinton era, a major component of United States collaborative engagement with Africa in order to prevent conflicts from escalating was the African Crisis Response Initiative (ACRI), initially called the African Crisis Response Force. The mission of this initiative was to help to create, out of African militaries, a peacekeeping force trained and equipped by the United States. Troops for this force were to be based in their home countries, but capable of rapid deployment to conflict areas. An idea that was first proposed in September 1996 at the wake of a possible outbreak of genocide in the Great Lakes region, ACRI was launched in October 1987 and was backed by a number of Western countries, principally Britain and France. The United States was consistent in emphasizing the African composition of the force and the essentially training character of America's participation. The operation of the force, command structure, and deployment were not intended to involve the United States military, but were considered the primary responsibility of the African states.[29]

To a large extent, ACRI was a project designed to relieve the United States of peacekeeping responsibility in Africa. Its hope of establishing a fully operational African force found immediate encouraging support from some African states. Seven states—Ethiopia, Ghana, Malawi, Mali, Senegal, Tunisia, and Uganda—signaled their intention to participate in the program. By mid-1997, in the first phase of the training program, troops from Senegal, Uganda, Malawi, and Ghana had undergone training with the Third Special Forces of the United States Army.[30] After this, Washington tried to enlist the support and participation of other African states. During his African trip, President Clinton canvassed for wider support for the program.

However, in general, many African governments remained rather cautious about ACRI. Regional powers such as Nigeria and South Africa, whose support was critical for the success of the project, opted not to participate. Nigeria was well experienced in regional and international peacekeeping, its troops having participated in a number of United Nations and African regional and subregional missions. Indeed, Nigeria was the backbone of ECOMOG. During the civil war in Liberia and Sierra Leone, it not only supplied the largest contingent of troops to the regional force, but also provided a great deal of its financial, material, and logistical support. In the same breath, South Africa was a dominant military power in the continent with capability that could well serve ACRI.

Nigeria's opposition to ACRI was on the grounds that Africa already had in the OAU and ECOWAS adequate peacekeeping mechanism.[31] Thus, its army high command was unreceptive to the initiative. Indeed, army chief Maj. Gen. Victor Malu reportedly described it as a "bit of an insult."[32] On his part, former President Nelson Mandela accused the United States of acting unilaterally.[33] But Pretoria's reluctance to be part of ACRI can be largely attributed to South Africa's limited experience in peacekeeping, and its unwillingness to burden its military with such operations.[34] Also, there was the question of lingering distrust of America's intentions given Washington's frosty relations with the ruling ANC during its struggle for black majority rule.

Post-Clinton Washington continued with cooperative engagement with Africa as a strategy for dealing with the continent's conflicts. The United States remained a major contributor to African peacekeeping initiatives through financial and logistical support as well as troop training programs. In October 2009, commenting on the United States' "investments in African peacekeeping," the American ambassador to the United Nations, Susan E. Rice, said Washington had "trained over 28 battalions from 15 African countries to prepare over 23,000 peacekeepers for deployment."[35]

Terrorism and New Engagements

The global war on terrorism that followed the terrorist attacks on the United States on September 11, 2001, introduced a new American engagement in Africa. Thereafter, Washington greatly expanded its security cooperation with Africa. This expanded initiative was part of America's global counterterrorism campaign. East Africa (discussed in Chapter 5), where states like Sudan and Somalia provided a breeding ground for radical Islamic and fundamentalist groups with links to al-Qaeda, was the center stage of the American counterterrorism campaign in Africa. Nevertheless, other parts of Africa have also featured in the American initiative.

In West Africa, the United States' counterterrorist project focused on shielding the states of the region from al-Qaeda's infiltration, thereby preventing the region from turning into a terrorist hot spot where attacks could be launched against Western and American interests. Links had already been suggested between al-Qaeda and Sierra Leone's brutal rebel movement, the Revolutionary United Front (RUF), accused of involvement in illegal diamond trade with the terrorist organization.[36] Indeed, in Western intelligence circles, Nigeria, regional power and Africa's most populous state and a major oil supplier to the United States, was believed to be vulnerable to terrorists' infiltration given the long history of Islamic militancy in its northern states. In the wake of the late July 2009 deadly attacks in the north by an Islamic sect led by Mohammed Yusuf, it was alleged that sect received financial support from an organization linked to al-Qaeda.[37]

Nigerian officials consistently denied any suggestion that al-Qaeda cells existed in their country. In any event, a botched terrorist attack by a Nigerian man, Umar Farouk Abdulmutallab, on a Northwest Airlines plane on December 25, 2009, brought the country under greater scrutiny for terrorism. In a flight from Amsterdam, the 23-year-old Abdulmutallab, wearing concealed explosives, had attempted to blow up the plane as it approached Detroit and possibly kill the almost 300 people on board. Initial investigations by United States officials suggested that the would-be suicide bomber had received terrorist training in Yemen, and that, indeed, he had been recruited there for this assignment by an al-Qaeda franchise. The United States swiftly responded by adding Nigeria to its list of states prone to terrorism. A new American policy consequently compelled passengers from Nigeria to stricter airport security scrutiny.

The Nigerian government protested against the American classification of Nigeria as "State Sponsors of Terrorism," alongside states like Sudan and Somalia. Nigeria's effort to deny any notion that it harbored al-Qaeda operatives was undercut by its incessant religious/ethnic violence. Indeed, a deadly three-day religiously motivated uprising occurred in its northern city of Jos, Plateau State, less than one month after Abdulmutallab's failed terrorist attack. The sectarian violence, a reenactment of similar mayhem in 2001 and 2008, began on January 20, 2010, and caused the death of over 300 people, the displacement of hundreds more, and the destruction of property. U.S. Secretary of State Hilary Clinton chided the Nigerian political class of fostering, by its corruption and neglect to deal with widespread poverty among the populace, the environment in which extremist elements flourish.[38]

As part of Washington's counterterrorism initiative in West and North Africa, the Pentagon embarked on counterterrorism training for the military forces of a number of the states in the regions and also equipped them to combat terrorist threats. Targeted for this training were Algeria, Chad, Mauritania, Mali, Morocco, Senegal, Niger, Nigeria, and Tunisia. However, this initiative also included a nonmilitary element in that it provided for job training for unemployed Muslim youths, often easy targets for recruitment into terrorist organizations.

The United States further expanded its security engagement with Africa as part of its counterterrorism campaign when on February 6, 2007, President George Bush announced his "decision to create a Department of Defense Unified Combatant Command for Africa," now popularly called Africa Command (AFRICOM). In this announcement, Bush defined this new initiative:

> This new command will strengthen our security cooperation with Africa and create new opportunities to bolster the capabilities of our partners in

Africa. Africa Command will enhance our efforts to bring peace and security to the people of Africa and promote our common goals of development, health, education, democracy, and economic growth in Africa.[39]

AFRICOM, established as a unit of the United States Department
of Defense (DOD), became operational in October 2008. Essentially, it
aimed at unifying and coordinating disparate American security programs in Africa.

The establishment of AFRICOM was widely criticized. In the United
States, fear was expressed that it would draw the country unnecessarily
into playing a leading role in African security. In Africa, there was the suspicion that it would result in the militarization of the continent as more
American military bases would be established. Nigeria, South Africa,
Libya, and many other African states roundly condemned the prospect of
new American bases on the continent.[40] AFRICOM was also criticized in
some quarters as an American endeavor to protect its oil and mineral
resource interests in Africa in the wake of growing Asian, particularly
Chinese, inroads into the continent.[41] However, American officials
insisted that AFRICOM was designed only to coordinate the already
existing American initiatives on the continent in such a way as to enhance
the capacity of African states and organizations to respond rapidly to continental security challenges and deal with them effectively.[42]

***

Violent, serious armed conflicts have certainly declined in number in
twenty-first-century Africa. This, of course, does not mean the elimina-
tion of such conflicts is evident in the DRC and Sudan. However, the
hot spots that dot every region of the continent generally manifest in
low-intensity conflicts. Kenya and Zimbabwe provide examples. The
end of the Cold War and the consequent unwillingness of foreign
powers to get involved in African conflicts have given African states
more leeway in the management of their own conflicts. Conflicts of
greater proportions and intensities like the Sudan genocidal war in Darfur
have, however, continued to be an issue for international response.

Predictably, incessant and devastating armed conflicts have had adverse
negative effects on all facets of life in Africa: political stability, economic
development, security, and living standard of the civil population.

Notes

1. See "Fifteen years of conflicts have cost Africa around $300bn," Oxfam
Press Release, October 11, 2007, http://www.oxfam.org/en/news/2007/
pr071011_control_arms_cost_conflict_africa.

2. For more on the *Mfecane*, see the following: David M. Westley, *The Mfecane: An Annotated Bibliography* (Madison: African Studies Program, University of Wisconsin-Madison, 1999); Warren R. Perry, *Landscape Transformations and the Archaeology of Impact: Social Disruption and State Formation in Southern Africa* (New York: Kluwer Academic/Plenum, 1999); Carolyn Hamilton, (ed.), *The Mfecane Aftermath: Reconstructive Debates in Southern African History* (Pietermaritzburg: University of Natal Press, 1995); and Said Kakese Dibinga, *Mfecane: Scattering of the People* (Boston: Omenana, 1995).

3. John K. Thornton, *Warfare in Atlantic Africa 1500–1800* (New York: Routledge, 1999), 27.

4. For more on the Amazons, see Robert B. Edgerton, *Warrior Women: The Amazons of Dahomey and the Nature of War* (Boulder, CO: Westview Press, 2000).

5. There are several works on African resistance to partition. For general works, see for instance, Michael Crowder (ed.), *West African Resistance: The Military Response to Colonial Occupation* (London: Hutchinson, 1978); and Gregory Maddox (ed.), *Conquest and Resistance to Colonialism in Africa* (New York: Garland, 1993). On the Ekumeku, see Don C. Ohadike, *The Ekumeku Movement: Western Igbo Resistance to the British Conquest of Nigeria, 1883–1914* (Athens: Ohio University Press, 1991).

6. See Gilbert Clement Kamana Gwassa, *The Outbreak and Development of the Maji Maji War, 1905–1907* (Köln: R. Köppe, 2005), and O. B. Mapunda and G. P. Mpangara, *The Maji Maji War in Ungoni* (Nairobi: East African Pub. House, 1969).

7. For more on this, see Gloria Chuku, *Igbo Women and Economic Transformation in Southeastern Nigeria, 1900–1960* (New York: Routledge, 2005), and Adiele E. Afigbo, *The Warrant Chiefs: Indirect Rule in Southeastern Nigeria, 1891–1929* (London: Longman, 1972).

8. Important works on decolonization include Toyin Falola, *Africa: The End of Colonial Rule: Nationalism and Decolonization, Volume 4* (Durham, NC: Carolina Academic Press, 2002); Ali Mazrui, *UNESCO General History of Africa, VIII: Africa Since 1935* (Paris: UNESCO, 1999); Prosser Gifford and Wm. Roger Louis (eds.), *The Transfer of Power in Africa: Decolonization, 1940–1960* (New Haven, CT: Yale University Press, 1982); W. H. Morris-Jones and Georges Fischer (eds.), *Decolonization and After: The British and French Experience* (London: F. Cass, 1980); A. H. M. Kirk-Greene (ed.), *The Transfer of Power: The Colonial Administrator in the Age of* Decolonisation (1979); J. D. Hargreaves, *The End of Colonial Rule in West Africa* (Oxford: University of Oxford Press, 1979).

9. See F. D. Corfield, *Historical Survey of the Origins and Growth of Mau Mau* (London: Her Majesty's Stationery Office, 1960), 316. Generally an overview of the Mau Mau uprising, see Wunyabari O. Maloba, *Mau Mau and Kenya: An Analysis of a Peasant Revolt* (Bloomington: Indiana University Press, 1993).

10. Americo Boavida, *Angola: Five Centuries of Portuguese Exploitation* (Richmond, VA: LSM Information Center, 1972), 31.

11. The literature on the Berlin Conference is extensive. See the following, for instance, Muriel E. Chamberlain, *The Scramble for Africa* (London: Longman, 1999); Sybil E. Crowe, *The Berlin West African Conference, 1884–1885* (New York: Longman, 1942); Stig Förster, Wolfgang J. Mommsen, and Ronald Edward Robinson, *Bismarck, Europe, and Africa: The Berlin Africa Conference 1884–1885 and the Onset of Partition* (Oxford, UK: Oxford University Press, 1989).

12. See Obafemi Awolowo, *Path to Nigerian Freedom* (London: Faber and Faber, 1947), 48.

13. OAU Charter, Article (3) 2, Addis Ababa, May 1963.

14. General Resolution on Border Disputes adopted by the Conference of Heads of States, Cairo, July 1964.

15. Ibid.

16. OAU Charter, Article 3 (3).

17. Good discussions of the causes of the war are provided in John de St. Jorre, *The Nigerian Civil War* (London: Hodder Stoughton, 1972); and A. H. M. Kirk-Greene, *Crisis and Conflict: A Documentary Sourcebook, Vols. I & II* (London: Oxford University Press, 1971). The literature on the war is quite extensive. See the following, for example, Emmanuel Okocha, *Blood on the Niger: The Untold Story of the Nigerian Civil War* (Port Harcourt, Nigeria: Sunray Publishers, 1994); Herbert Ekwe-Ekwe, *The Biafra War: Nigeria and the Aftermath* (Lewiston, NY: Edwin Mellen Press, 1990); Olusegun Obasanjo, *My Command: An Account of the Nigerian Civil War, 1967–1970* (Ibadan, Nigeria: Heinemann, 1980); John J. Stremlau, *The International Politics of the Nigerian Civil War, 1967–1970* (Princeton, NJ: Princeton University Press, 1977); and Zdenek Cervenka, *The Nigerian War, 1967–1970* (Ibadan, Nigeria: Onibonoje Press, 1972).

18. For a critical discourse on this subject, see Adebayo Oyebade, "The Role of the Organization of African Unity in the Civil War," in Toyin Falola (ed.), *Nigeria in the Twentieth Century* (Durham, NC: Carolina Academic Press, 2002), 413–424.

19. For details on the alleged secession attempt, see "Secession du Katanga, Premier Mai 2005," *Action Contre l'Impunité pour les Droits Humans*, May 2005, cited in "The Congo's Forgotten Crisis," *Africa Report*, Vol. 103 (January 9, 2006), at: http://www.grandslacs.net/doc/3987.pdf.

20. For the roles of the superpowers in Africa during the Cold War, see the following: Edmond J. Keller and Donald Rothschild (eds.), *Africa in the New International Order* (Boulder, CO: Lynne Rienner, 1996); George W. Breslauer (ed.), *Soviet Policy in Africa* (Berkeley: University of California Press, 1992); Thomas J. Noer, *Cold War and Black Liberation: The United States and White Rule in Africa, 1948–1968* (Columbia: University of Missouri Press, 1985); Craig R. Nation and Mark V. Kauppi, *The Soviet Impact in Africa* (Lexington, MA: Lexington Books, 1984); Bruce E. Arlinghaus (ed.), *Arms for Africa: Military Assistance and Foreign Policy in the Developing World* (Lexington, MA: Lexington Books, 1983); and Henry F. Jackson, *From the Congo to Soweto: U.S. Foreign Policy toward Africa since 1960* (New York: Morrow, 1982).

21. CIA's declassified papers released in 2007 implicated the organization in the plot to assassinate Lumumba.

22. See "The Failed States Index, 2008: The Ranking," http://www.foreign policy.com/story/cms.php?story_id=4350&page=1.

23. See Peter da Costa, "Keeping the Peace," *Africa Report*, Vol. 40, No. 3 (May–June 1995: 28). Quoted in Richard S. Mukisa, "Toward a Peaceful Resolution of Africa's Colonial Boundaries," *Africa Today*, Vol. 44, No. 1 (January–March 1997: 12).

24. ECOWAS Treaty, Article 2 (1).

25. The African Union, Consultative Act, http://www.africa-union.org/organs/pan%20african%20parliament/AbConstitutive_Act.htm#Article1.

26. For an analysis of the OAU principle of noninterference in regard to the Nigerian Civil War, see Adebayo Oyebade, "The Role of the Organization of African Unity in the Civil War," in Toyin Falola (ed.), *Nigeria in the Twentieth Century* (Durham, NC: Carolina Academic Press, 2002), 413–424.

27. For ECOWAS' role in the Liberian war, see Margaret A. Vogt (ed.), *The Liberian Crisis and ECOMOG: A Bold Attempt at Regional Peace Keeping* (Lagos, Nigeria: Gabumo Publishing Co. Ltd., 1992), and Karl P. Magyar and Earl Conteh-Morgan, *Peacekeeping in Africa: ECOMOG in Liberia* (New York: St. Martin's Press, 1998).

28. George E. Moose, "U.S. Commitment to Conflict Resolution in Africa," *U.S. Department of State Dispatch*, Vol. 5, No. 25 (1994: 412).

29. See Marshall F. McCallie, "The African Crisis Response Initiative: America's Engagement for Peace in Africa," *Special Warfare*, Vol. 11, No. 3 (Summer, 1998: 6).

30. For a brief discussion of the training in these countries, see Mark T. Alexander, "Getting the Word out: The Role of PSYOP in the ACRI," *Special Warfare*, Vol. 1, No. 3 (Summer 1998: 18–21). See also, "U.S. Troops Teach Peacekeeping to Africans," *Washington Post* (September 26, 1997) and "Joint U.S.-African Peacekeeping Training Kicks off in Mali," United States Information Service (USIS), Washington File, February 26, 1998.

31. See "Nigeria Opposes U.S. Crisis Response Initiative," *Nigeria.Com News*, at http://london.nigeria. See also, "Lagos Not Impressed by U.S. Proposal for an African Force," *Panafrican News Agency*, October 16, 1996.

32. See "Nigerian Army Balks at U.S. Training," *Philadelphia Inquirer* (November 15, 2000).

33. *Washington Post* (September 26, 1997: A16).

34. Rocky Williams, "Brothers' Keepers," How African Countries Can Pull Together an African Crisis Reaction Force, *Track Two* (April 1997: 27).

35. U.S. Mission to the United Nations, "Remarks by Ambassador Susan E. Rice, U.S. Permanent Representative to the United Nations, on Support for African Union Peacekeeping, in the Security Council Chamber," New York, NY, October 26, 2009, retrieved on November 16, 2009, from: http://www.usun.state.gov/briefing/statements/2009/130928.htm.

36. See for instance, Douglas Farah, "Al Qaeda Cash Tied to Diamond Trade," *Washington Post* (November 2, 2001), retrieved on November 12, 2009, from: http://www.washingtonpost.com/ac2/wp-dyn/A27281-2001Nov1.

37. Andrew Walker, "Is al-Qaeda Working in Nigeria?" *BBC Online* (August 4., 2009), retrieved on November 12, 2009, from: http://news.bbc. co.uk/2/hi/africa/8182289.stm.

38. "Hillary Clinton Blames Nigeria Leaders for Extremism," *BBC News Online* (January 27, 2010), retrieved on January 27, 2010, from: http://news. bbc.co.uk/2/hi/africa/8482420.stm.

39. Office of the Press Secretary, the White House, "President Bush Creates a Department of Defense Unified Combatant Command for Africa," February 6, 2007, retrieved on November 19, 20, 2009, from: http://georgewbush-whitehouse. archives.gov/news/releases/2007/02/20070206-3.html.

40. See "Nigerian Doubts over Africom Base," *BBC News Online* (November 20, 2007), retrieved on November 20, 2009, from: http://news.bbc.co.uk/2/hi/africa/7104215.stm.

41. Ibid.

42. See, for instance, U.S. AFRICOM Public Affairs Office, "FACT SHEET: United States Africa Command," October 18, 2008, retrieved on November 20, 2009, from: http://www.africom.mil/getArticle.asp?art=1644. For further readings on AFRICOM, see David J. Francis (ed.), *US Strategy in Africa: AFRICOM, Terrorism, and Security Challenges* (New York: Routledge, 2010); Russell L. Barkely (ed.), *AFRICOM: Security, Development, and Humanitarian Functions* (New York: Nova Science Publishers, 2009); Olayiwola Abegunrin, *Africa in Global Politics in the Twenty-First Century: A Pan African Perspective* (New York: Palgrave Macmillan, 2009); Philip Seib (ed.), *Africom: The American Military and Public Diplomacy in Africa* (Los Angeles: Figueroa Press, 2008); and Robert G. Berschinski, *AFRICOM's Dilemma: The "Global War on Terrorism," "Capacity Building," Humanitarianism, and the Future of U.S. Security Policy in Africa* (Carlisle, PA: Strategic Studies Institute, U.S. Army War College, 2007).

CHAPTER 2

West Africa: The Mano River Basin Conflicts

The past dozen years of warfare in West Africa have led to the death, injury, and mutilation of hundreds of thousands of people and the displacement of millions more.

USIP Special Report[1]

There are some of us who can't seem to live without a weapon— anywhere we hear about fighting, we have to go. It's because of the way we grew up—and now it's in our blood. A warrior can't sit down when war is on.

Mohammed, 24-year-old Liberian who fought in Liberia, Sierra Leone, Guinea, and Côte d'Ivoire[2]

If you see a next-door neighbour's house on fire, you must act speedily to help put it out, because you do not know when the resulting conflagration may spread to your home.

President Gnassingbé Eyadéma of Togo[3]

The subregion of West Africa is made up of 16 countries over a land area of about 2.37 million square miles (6.14 million square kilometers).[4] Reflecting the legacy of European colonial rule, Benin, Burkina Faso, Côte d'Ivoire, Guinea, Mali, Mauritania, Niger, Senegal, and Togo are Francophone; Gambia, Ghana, Liberia (never colonized), Nigeria, and Sierra Leone are Anglophone; and Cape Verde and Guinea-Bissau are Lusophone. The Economic Community of West African States (ECOWAS), a regional body to which these countries

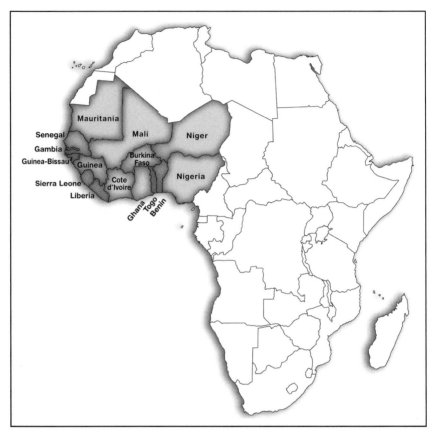

Political Map of West Africa. (Courtesy of Sam Saverance.)

belong, except Mauritania, has been an attempt at economic integration and regional security.

Ghana, called the Gold Coast during the colonial era, became in 1957 the first state in West Africa to be independent. In 1960, the rest of the countries in the region obtained independence, except the Portuguese territories, Guinea-Bissau and Cape Verde, whose independence did not come until 1974 and 1975, respectively, only after wars of national liberation. Apart from Nigeria, which went through a bloody civil war from 1967 to 1970, most of West Africa managed to avoid violent conflicts in the immediate post-independence years. A number of states such as Senegal, Côte d'Ivoire, and Guinea experienced relative peace and political stability. However, in the last 20 years, West Africa has emerged a crisis-ridden region and thus a major hot spot in Africa. Some of the continent's most brutal conflicts have occurred in the region. The civil wars in Nigeria, Liberia, Sierra Leone, Guinea, Guinea-Bissau, and Côte d'Ivoire are some of the most devastating on the continent. In some instances, internal conflicts such as the Liberian and Sierra Leonean wars became a major destabilizing force and threat to the security of the entire region.

Conflicts that have occurred in West Africa are of varying proportions, from low-level intercommunal clashes to complex, protracted, and devastating civil and cross-border wars. As in the rest of the continent, conflicts in West Africa are multifaceted and the product of many causes. There is the historical legacy of the European arbitrarily drawn borders and colonial rule. As colonial creations, modern West African states are characterized by the existence of disparate groups within a single polity. The result is incessant ethno-religious antagonism that has, in many of the states, given rise to sectional conflicts.

Conflicts have also emanated from post-colonial political and economic realities. The prevalence of bad governance virtually throughout West Africa as demonstrated in political corruption, graft, oppressive rule, and economic mismanagement, has created conditions for internal turmoil. Political instability is compounded by the failure of many states to achieve economic development and provide a meaningful level of livelihood for their people. The correlation between economic underdevelopment and civil strife has often been underscored.[5] In the West African context, the major hot spots where conflicts have been violent and prolonged are also some of the poorest nations in the world. Recent Human Development Indices (HDI) ranks 12 of the 16 countries in West Africa in Low Human Development (LHD).[6] Thus, economic underdevelopment in West African states has made them particularly prone to conflict. Where conflict was vicious and prolonged, as in Liberia and Sierra Leone, for example, it contributed significantly to further economic decline. The inability of the state to meet the social and economic costs of war provided fuel for further strife. Collapsed infrastructure and massive decline in standards of living as a result of ailing economy often caused civil tension and strife and, ultimately, violent conflicts.

This chapter examines the hot spots of West Africa during the post-independence period. The focus is on the major conflicts that have defined the region as a volatile one. The chapter, however, excludes Nigeria, a subject fully explored in Chapter 3. However, as a major power in the subregion, Nigeria's role in conflict resolution in the region, especially within the framework of ECOWAS, is discussed.

THE MANO RIVER BASIN

At the beginning of the last decade of the twentieth century, the Mano River Basin, a region consisting of mainly the three countries of Guinea, Liberia, and Sierra Leone emerged as the most crisis-ridden spot in West Africa. Hostilities began in the region in 1989 when a guerrilla invasion of Liberia from neighboring Côte d'Ivoire by a hitherto unknown Liberian rebel organization sparked a civil war in the country. The Liberian war was to significantly have adverse repercussions on the Mano River Basin, and indeed, the entire West Africa.

Protracted Civil War in Liberia

The Liberian state was founded in 1822 under the auspices of the American Colonization Society (ACS) as a colony for free American blacks who chose to immigrate to Africa under the conviction that free life in racist America was unattainable. After initial existence as a commonwealth under the ACS, Liberia declared independence on July 26, 1847, making it the first sovereign state in West Africa.[7] Although the United States did not immediately recognize its independence, by the early twentieth century Liberia had become virtually America's informal colony. Liberia's rubber economy was practically, wholly controlled by the United States. During World War II, Liberia played an important strategic role in America's war effort in Africa.

Prior to 1980, Liberia demonstrated a long history of relative political stability. It was an example of a stable state very much lacking in the political dictionary of Africa. However, underneath this façade of political stability was the inherent contradiction in its political and socioeconomic constitution. For about 200 years, the Americo-Liberians, descendants of the émigrés from America, held exclusive economic and political power to the detriment of the indigenous groups. The Americo-Liberian dominance, however, was terminated on April 12, 1980, when a bloody coup d'état led by MSgt. Samuel Kayon Doe of the Krahn ethnic group toppled the ruling True Whig Party. The widespread support for the coup was an indication of the discontentment of the people toward Americo-Liberian rule.

Doe's rule, first as a military head of state and subsequently as civilian president after winning a flawed election in October 1985, however, contributed to the descent of Liberia into abyss. The president not only led an authoritarian and repressive regime that was intolerant of dissent, he also played the ethnic card by favoring his own Krahn group over others. After an attempted coup against him in 1985, Doe directed his repressive energy against the Gio and the Mano in Nimba County, the region from which the coup leader, Thomas Quiwonkpa, came. Doe's political woes were further compounded by the increasingly crumbling Liberian economy, accentuating civil discontent. It was this adverse political and economic condition in Liberia that provided the environment for the devastating war that would engulf the country for 14 years.[8]

The Liberian war began the trend of regionalized conflicts that plagued West Africa from the later part of the twentieth century. The genesis of the war could be traced to the December 1989 invasion of the country from Côte d'Ivoire by a rebel insurgent group, the National Patriotic Front of Liberia (NPFL) led by a former Doe ally, Charles McArthur Ghankay Taylor. The primary objective of this invasion was to overthrow the Doe regime, which had become rather unpopular as a result of its authoritarianism and the worsening economic problems the nation faced.

In the quest to topple Doe's government, the NPFL insurgency rapidly intensified and degenerated into a full-scale civil war. By mid-1999, Taylor was in control of three-quarters of the Liberian territory. The war became more complicated with proliferation of armed rebel factions. By the time the war finally ended in 2003, about a dozen warring factions had become involved in it. These included:

1. Armed Forces of Liberia (AFL)
2. Government of Liberia Forces (GOL)
3. Independent National Patriotic Front of Liberia (INPFL)
4. Liberia Peace Council (LPC)
5. Liberians United for Reconciliation and Democracy (LURD)
6. Lofa Defense Force (LDF)
7. National Patriotic Front of Liberia (NPFL)
8. Movement for Democracy in Liberia (MODEL)
9. National Patriotic Front of Liberia-Central Revolutionary Council (NPFL-CRC)
10. United Liberation Movement of Liberia for Democracy (ULIMO)
11. United Liberation Movement of Liberia for Democracy-Johnson Faction (ULIMO-J)
12. United Liberation Movement of Liberia for Democracy-Kromah Faction (ULIMO-K)[9]

The proliferation of rebel factions partly emanated from internal wrangling within some of the groups. For example, the INPFL led by Prince Yomie Johnson was a splinter group of the NPFL; ULIMO-J and ULIMO-K, led by Roosevelt Johnson and Alhaji G. V. Kromah, respectively, were breakaway factions of ULIMO; and MODEL was a faction that broke away from LURD. In most cases, the factions were divided along ethnic lines, making the war also a fratricidal ethnic conflict. Taylor's NPFL had its stronghold among the Gio/Mano; ULIMO-J had the support of the Krahn, while ULIMO-K was based among the Mandingo.

The war occurred in two phases. The first phase, often called the "First Liberian Civil War," began with Taylor's insurgency in December 1989. In August 1990, the regional organization, ECOWAS, intervened in the conflict to bring a peaceful resolution to it and restore normalcy to the country. The organization deployed its military force, the ECOWAS Monitoring Group (ECOMOG), to Monrovia to help achieve a cease-fire necessary for the establishment of a broad-based interim government as a precursor for elections expected to restore democratic rule. ECOWAS initiated peace talks involving some of the rebel factions and eventually produced a cease-fire that paved the way for the formation of the Interim Government of National Unity (IGNU) in November 1990. However, violence continued under the new government, and it was never able to exercise control over the rest of the country beyond Monrovia. Amidst the violence, elections originally slated for 1994 could not be held until July 1997, after a peace agreement had been brokered the previous year. Taylor's National Patriotic Party (NPP) won the election, turning the former rebel leader and warlord into president.

The election of a democratically elected government brought about a lull in the devastating Liberian war. Violence was reduced considerably, and relative peace returned to the country. However, Taylor failed to bring about national reconciliation necessary for sustaining peace. Authoritarian, corrupt, and facing a deteriorating economy and hardly in control of the whole country, the government proved unable to bring a permanent end to the civil war.

The unstable peace buckled and collapsed in 1999 when a new rebel group, the Liberians United for Reconciliation and Democracy (LURD), began an insurgence in Lofa County in the northern part of the country. What is usually dubbed the "Second Liberian War," had thus begun. LURD's aim was ostensibly to bring about a stable democracy in Liberia by overthrowing President Taylor's government. In early 2003, another rebel group operating in the south of the country, the Movement for Democracy in Liberia (MODEL), joined the armed insurrection against the government, further complicating the civil war and raising its level of violence and brutality. In June, a rebel assault on Monrovia led to serious disorder and killings in the city. The siege on Monrovia prompted the United States to send a limited force to secure its embassy, and also to help evacuate foreign nationals trapped in the fighting. ECOWAS also sent a peacekeeping force to Monrovia to buoy security. Meanwhile, the international community, championed by the American president, George Bush, pressed for Taylor's resignation, convinced he posed a stumbling block to peace. After initially resisting the demand to step down, Taylor eventually resigned on August 11, 2003, and went into exile in Nigeria. His departure from Liberia undoubtedly played an important part in bringing an end to the war that had for almost 15 years torn the country apart.

The Liberian Civil War was one of the most violent conflicts in modern Africa. Its brutality is evident in that hundreds of thousands of people were injured; a quarter-of-a-million people, mostly innocent civilians, were killed, about 150,000 of them within the first seven years of the conflict.[10] The war also created a massive refugee crisis, not only for Liberia, but also for other Mano River Union (MRU) states. The country was inundated by an unprecedented number of internally displaced persons (IDPs), estimated in 2003 to be about half a million.[11] Many Liberians were forced to flee to refugee camps in neighboring countries, including Côte d'Ivoire, Guinea, Sierra Leone, and Ghana, orchestrating a refugee predicament for those countries. The post-war mass migration and resettlement of nearly one million returning refugees from neighboring countries also became a major challenge for the Liberian government.

The war touched practically every region of Liberia, traumatizing its entire population of about 3.1 million people. Apart from the enormous death toll, the war devastated the countryside and disrupted rural life and livelihoods. Urban areas saw a good dose of destruction of physical infrastructure and social institutions such as education and health care. In search of relative safety, large-scale refugee movement to Monrovia stretched thin facilities in the city. Access to basic human needs such as shelter, food, and good drinking water became severely limited, leaving large numbers of people in abject squalor and intense human suffering. In an economy that was almost crippled, unemployment spiraled, crime rates rose dramatically, and general rampant lawlessness made life and property insecure. Given the prolonged war and the inability of the government to protect life and property, by 1999, many observers had concluded that Liberia was a collapsed state.[12]

FROM LIBERIA TO SIERRA LEONE

The Liberian war assumed a cross-border character right from inception. The NPFL insurgency did not originate inside Liberia; it took root in neighboring Côte d'Ivoire where Taylor had organized and trained anti-Doe Liberian exiles. The insurgent movement that emerged out of this was somewhat multinational in character. Although it primarily comprised Liberian nationals, elements from Sierra Leone, Gambia, Guinea, and Burkina Faso were also a part of it, and Côte d'Ivoire was its launching base.[13]

Few observers could have predicted that the insurgency that began in late 1989, ostensibly to overthrow the Liberian government, would be the genesis of a long, vicious civil war that would last 14 years and nearly destroy the country. Fewer still could have predicted that the war would have serious repercussions beyond Liberia's borders. The war soon spilled over to neighboring Sierra Leone, and became linked with conflicts in Côte d'Ivoire and Guinea. The Liberian war was thus instrumental to the regionalization of conflict in the Mano River Basin. The regional conflict assumed such a proportion that it threatened to destabilize the entire subregion of West Africa.

The highly destructive and bloody civil war in Sierra Leone began in 1991 when a rebel movement, the Revolutionary United Front (RUF), invaded the country from Liberia, aided by Charles Taylor. The RUF was led by Foday Sankoh, an ex-army corporal who emerged to become one of the most brutal warlords in West Africa's hot spots. It was an insurgency with a disguised political and economic agenda—to acquire power for selfish end, and as means to control Sierra Leone's mineral wealth. Largely constituted by riffraff, the RUF had no progressive ideological bearing. Initially, by its propaganda, it purported to be fighting to save the people of Sierra Leone from the shackles of successive oppressive and corrupt governments. However, this altruistic objective proved to be a facade. Its open penchant for the worst kind of violence against the very people whose interest it purported to be fighting for was a contradiction of its rhetoric of giving back "power to the people." For seven years, the RUF engaged successive governments of Sierra Leone in a most vicious war.[14]

The outbreak of civil war in Sierra Leone was a culmination of fundamental contradictions in the post-colonial history of the country. Sierra Leone achieved independence in April 1961, with great potential to become a stable democratic state. However, the country soon entered a long era of dictatorship, beginning with the administration of its founding leader, President Siaka Stevens. An authoritarian state emerged under him just as an underdeveloped economy was gradually taking shape. Successive governments in the post-Stevens era remained corrupt and oppressive, and the ruling elite was indifferent to the plight of the civil population as the economy steadily declined. It was out of this atmosphere of failed governance, political instability, a virtually collapsed economy, and the decline of the army as a disciplined force that the RUF emerged.[15] On the eve of the insurgency, the Sierra Leonean society was characterized by high unemployment, a drastic fallen living standard, crumbled public infrastructure, and almost non-existent medical facilities.

The RUF insurgency quickly escalated into a major war, which the Sierra Leone Army (SLA) proved ill equipped to counter. The failure of the army to decisively contain the rebels could be partly attributed to its decline as an effective fighting force. The army, indeed, suffered from a number of ailments. It was inadequately armed and poorly paid, which explained its low morale. When the war began, its rank and file had swelled by recruitment of all sorts of undesirable elements: hooligans, thieves, thugs, riffraff, and the like. Little wonder, then, that it became a force plagued by corruption, division, and gross indiscipline. Its corruption was glaringly displayed in the *Sobel* phenomenon. *Sobels*, in the words of Alfred Zack-Williams, were "renegade elements of the national army who would loot private property and work the diamond fields in addition to military activities."[16] Lansana Gberie describes them as "soldiers by day and rebels by night."[17] Underpaid and generally lacking good welfare, regular soldiers were often pushed to collude with rebels to loot as a way of augmenting their meager salaries.

An important dimension was introduced into the conflict when the Kamajors, a civil defense force (CDF), entered the combat scene in 1993. Although members of this paramilitary force have often been seen as traditional hunters, it was essentially made up of youths from Sierra Leone's largest ethnic group, the Mende of the southern and eastern parts of the country, areas that particularly bore the brunt of rebel atrocity.[18]

The Kamajors' entry into the war to fight alongside the SLA in defense of their communities, particularly in the southeast, was precipitated by the latter's apparent inability to defeat the RUF. Indeed, many elements of the SLA were already cooperating with the rebels as they continued their brutal and terror campaigns against defenseless civilians. The RUF attacks on the people, particularly in the countryside, were devastating, marked by looting of households; raping of young girls and women; indiscriminate amputation of people's limbs, especially those they perceived as opposed to them; and kidnapping and induction of children into its ranks. The entrance of the Kamajors into the war soon began to change the balance of the military equation of the conflict. By the mid-1990s, the Kamajors, although once described as "a ragtag militia of men and boys who often wear mirrors on their chests in the belief that this will ward off bullets,"[19] had constituted itself as a formidable challenge to the RUF, posing a significant military threat to it. In the mid-1990s, the paramilitary force had grown stronger, having undergone large-scale recruitment and more structured training. In response to the Kamajors' effective challenge to the alleged RUF superiority, the rebels stepped up their horrendous and crude practice of hacking off people's limbs.[20]

The civil war entered a new phase in 1997 when dissident elements of the SLA overthrew the one-year-old civilian government of President Ahmad Tejan Kabbah. The new military elite, the Armed Forces Ruling Council (AFRC) led by Maj. Johnny Paul Koroma, quickly allied with the RUF. Koroma appointed some of the rebel commanders as members of the council including its leader, Foday Sankoh, who was named vice chairman. The AFRC/RUF rule, lasting about one year, was characterized by political and economic ineptitude. More than failure at governance, the regime was a disaster in safeguarding national security. The period witnessed government soldiers and their rebel allies committing atrocities with reckless abandon. Indiscriminate killings, rape, torture, and looting continued. However, the AFRC/RUF usurpation of power ended in February 1989 when Nigerian and other support forces launched an offensive on Freetown, the capital, and routed the regime from power.[21]

The expulsion of the Koroma junta and his RUF allies from power did not end the bloody conflict. Beginning in December 1998, in military campaigns code-named "Operation No Living Thing," the rebels and renegade elements of the SLA who had defected to the RUF[22] launched very bloody attacks on towns and villages before entering their prized target, Freetown. The attacks led to the capture and devastation of important cities like Koidu in the diamond-rich Kono District, Makeni, Waterloo, and Benguema. Hundreds of innocent civilians, as well as recognized opponents of the rebels like Nigerian ECOMOG soldiers, were murdered in the rebel rampage. However, the worst terror and the most horrific atrocities of the whole war experience were reserved for Freetown. In a two-week occupation of the city in January 1999, following its capture from the remnants of the SLA and ECOMOG troops defending it, the rebels unleashed a macabre orgy of violence on its inhabitants. They murdered indiscriminately, burned down homes and entire neighborhoods, committed sexual violence against girls and women, and abducted hundreds of children and women. During these attacks, the RUF took the practice of amputation, which had become its diabolic trademark, to an unprecedented height. Victims had noses, ears, lips, arms, hands, and legs gruesomely cut off. A Human Rights Watch report provides a vivid picture of the Freetown onslaught. Excerpts from the report read:

> The battle for Freetown and the ensuing three week rebel occupation of the capital was characterized by the systematic and widespread

perpetration of all classes of atrocities against the civilian population, of over one million inhabitants, and marked the most intensive and concentrated period of human rights violations in Sierra Leone's eight-year civil war.

As the rebels took control of street after street, they turned their weapons on the civilian population. By the end of January, both government and independent sources estimated that several thousands of civilians had been killed. The rebels dragged entire family units out of their homes and murdered them, hacked off the hands of children and adults, burned people alive in their houses, and rounded up hundreds of young women, took them to urban rebel bases, and sexually abused them. As the ECOMOG forces counterattacked and the RUF retreated through the capital, the rebels set fire to neighborhoods, leaving entire city blocks in ashes and over 51,000 people homeless . . .

Upon gaining control of a neighborhood or suburb, the rebels went on systematic looting raids in which families were hit by wave after wave of rebels demanding money and valuables. Those who didn't have what the rebels demanded were frequently murdered. Civilians were also executed for resisting rape or abduction, trying to flee, trying to protect a friend or family member, or for refusing to follow instructions.

The largest number of killings took place within the context of attacks on civilians gathered in houses, compounds, and places of refuge such as churches and mosques. A study carried out in Freetown's biggest hospital found that some 80 percent of all war-wounded were survivors of mass killings and massacres . . .

There were also frequent accounts of people being burned alive in their houses, often after having been wounded. Children and the elderly were particularly vulnerable. Witnesses described rebels throwing civilians, sometimes children, into burning houses and shooting at those trying to escape. Family members trying to rescue their children or other relatives from a burning house were threatened with death and forced to abandon them to the fire.

The rebels carried out large numbers of mutilations, in particular, amputation of hands, arms, legs, and other parts of the body—a horrific practice developed during offensives in the rural parts of Sierra Leone . . .

Throughout the occupation, the rebels perpetrated organized and widespread sexual violence against girls and women. The rebels launched operations in which they rounded up girls and women, brought them to rebel command centers, and then subjected them to individual and gang-rape. The sexual abuse was frequently characterized by extreme brutality. Young girls under seventeen, and particularly virgins, were specifically targeted, and hundreds of them were later abducted by the rebels.[23]

The RUF undoubtedly represented the worst in the bands of armed rebels in West African conflicts. For eight years, the rebels turned

Sierra Leone into a living hell for the mass of its people. It initially pillaged rural provinces, but as Freetown showed in January 1999, its horrendous atrocities became urbanized. Conservative estimates put the number of war casualties at 50,000, the displaced at over one million,[24] many of whom fled to neighboring states especially Guinea.

CÔTE D'IVOIRE

Post-colonial Côte d'Ivoire enjoyed national stability for a long period, although under a dictatorship. Its long-term president, Félix Houphouët-Boigny, ruled the Francophone state from independence in 1960 until his death in 1993. In the late 1990s, however, political instability set in. First, a military coup d'état in 1999 toppled the regime of Aimé Henri Konan Bédié, Houphouët-Boigny's successor. Political intrigue and manipulation of ethnic and religious differences by the political class, thereafter, plunged the state into a violent civil war. The war commenced in September 2002 following a violent uprising within the Ivorian military in which the former military ruler, Gen. Robert Guéï, was killed, along with hundreds more people in several cities.

By late 2002, the civil war had effectively split the country into two. A rebel coalition called the *Forces Nouvelles de Côte d'Ivoire* (New Forces; FN), held control of the northern part of the country while the south was under the control of the government. International efforts such as an ECOWAS initiative, French forces' intervention, and a United Nations peace operation contributed to progress toward peace but did not bring about national reconciliation. Peace talks in March 2007 produced a peace accord, the Ouagadougou Political Agreement (OPA), signed by President Laurent Gbagbo and Guillaume Soro, the FN leader. Under the agreement, a new government was established with Soro as prime minister.

Although violence had greatly subsided, by late 2009 Côte d'Ivoire still remained a divided country. The government was still not able to exercise full control over the rebel-held north. Like the rest of the war-torn countries in West Africa, the Côte d'Ivoire conflict has had a devastating effect on the hitherto stable state. Apart from institutional and infrastructural damage, the war has greatly accentuated political, religious, and ethnic divisions in the country. While the fighting lasted, it was characterized by various forms of human rights abuses and atrocities against the civil population. For example, sexual violence against women was rampant, perpetrated by both rebel and government forces.[25]

WARLORDISM: THE CASE OF CHARLES TAYLOR

A major development in the wake of the violent conflicts in the Mano River Basin was the rise of warlords. Warlordism is the phenomenon by which a leader of an armed rebel movement, driven, often by personal ambition, seeks to overthrow the central authority of a state or exercise control over parts of its territory. Warlordism thrives best in failed states where the national government has little or no control over significant portions of its territory or is unable to perform its basic functions of maintaining law and order and safeguarding security of life and property. Years of political maladministration and economic failure followed by prolonged, violent conflicts easily made Liberia and Sierra Leone susceptible to warlordism.[26] Thus, they produced some of the most vicious warlords in modern African history. Adebajo has identified the quartet of Charles Taylor (Liberia), Foday Sankoh, Sam Bockarie, and Johnny Paul Koroma (Sierra Leone) as "West Africa's most ruthless warlords."[27]

Taylor is undoubtedly the most notorious of these warlords. His desperate quest for power and wealth, and the predatory politics he played in the complex Mano River states' conflicts led to the destabilization of the entire region and the perpetration of the most despicable war crimes to be committed in the history of modern conflicts in Africa.

Taylor's notorious career as a warlord began with the NPFL-led insurrection in December 1989. Born of an Americo-Liberian father, Taylor had studied in the United States, graduating with a degree in economics from Bentley College, Waltham, Massachusetts, in 1977. The future warlord returned to Liberia in 1980, and after the termination of President William R. Tolbert's regime, managed to become a part of Samuel Doe's government that succeeded it. Taylor served under Doe as a junior minister in the ministry of commerce, a position in which he was later accused of embezzling nearly a million dollars of state funds. To avoid arrest, Taylor fled to the United States in 1983 and was later arrested and detained by the American authorities pending extradition to Liberia. Fugitive Taylor, however, managed to escape from the Massachusetts detention facility where he was being held; he later re-emerged in Libya, a state that had become a haven for dissident elements from various parts of West Africa. Taylor traversed West Africa in the next five years, conferring with anti-Doe dissidents. He later made Côte d'Ivoire his base, where he organized his followers into an armed militia, ostensibly with the aim of overthrowing the regime of President Doe.

Taylor's insurgency, it has been noted, probably transcended merely overthrowing the Doe government. Sierra Leonean scholar and journalist Lansana Gberie argues that the warlord might have also intended to destabilize West Africa for his own purpose of achieving "broader hegemonic control" over the region.[28] This assertion seems plausible, given, first, the multinational composition of his rebel movement, and second, by the prominent role he played in spreading the Liberian war to neighboring states and in the process destabilizing the region.

As a warlord, Taylor was a skillful manipulator, a master at intrigue, and widely known for showmanship and theatrics. To buoy his own position, he exploited Doe's unpopularity especially among the Gio and the Mano of Nimba County, who had been a target of the president's persecution. He played on ethnic distrust in Liberia and curried support from foreign leaders, particularly those disdainful of Doe. Even beyond the region, Taylor had the backing of the Libyan dictator Muammar Gaddafi, believed to harbor a hegemonic interest in West Africa, which its stabilization through conflicts could bring about.[29] Gaddafi, indeed, provided the NPFL with training bases as well as arms.

In the battle for Monrovia, Taylor, the warlord, orchestrated a most ugly war characterized by interethnic killings, tortures, kidnappings, and widespread human rights violations. By July 1990, NPFL forces and those of its splinter group, INPFL, had fought their way into Monrovia. Although Doe was subsequently toppled and assassinated (in a most gruesome way), Taylor's attempt at grabbing power was thwarted by ECOMOG intervention in the ensuing civil war.

Like most warlords, Taylor presided over a most ruthless rebel movement with no clearly discernible ideology.[30] The NPFL consisted of several thousand irregular guerrilla fighters that launched Liberia on one of the bloodiest wars in African history. As elected president, from 1997 until forced to resign in 2003, Taylor did not shed the garb of a warlord. His role in the civil war in Sierra Leone epitomized warlord politics. His backing of the RUF rebels in the insurgency against the Freetown government was the most visible manifestation of the readiness, apparent in the cross-border conflicts in the Mano River Basin, of one government to support rebel movement(s) in the neighboring state. The critical support in the form of arms supply that the Liberian president-cum-warlord provided the RUF helped to sustain the rebel movement and prolong the Sierra Leonean Civil War. The support also played a major role in the rebels' capability to commit untold atrocities in the course of the war. In March 2006, Taylor, now ex-president exiled in Nigeria after his forced resignation, was arrested for alleged war crimes committed as a result of his role in the RUF war. After spending sometime in detention, the former president's trial by a special tribunal for Sierra Leone, meeting in The Hague, formally began on January 7, 2008.

The Rapid Increase of Regional Combatants

The phenomenon of cross-border combatants was one of the most significant characteristics of the interwoven conflicts in the Mano River Basin.[31] The regionalized set of conflicts produced numerous cross-border armies, both government sponsored and rebel controlled. These armed factions employed hundreds of thousands of regional fighters drawn from several parts of West Africa. Liberians, given the long war in their country, constituted the largest number of cross-border fighters in West Africa. However, a good number of regional fighters were Sierra Leoneans, Guineans, Ivoirians, Malians, Burkinabes, Gambians, and Senegalese. Yet some of these combatants came from as far away as Ghana and Nigeria. The porous borders characteristic of the states in the region aided easy and free movement of foreign fighters.

The use of cross-border combatants in the Mano River Basin began with the NPFL's recruitment of fighters from Burkina Faso, Gambia, and Sierra Leone, during its initial invasion of Liberia in 1989.[32] But in the course of the country's long civil war, all the other rebel groups as well as the AFL recruited foreign fighters. Likewise, the civil war in Sierra Leone saw the use of mercenaries by the SLA, the different civil defense militias, and the rebel RUF, which used Liberians and Burkinabes. Côte d'Ivoire was not left out; the outbreak of civil war there in September 2002 saw the employment of foreign fighters by the Ivorian Popular Movement of the Great West (*Mouvement Populaire Ivoirien du Grand Ouest*; MPIGO), and the Movement for Justice and Peace (*Mouvement pour la Justice et la Paix*; MJP).

Many of the migrant fighters in the cross-border conflicts had fought for as many as four armed groups. Most, often unemployed youths, hired themselves for military service, generally driven by their dismal condition of grinding poverty. The depressed economy of their countries offered them no hope for betterment of livelihood, and thus conflict provided them the opportunity for economic advancement. The liberty to rob people, loot their property, and exhort money from them with impunity afforded by a conflict environment became a prime attraction for membership in armed groups.

While economic deprivation had pushed many of the regional fighters into the arms of warlords, others had been victims of impressments. Abduction of adults, and especially children, and their impressments into armed groups, was very common. As will be seen later, this was practiced by virtually all the armed sides in the regional conflicts. However, whether they volunteered or were forced into armed conflicts, and whether they were young or old, the roving bands of mercenary fighters in the regional wars committed unspeakable war crimes. Fighters in the rebel armies in Liberia and Sierra Leone, for example, essentially constituted themselves into brutal, lawless, terrorizing squads of marauding brigands. They senselessly killed innocent and defenseless civilians, viciously raped women and young girls, mutilated their victims, and looted properties. Although they were perpetrators of evil, these fighters themselves, especially children, lived a life of hardship in military camps, suffering both physical and mental abuse.

The free movement of migrant combatants in the porous borders between states in the Mano River Basin was accompanied by the free flow of arms. Arms dealers such as Charles Taylor had a field day and injected huge amounts of weapons into the region. Taylor's arms dealings were, indeed, interlocked with the illicit diamond trade. The RUF obtained a great deal of its weapons from the Liberian president in a diamonds-for-arms deal. The rebels' exchange of diamonds for weapons was enhanced by their control of Sierra Leone's diamond fields at some stages of the conflict.

Child Soldiers

The use of child soldiers in armed conflicts around the world is not a new phenomenon, but has become more prevalent since the end of the Cold War. The post–Cold War period, rather than ushering in an era of peace and tranquility as widely expected, has, on the contrary, seen an upsurge of conflicts around the globe. One of the important by-products of increased armed conflicts is an escalated use of children. Child soldiers have increasingly been employed in various capacities in wars in Asia, Latin America, the Middle East, Europe, and Africa. By the end of the last century, over 300,000 children below the age of 18 were estimated to have taken part in conflicts around the world.[33]

Perhaps the most profound act of human rights violation in African conflicts is the conscription and use of children in combat and in other military formations. It is useful to note that child soldiering is not a new phenomenon in Africa. During the bloody Nigerian Civil War, Biafra made use of children as soldiers. Children were a part of the protracted post-independence wars in Angola and Mozambique. Also, children were utilized in combat in conflicts in Algeria, Eritrea, Sudan, and Ethiopia. What has changed in the post–Cold War period is the magnitude of the use of children in conflicts.

African conflicts have become more violent and more protracted. They have also increasingly become less conventional and more guerrilla in nature. With battle lines less defined, defenseless civilian populations including children are easily drawn into violent conflicts. This changing dynamic of conflict is very evident in West Africa from the late 1990s to the early twenty-first century. The subregion, therefore, provides a case study for the understanding of the phenomenon of child soldiers in Africa.

The use of children as soldiers prevalent in the Mano River Basin dates to the beginning of the Liberian Civil War at the end of 1989. The NPFL actively recruited children, often by force, to perform military duties, including combat. Other insurgent factions that emerged as the war deepened, the LURD and MODEL, in particular, extensively conscripted children.[34] When the Liberian war spilled over to Sierra Leone, the RUF also extensively employed child soldiers.[35] It must be noted that child soldiers were not only recruited into armies of opposition or rebel groups, they were quite as often employed in national armed forces such as the AFL and the SLA.

Many of the child recruits were below the age of 15, the internationally sanctioned age of participation in armed conflict.[36] In Liberia and Sierra Leone, some of the combatants were as young as eight years old. Boys generally formed the bulk of these child soldiers. Typically trained in the use of weapons, they served as combatants. But they also served as porters, bodyguards, spies, informants, and in other paramilitary duties. However, the use of children as soldiers is by no means reserved for boys alone; girls were also recruited into armed groups, sometimes as combatants, but most often to perform chores such as cooking. Both boys and girls were subjected to various forms of abuses including forced illicit drug taking, primarily to harden them and make them impervious to killings and other atrocities they were compelled to do. Girls, typically, were subjected to sexual abuse, used as "wives" of commanders, and sex slaves to older soldiers.

REGIONAL CONFLICT AND INTERNATIONAL RAMIFICATIONS

The destructive magnitude of the cross-border conflicts and the security threat they posed to the security of the West Africa subregion compelled the intervention of the regional organization ECOWAS and the United Nations peacekeeping or peace-enforcing forces. ECOWAS, in particular, launched extensive operations in Liberia and Sierra Leone, and also in Guinea Bissau.

ECOWAS Intervention: Liberia and Sierra Leone

Essentially an economic arrangement, ECOWAS expanded its mandate when it began to take on security matters through its intervention in the Liberian and Sierra Leonean wars. Indeed, ECOMOG as peace monitoring force was formed by ECOWAS in August 1990, and subsequently deployed to Liberia to broker and monitor a cease-fire in the country's civil conflict. Apart from helping to improve the security situation in the country, its mandate also included assisting the Liberians to establish an interim government and to subsequently hold elections to elect a democratic government. Consisting of predominantly Nigerian troops but also from other ECOWAS countries, the force's mandate soon expanded from peace monitoring to counterinsurgency, peacekeeping, and peace enforcement. The 4,000-strong force, consequently, played one of the most important roles in the Liberian conflict. Despite its inadequacies and failures, to a large extent it contributed to the establishment of a more secure environment that paved the way for subsequent intervention of a UN mission in 2003.

In Sierra Leone, almost since the inception of its civil war, ECOWAS had followed the conflict with keen interest given its potential destabilization effect on the subregion. In particular, regional power, Nigeria, was more insistent on full-scale ECOWAS intervention. In April 1991, as the RUF incursions began, the Nigerian government had sent a military force to the country to assist the government in containing the rebels.

However, ECOWAS full intervention in the Sierra Leone conflict came in February 1998 when Nigerian forces, ostensibly acting under the auspices of ECOMOG, sent its troops to Freetown to drive the AFRC out of power and restore to power the deposed democratic government of President Kabbah. As noted earlier on, Nigerian troops achieved this immediate objective. However, the restoration of Kabbah did not end the war. Nigerian troops continued to battle the remnants of the AFRC and its rebel allies. Indeed, in January 1999, following a devastating invasion of Freetown in which thousands of people were killed, the rebels succeeded in wresting parts of the city from ECOMOG forces.

If ECOMOG performed a noble role in the civil wars in Liberia and Sierra Leone, the regional force was not immune from atrocities, although not on the same scale as an insurgent group like the RUF. In Sierra Leone, in particular, during the rebels' January 1999 infiltration of Freetown, Nigerian ECOMOG troops allegedly summarily executed scores of captured RUF fighters and others suspected of being their collaborators or sympathizers. Some of these victims were said to be children and women.[37]

United Nations Intervention

The inability of the state to meet the challenges of conflict was clearly evident in Liberia and Sierra Leone. In Liberia, ECOWAS' efforts in establishing peace in the war-torn country were buoyed by the intervention of the United Nations. Following ECOWAS' success in brokering the Cotonou Peace Agreement between Liberia's interim government (IGNU), NPFL, and ULIMO in July 1993, the UN established the United Nations Observer Mission in Liberia (UNOMIL) to supervise and monitor, along with ECOWAS, the implementation of the agreement.[38]

With the war persisting, in October 2003, following the Secretary General's recommendation, the UN deployed a peacekeeping mission, the United Nations Mission in Liberia (UNMIL) to Liberia to replace ECOMOG.[39] About 15,000 strong, consisting of armed soldiers, police officers, civilian political advisers, and aid workers, UNMIL had the task of monitoring the cease-fire achieved under the Comprehensive Peace Agreement (CPA), which had been signed following President Taylor's resignation. UNMIL's mandate also included promoting the peace process and human rights activities, supporting humanitarian endeavors, and helping in the task of national security reform that involved creating a new national army and training of the police force.[40] By 2005, UNMIL had recorded a high level of success in the arduous task of post-war reconstruction. The mission was largely credited for the success of the 2005 election, which was widely acclaimed as free and fair, and which installed Ellen Johnson-Serleaf as the first woman to be elected as president in Africa. Although rehabilitation and integration still pose major problems, UNMIL has recoded some success in disarming hundreds of thousands of former combatants in the bloody conflict.

The RUF war in Sierra Leone also invited UN intervention. In July 1998, the organization established the United Nations Observer Mission in Sierra Leone (UNOMSIL), with a broad mandate that included monitoring the military and security condition in Sierra Leone, and disarming and demobilizing former combatants. However, the regime of UNOMSIL ended in October 1999, when the UN replaced it with a more expanded peacekeeping mission, the United Nations Mission in Sierra Leone (UNAMSIL). The new mission's mandate was essentially to help Sierra Leone in the implementation of a controversial peace agreement, the Lomé Accord that had been signed by the Government of Sierra Leone, the RUF, and the other warring groups. In spite of the accord that was expected to bring about the end of the civil war, the conflict lingered on as a new group, the West Side Boys (sometimes regarded as a splinter of the RUF) refused to disarm, in accordance with the accord. Hostilities continued until 2001, when the new rebels were finally routed with the help of British forces. UNAMSIL's mandate ended in 2005.

Foreign Private Military Forces

An important element of the conflict in Sierra Leone was the role played by foreign private military forces. The RUF control of diamond-mining areas in the early years of the conflict and the failure of the SLA to defeat the rebels caused the government to employ the services of private security companies. The first firm hired to provide military training to the SLA was Gurkhe Security Guards (GSG). In 1995, GSG was replaced by Executive Outcomes (EO), founded in South Africa, to perform the same task. Later, in the civil war in 1998, another private military firm, the London-based Sandline International, was recruited by President Kabbah to help ensure security in the country. At the tail end of the civil war in Liberia, Sandline also served the government of Charles Taylor.

The history of foreign mercenaries in modern West African conflicts can be traced to the Nigerian Civil War of 1967–1970. During the war, Biafra engaged the military services of a few white mercenaries. In Sierra Leone, it is widely believed that EO soldiers actively participated in fighting against RUF rebels, and, indeed, were instrumental to the government forces' recapture by mid-1995 of some of the diamond-rich areas from the rebels.

***

Regional conflicts in West Africa have been waged at great costs, not only for the countries directly involved, but also for the entire subregion. Civil wars in countries like Liberia and Sierra Leone, where they were intense, brutal, and prolonged, have, in human terms, resulted in colossal loss of lives, massive displacement of populations, and refugee crises in and across borders. The wars also virtually destroyed the nations' economies. Economic failure has also exacerbated political instability. Both Liberia and Sierra Leone were failed states for the greater part of the 1990s and the early twenty-first century.

Although the wars had ended, both Liberia and Sierra Leone still faced an uphill task of economic and political reconstruction. Fundamental to the post-war reconstruction has been the problem of rehabilitation of hundreds of child soldiers and other combatants into civil society.

Notes

1. Cited in United States Institute of Peace (USIP), "Responding to War and State Collapse in West Africa," *Special Report* (January 21, 2002: 1).

2. Cited in Human Rights Watch, "Youth, Poverty and Blood: The Lethal Legacy of West Africa's Regional Warriors," April 13, 2005, retrieved on January 18, 2009, from: http://www.hrw.org/en/node/11795/section/2.

3. Cited in Adekeye Adebajo, *Liberia's Civil War: Nigeria, ECOMOG, and Regional Security in West Africa* (Boulder, CO: Lynne Rienner, 2002), 41.

4. William Adams Hance, *The Geography of Modern Africa* (New York: Columbia University Press, 1975), 173.

5. See, for instance, George Klay Kieh and Ida Rousseau Mukenge (eds.), *Zones of Conflict in Africa: Theories and Cases* (Westport. CT: Praeger, 2002).

6. These countries include: Nigeria, Togo, Gambia, Benin, Côte d'Ivoire, Guinea, Mali, Guinea-Bissau, Burkina Faso, Niger, Liberia, and Sierra Leone. See "Human Development Indices: A Statistical Update, 2008—HDI Rankings," retrieved on February 3, 2009, from: http://hdr.undp.org/en/statistics/.

7. For more on the foundation of Liberia, see John David Smith (ed.), *The American Colonization Society and Emigration: Solutions to "The Negro Problem"* (New York: Garland Publishers, 1993); and James Wesley Smith, *Sojourners in Search of Freedom: The Settlement of Liberia of Black Americans* (Lanham, MD: University Press of America, 1987). For general history of Liberia's development, see J. Gus Liebenow, *Liberia: The Evolution of Privilege* (Ithaca, NY: Cornell University Press, 1969).

8. For more detailed examination of the causes of the conflict, see the following works: Sikiru Taiwo Kassim, "Civil Wars and the Refugee Crisis in West Africa: A Case Study of Liberian Refugees in Nigeria," in W. Alade Fawole and Charles Ukeje (eds.), *The Crisis of the State and Regionalism in West Africa: Identity, Citizenship and Conflict* (Dakar, Senegal: Council for the Development of Social Science Research in Africa, 2005), 175–190; Ahmadu Sesay, "Historical Background to the Liberian Civil War," in Margaret Vogt (ed.), *The Liberian Crisis and ECOMOG: A Bold Attempt at Regional Peace Keeping* (Lagos, Nigeria: Gabumo Press, 1992); Abiodun Alao, *The Burden of Collective Goodwill: The International Involvement in the Liberian Civil War* (Aldershot, UK: Ashgate, 1998), 1–21.

9. Note that the factions are arranged alphabetically, not in order of their formation.

10. Similar estimates of war-related casualties have been provided. See for instance, USIP, "Responding to War and State Collapse," 2; Kassim, "Civil Wars and the Refugee Crisis," 180.

11. This figure seems to be a general consensus. See, for instance, United Nations, *Consolidated Appeal Process, Liberia 2004* (Geneva: UN Office for the Coordination of Humanitarian Affairs, 2003), 1.

12. For an examination of Liberia as a collapsed state, see Jeremy Levitt, *The Evolution of Deadly Conflict in Liberia: From "Paternaltarianism" to State Collapse* (Durham, NC: Carolina Academic Press, 2005).

13. See William Reno, *Warlord Politics and African States* (Boulder, CO: Lynne Rienner, 1998) 92. More details on the support given to the NPFL by Côte d'Ivoire and Burkina Faso are provided in Adebajo, *Liberia's Civil War*, 54–55.

14. Important studies of the RUF include Lansana Gberie, *A Dirty War in West Africa: The RUF and the Destruction of Sierra Leone* (Bloomington: Indiana University Press, 2005); Paul Richards, *Fighting for the Rain Forest: War, Youth and Resources in Sierra Leone* (Portsmouth, NH: Heinemann, 1996); Ibrahim Abdullah, "Bush Path to Destruction: The Origin and Character of the Revolutionary United Front/Sierra Leone," *Journal of Modern African Studies*, Vol. 36, No. 2 (1998: 203–235); Ibrahim Abdullah and Patrick Muana, "The Revolutionary United Front of Sierra Leone: A Revolt of the Lumpen-proletariat," in Christopher Clapham (ed.), *African Guerrillas* (Bloomington: Indiana University Press, 1998).

15. For more analysis of the economic mismanagement, see S. W. Reno, *Corruption and State Politics in Sierra Leone* (Cambridge, UK: University Press, 1995); Alfred B. Zack-Williams, "Sierra Leone: The Political Economy of Civil War, 1991–1998," *Third World Quarterly*, Vol. 20, No. 1 (1999)," and Alfred B. Zack-Williams, "Sierra Leone: The Deepening Crisis," *Review of African Political Economy*, Vol. 49 (1990).

16. Zack-Williams, "Sierra Leone: The Political Economy, 152.

17. Lansana Gberie, "The May 25 Coup d'état in Sierra Leone: A Militariat Revolt?" *Africa Development*, Vol. 22, Nos. 3 & 4 (1997: 150).

18. The Kamajor militia has been extensively studied. See, for example, Patrick K. Muana, "The Kamajor Militia: Civil War, Internal Displacement and the Politics of Counter-Insurgency," *Africa Development*, Vol. 22, Nos. 3 & 4 (1997).

19. Norimitsu Onishi, "What War Has Wrought: Sierra Leone's Sad State," *New York Times* (January 31, 1999).

20. Gberie, *A Dirty War in West Africa*, 14–15.

21. For Nigeria's role in ECOWAS and Nigeria's intervention, see Adebayo Oyeabde, "Restoring Democracy in Sierra Leone: Nigeria's Hegemonic Foreign Policy in West Africa, 1993–1998," in Olayiwola Abegunrin and Olusoji Akomolafe (eds.), *Nigeria in Global Politics: Twentieth Century and Beyond* (New York: Nova Science Publishers, 2006), 95–106.

22. About 80 percent of the members of the SLA were reported to have defected to the RUF by 1997. See Ibrahim Abdullah and Ismail Rashid, "Rebel Movement," in Adekeye Adebajo and Ismail Rashid (eds.), *West Africa's Security Challenges: Building Peace in a Troubled Region* (Boulder, CO: Lynne Rienner, 2004), 187.

23. Human Rights Watch, "Getting Away with Murder, Mutilation, Rape: New Testimony from Sierra Leone," Vol. 11, No. 3A (July 1999), retrieved on April 9, 2009, from: http://www.hrw.org/legacy/reports/1999/sierra/SIERLE99.htm#P2_0.

24. Figures provided by Human Rights Watch. See "Getting Away with Murder."

25. On this subject, see, for instance, "Côte d'Ivoire, Silence and Impunity: The Only Response to Sexual Violence against Women," Amnesty International, Public Statement, AI Index: AFR 31/002/2008, December 16. 2008, retrieved on November 23, 2009, from: http://www.amnesty.org/en/library/asset/AFR31/002/2008/en/3be286d6-ccf8-11dd-9047-0dd649cecd02/afr310022008 en.pdf.

26. On this subject, see A. J. Christopher, "'Nation-States,' 'Quasi-States,' and 'Collapsed-States' in Contemporary Africa," *GeoJournal*, Vol. 43, No. 1 (September 1997: 91–97); and Adam Groves, "Explaining African State 'Failure': Does the State Make the Nation or the Nation Make the State?" *e-International Relations* (June 2008), retrieved on March 9, 2009, from: http://www.e-ir.info/?p=495. For a report on failed and collapsed states in the contemporary international system, see "Failed and Collapsed States in the International System," The African Studies Centre, Leiden; The Transnational Institute, Amsterdam; The Center of Social Studies, Coimbra University, and The Peace Research Center—CIP-FUHEM, Madrid; December 2003, retrieved on March 9, 2009, from: http://www.globalpolicy.org/nations/sovereign/failed/2003/12failedcollapsedstates.pdf.

27. Adekeye Adebajo, "West Africa: Of Warlords, Sobels, Politicians, and Peacekeepers," retrieved on March 9, 2009, from: http://ccrweb.ccr.uct.ac.za/fileadmin/template/ccr/pdf/warlords_peacekeepers_adebajo_feb2004.pdf. Bockarie (a.k.a. Mastika or mosquito) became the commander of RUF forces in 1997, following the arrest and detention of Foday Sankoh by the Nigerian government. For a detailed discourse on warlordism in African states involved in conflicts including Liberia and Sierra Leone, see William Reno, *Warlord Politics and African States* (Boulder, CO: Lynne Rienner, 1998).

28. Lansana Gberie, *A Dirty War in West Africa: The RUF and the Destruction of Sierra Leone* (Bloomington: Indiana University Press, 2005), 54.

29. Adebajo, *Liberia's Civil War*, 55.

30. Ibid., 58.

31. New York-based Human Rights Watch has published a report on this phenomenon based on interviews with about 60 veterans of the cross-border conflicts. See "Youth, Poverty and Blood: The Lethal Legacy of West Africa's Regional Warriors," April 13, 2005, retrieved on March 17, 2009, from: http://www.hrw.org/en/node/11795/section/1.

32. Alao, *The Burden of Collective Goodwill*, 23.

33. International Save the Children Alliance, *Stop Using Child Soldiers* (London: Radda Barnen, 1998), 1.

34. An informative narrative on child soldiers in Liberia, based on *Human Rights Watch* research conducted in the country in 2003, is provided in "How to Fight, How to Kill: Child Soldiers in Liberia," *Human Rights Watch*, Vol. 16, No. 2A (February 2, 2004), retrieved on March 27, 2009, from: http://www.hrw.org/en/node/12180/section/1.

35. For the use of children as combatants in the war, see Richards, *Fighting for the Rain Forest*; and Krijn Peters and Paul Richards, "Why We Fight:

Voices of Youth Combatants in Sierra Leone," *Africa*, Vol. 68, No. 2 (1998: 183–210).

36. However, there has been a strong international movement—championed by the International Red Cross and Red Crescent Movement, the United Nations Children's Fund (UNICEF), and the Office of the United Nations High Commissioner for Refugees (UNHCR)—to make 18 the minimum age of recruitment into armed forces.

37. Human Rights Watch, "Getting Away with Murder."

38. Details of the agreement are provided in United States Institute of Peace, "Peace Agreements Digital Collection: Liberia.," Retrieved on April 12, 2009, from: http://www.usip.org/library/pa/liberia/liberia_07251993.html#I-A.

39. ECOWAS countries, namely Benin, Gambia, Ghana, Guinea-Bissau, Mali, Nigeria, Senegal, and Togo, also contributed troops to UNMIL.

40. See UN Security Council Resolution 1509 (2003), adopted September 19, 2003, accessed on April 12, 2009, at: http://daccessdds.un.org/doc/UNDOC/GEN/N03/525/70/PDF/N0352570.pdf?OpenElement.

CHAPTER 3

Nigeria

To Keep Nigeria One Is A Task That Must Be Done!
Radio jingo in Nigeria, constantly aired
during its civil war of 1967–1970.

Instead of guaranteeing citizens' basic right to vote freely, Nigerian government and electoral officials actively colluded in the fraud and violence that marred the presidential polls in some areas.
Peter Takirambudde, Africa Director,
Human Rights Watch, commenting on the 2007 elections.

The Federal Republic of Nigeria, as the country is officially known, is one of the most prominent states, not only in the subregion of West Africa where it is located, but in the entire continent. The country shares boundaries with Benin Republic in the west, Niger Republic in the north, Chad in the northeast, Cameroon in the east, and the Atlantic Ocean in the south. A big country occupying an area totaling 356,667 square miles (923,768 sq km), Nigeria is about two and a half times the size of the state of California and three times larger than the United Kingdom. It is a country of diverse cultures with over 250 different ethno-linguistic groups. The three largest and dominant of these groups are the Hausa-Fulani of the North, the Yoruba of the West, and the Igbo (also called Ibo) of the East. There is also a host of smaller groups, sometimes referred to as minorities. Among these are the Tiv, Nupe, Ibibio, Kanuri, Ijo, Efik, Edo, Kalabari, Igala, Itshekiri, Idoma and Uhrobo. Many of the ethnic groups consist of a number of sub-groups, each with its own dialect.

Nigeria boasts having the largest population in Africa, reporting a census figure of 140 million in 2006.[1] A considerable portion of its population is rural, but steady streams of rural-urban migrations have continued to buoy urbanization. The nation's capital city since 1991 is Abuja, centrally located in the heart of the country. Lagos, the former capital, is a sprawling metropolis in the southwest, and is the commercial nerve center of the nation. Some of the other large cities include Ibadan, Kano, Kaduna, Jos, Benin City, Port Harcourt, Calabar, Enugu, and Warri.

Religion is a key element of the Nigerian culture and has often been a major source of conflict among the people. Islam, representing about 50 percent of the population, is strong in the north among the Hausa-Fulani. In the south, the Igbo and the Yoruba are predominantly Christian and make up about 40 percent of the population. About 10 percent of the people practice various forms of traditional religions. Religious antagonism and incessant violent conflicts have often been between Christians and Muslims, occurring mainly in the Muslim-dominated north.

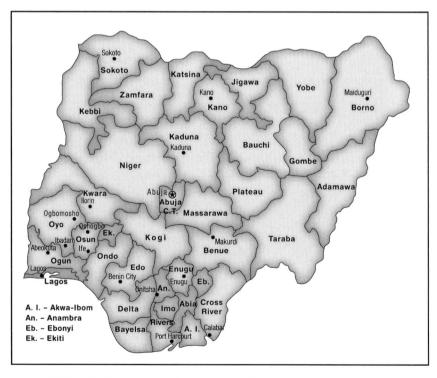

States of Nigeria. (Courtesy of Sam Saverance.)

As a large state, varied climatic conditions and topography also define Nigeria's diversity. The climate is wet and tropical in the south and becomes progressively drier to the north. The moist weather of the coast is derived from the Atlantic Ocean's maritime winds. The drier north is more susceptible to the dry southbound Harmattan wind from the Sahara Desert. There are two main seasons, the rainy and the dry seasons. Roughly, the rainy season lasts from March to October, and the dry season from November to February. In terms of topography, the terrain rises from the mangrove swamp of the deep south in the Niger Delta area to the tropical rain forest further inland, and to the vast savanna grassland of the middle belt and the north. The topography is also dotted with hilly formations such as the Jos Plateau, located in the center of the vast region north of the Niger and Benue rivers. The Niger, which takes its source from the Futa Jalon Highlands in Guinea, flows into Nigeria from the northwest discharging its waters into the Atlantic through a delta. The Niger is Africa's third longest river, running about 2,500 miles and joined by its main tributary, the Benue, at the Lokoja confluence.

Nigeria is richly endowed with natural resources among which are petroleum, tin, iron ore, coal, limestone, lead, zinc, and columbite. Nigeria's economy has been driven largely by oil export for the greater part of its post-colonial history. In the 1970s and early 1980s during the so-called "oil boom," oil exports soared dramatically and brought enormous wealth to Nigeria. As the largest oil-producing country in Africa, in 1971 Nigeria became a member of the Organization of Petroleum Exporting Countries (OPEC). Its major export partner is the United States. Indeed, Nigeria reportedly surpassed Venezuela as the fourth largest supplier of crude oil to the United States during the first five months of 2008.[2] Oil interest has thus made Nigeria of strategic value to the United States.

Nigeria is a potentially great country. Despite economic recession that became pronounced from the early 1980s, it is still the second largest economy in Africa (after South Africa). As an emerging democracy, having transitioned in 1999 from decades of retrogressive and sometimes oppressive military rule, Nigeria, for many, still holds the hope of providing for Africa an example of a viable polity. The idea has always been held that Nigeria has a manifest destiny to play a leadership role in Africa, a perception that rests on claims of enormous population, considerable landmass, and potential wealth.[3]

Although dwindling economic fortunes have severely curtailed Nigeria's leadership ability, it has, nevertheless, demonstrated its capability to be a power in West Africa and, indeed, to be a key player in continental affairs. It has played a significant role in promoting economic integration, cooperation, and conflict resolution in the subregion, particularly through the regional organization the Economic Community of West African States (ECOWAS), whose establishment it championed. Specifically, Nigeria was instrumental in dealing with the complex, long conflicts that ravaged Liberia and Sierra Leone. In the 1970s, Nigeria's vibrant economy allowed the nation to play a major role in continent-wide affairs. For instance, Nigeria provided unwavering support for the liberation struggles in Southern Africa to end the remaining vestiges of colonialism and supremacist white rule in Africa.[4] Beyond being a major force in Africa, Nigeria has also made some impressions in the global arena. The Nigerian military, more than any other force in Africa, has most extensively participated in United Nations–sponsored peacekeeping missions in various hot spots of the world, from the Congo in 1960 to Aouzou Strip (Chad) in 1994.[5]

Despite its regional power status, sadly, Nigeria has been unable to sufficiently marshal its enormous human and material resources to achieve lasting political stability, sustainable development, and economic growth. Almost since independence, the country has witnessed political instability as indicated by a brutal civil war that almost dismembered the nation; incessant, sometimes bloody military coups; and years of repressive dictatorships with dismal human rights records. Political instability has been compounded by economic underdevelopment brought about largely by massive and rampant corruption, graft, waste, and gross fiscal mismanagement by the political class. In the prevailing political and economic climate, divisible ethnic conflicts and recurring, devastating religious conflicts have been rife. In particular, the economic crunch has brought about hardship among the citizenry, thus creating dissatisfaction and discontentment that has found expression in civil strife, sectarian violence, insurgencies, political assassinations, and extra-judicial killings, as well as antisocial behaviors such as armed robbery, banditry, drug trade, and scams.

BRIEF HISTORICAL OVERVIEW

The peoples of the area that later became Nigeria have a long history dating to antiquity as supported by Stone Age evidence unearthed in a number of places. By 1000 CE, the process of state formation had begun, resulting in the establishment in the next half a century of some of the most prominent West African states such as Benin, Oyo, Kanem-Borno, and the Hausa states.

As indicated in Chapter 1, pre-colonial African states were not immune to conflicts. In what was to become Nigeria, interstate and communal conflicts occurred everywhere. In the north, the Hausa states of Kano,

Katsina, Zazzau, Zamfara, and Gobir were for much of the seventeenth and eighteenth centuries constantly at each other's throats often due to trade rivalries. The internecine warfare ended only when the fragmented states were united in 1804 after the Fulani Jihad, an Islamic revolution of Fulani *Mujahideen*, turned the region into an Islamic empire, the Sokoto Caliphate. East of the Hausa states in the Lake Chad region, Borno, a large state by the late sixteenth century, expanded principally through military conquests achieved by its great emperors, most notably Idris Alooma. Following the success of the Fulani Jihad in the north, the jihadists turned their expansionist and Islamization project southward.

In the southwest, the cavalry state of Oyo, the most powerful of the Yoruba states up to the late eighteenth century, waged wars with its Yoruba neighbors such as the Egbado, and with other surrounding states including the kingdoms of Nupe, Allada, and Dahomey. Oyo itself soon fell prey to the Fulani jihadists whose invasion led to the desertion of Old Oyo, its capital, in about 1837. Meanwhile, the decline of the great Oyo Empire had been accompanied by protracted warfare in the whole of Yorubaland with significant consequences for the region.[6] The Yoruba states were severely weakened by the conflicts; new polities emerged out of the ashes of Oyo, the most prominent being Ibadan, a militarist center that pursued a hegemonic foreign policy; and then a refugee crisis engulfed the region.[7] Not only did the wars create thousands of refugees, but captives and war prisoners often fed the Atlantic slave market.

The European advent in West Africa could be dated to the fifteenth century. Initially they pursued a three-fold interest in the region: exploration, the spread of the Christian gospel, and commerce. In time, before the mid-nineteenth century, the slave trade was the most enduring component of Britain's relations with pre-colonial Nigeria. Britain, which was to later colonize Nigeria, was the largest slave-trading nation in the Bight of Benin in the eighteenth century. In 1807, however, the British abolished the slave trade, and then slavery itself in 1833. Slave traffic on the Atlantic continued, in any case, which caused the British to institute an anti-slavery naval squadron to police the West African seas and arrest persistent slave trafficking ships and free their human cargoes. The British newfound anti-slavery attitude was partly designed to promote a new form of trade, the so-called "legitimate trade." This was commerce in African products such as palm oil and kernels. Their desire to protect their new trading enterprise, which was essential to the success of the emerging industrial economy of Europe, called for colonial occupation of Africa.

The process of the British occupation of Nigeria was essentially a violent one. That process could be said to have begun in earnest in

1861 when a consulate was established in Lagos after its annexation. Thereafter, the British slowly expanded their authority, which extended to the Niger Delta by 1880. In the early twentieth century, the British embarked on a large-scale imperial project through military conquests in most places. One after the other, states and peoples succumbed to the superior conquering forces of the British who were equipped with Maxim and Gatling guns. By 1912, virtually all the pre-colonial states had lost their sovereignty to the British.[8] The colonial state of Nigeria was officially born on January 1, 1914, when the hitherto separately governed Protectorate of Southern Nigeria and Protectorate of Northern Nigeria were amalgamated under one government. Thus Nigeria entered a new political dispensation in which hundreds of ethno-linguistic groups now existed under a common boundary and were subject to a common administrative system. This was the most profound legacy of colonialism.

The conquest and subjugation of the Nigerian peoples and the creation of a colonial administration did not mean the end of conflict in the colonial state. Although colonialism was largely adjusted to, Nigerians often reacted violently to foreign domination during the colonial era. The British thus had to engage Nigerians in pacification wars in many places, especially during the early period of colonial rule.[9] The British colonial administrative system, indirect rule, introduced by the governor-general, Lord Frederick Lugard, met vehement opposition in eastern and western Nigeria where uprisings occurred.[10] The colonial government put to good use the military and the police to put down pockets of opposition wherever they occurred, and to ensure compliance with colonial policies such as taxation demand.

ETHNICITY, POLITICS, AND CONFLICT

Ethnicity is the affiliation of a group of people to a particular identity based on common ties, shared historical affinity, cultural identity, common language, and identifiable geographical location as homeland. Ethnic identity is extremely strong in Nigeria; in fact, it is stronger than national identity. Indeed, as a multiethnic state, Nigeria's social, political, and economic life has been propelled by ethnicity. Particularly, ethnicity has been a dominant factor in the nation's politics and a source of constant conflicts.[11]

In pre-colonial times, the territory that later became Nigeria was made up of numerous ethnolinguistic groups, some big and powerful enough to establish large states. During the colonial period, the British made little, if any attempt, to forge unity among the disparate peoples of Nigeria. Colonial policy was not intended to create a nation out of the many ethnic groups. Indeed, as a way of achieving colonial end, the British adopted a strategy of divide and rule, which further entrenched ethnic differences. The constitution of the disparate peoples and states into a single geographical entity called Nigeria made the modern state an artificial creation.

The exigency of the independence movement of the post-1945 period compelled the diverse peoples of Nigeria to temporarily eschew their ethnic differences and confront the common enemy, the colonial master. However, the fragile ethnic alliance quickly dissipated in the early post-colonial period. The failure of the colonial state to resolve ethnic differences and forge national unity inevitably laid the foundation for post-independence ethnic antagonism. Nigeria did have high hopes for unity among its various peoples. This was eloquently expressed in the first stanza of its national anthem adopted at independence in 1960:

Nigeria we hail thee,
Our own dear native land,
Though tribe and tongue may differ,
In brotherhood we stand,
Nigerians all, and proud to serve
Our sovereign Motherland.[12]

Nigeria is yet to successfully forge a nation where national identity has replaced the ethnic one. The first rude indication of the failure of this project was the violence that attended the politics of the first republic and which ultimately brought it down in January 1966.

The First Republic and Political Crisis (1960–1966)

Nigeria's First Republic was inaugurated at the attainment of independence in 1960. Mutual ethnic distrust and rivalry, especially among the major ethnic groups—the Hausa-Fulani, the Yoruba, and the Igbo—never resolved before independence quickly became the defining dynamic of the new political order. The First Republic would be plagued by interethnic tension, so toxic as to eventually orchestrate the collapse of the republic on January 15, 1966, through a military coup d'état.

Regionalism and ethnicity underlined politics in the First Republic. Politics largely revolved around ethnic-based regional political parties, particularly three dominant ones: the Northern People's Congress (NPC), the Action Group (AG), and the National Council of Nigerian Citizens (NCNC). The NPC, as its name implies, was a northern-based,

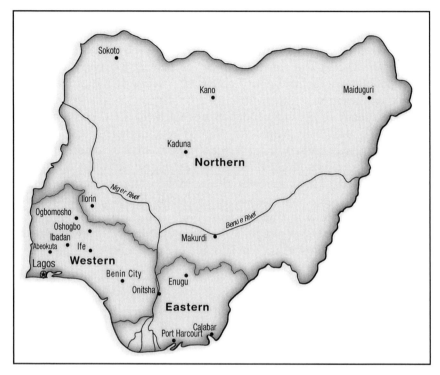

Regions of Nigeria in 1960. (Courtesy of Sam Saverance.)

aristocratic, Islamic-oriented party clearly identified with the Hausa-Fulani and established to defend its interests. The AG was equally regionally based—a party of Yoruba origin predominant in the west. The NCNC was originally nationalistic in outlook, but soon acquired Igbo identity and increasingly became a party of eastern interests.[13]

Party politics in Nigeria, thus, necessarily focused on achieving narrow regional and ethnic political security, and not national interest. In the prevailing atmosphere of mutual suspicion and antagonism, regional politics inevitably led to destructive power struggles among the dominant ethnic parties to gain control of federal power for their respective regions. Given this political dynamic, Nigeria drifted from one political crisis to another, compromising national stability, unity, and development.

The long crisis in the Western Region began in 1962 and was caused by the split in the AG, the party in power in the region, which had also formed the opposition in the federal parliament. This was, perhaps, the most debilitating of the succession of conflicts that bedeviled Nigeria's First Republic. Olufemi Vaughan rightly qualified this crisis as a "benchmark in Nigerian history."[14] The crisis would prove the beginning of the end of the First Republic.

The genesis of the Western Crisis was the ideological tension within the party. Its leader, Chief Obafemi Awolowo, who was also the opposition leader in the federal parliament, had begun to steer the party to a new ideological direction by espousing democratic socialism and promoting populist ideals. This ideological shift did not go well with his deputy, Chief S. L. Akintola, the premier of the region and an ardent promoter of regionalism. Akintola and his supporters also opposed the party's decision not to cooperate with the ruling NPC. The brewing tension between the two party chieftains and their supporters came to the fore in February 1962 at the party's annual congress held in Jos, when the Awolowo faction, the "progressives," prevailed over the conservative Akintola faction to clinch control of the party platform. What followed was a volley of bitter charges, counter-charges, and smear campaigns against each other by the two prominent Yoruba politicians. The deteriorating situation in the AG was clearly becoming a threat to peace and order in the West, and thus invited mediation efforts, for example, by some prominent Yoruba traditional rulers and eminent Yoruba leaders. These peace initiatives were to no avail, and the crisis deepened, taking a sharp turn in May when, goaded by Awolowo, the party deposed Chief Akintola as premier of the Western Region. Awolowo had earlier accused his estranged deputy of disloyalty to the party, mismanagement, and indiscipline. Akintola refused to go down and challenged his dismissal in the courts on the ground that it was unconstitutional. Meanwhile the AG appointed a new premier for the region.

The disputed dismissal of Akintola orchestrated violent rioting in the Western Region. The disturbances in the region even reached its House of Assembly on May 25 when the legislative body attempted, twice, to meet in sessions to ratify the appointment of the new premier. Fighting broke out among the lawmakers on the floor of the assembly; injuries were recorded, and damage was done to government property. The federation's prime minister, Sir Abubakar Tafawa Balewa, gave a rather graphic description of the event. According to him, "The Whole House was shattered, every bit of furniture there was broken; the people broke their heads, some persons were stabbed."[15] In the wake of this fracas, the federal government swiftly intervened in the crisis. Prime Minister Balewa, who was of the NPC, declared a state of emergency in the region on May 29, which was to last for six months. Also, the federal government dissolved the western legislature, and appointed a new administrator for the region.

The federal government's intervention has sometimes been explained as motivated, at least in part, by the desire of the ultraconservative

NPC/NCNC coalition government to curtail the growing influence of the radical Awolowo faction of the AG in the Western Region, and even outside the region. In its pursuit of radical changes to Nigeria's body politic, the Awolowo faction constituted a threat to the interests of the NPC/NCNC coalition government. Larry Diamond has provided some ways in which the Awolowo faction posed a threat to the federal coalition: its attacks on "political corruption and high living . . . its commitments to radical change . . . its political forays into [NPC/NCNC] minority areas . . . and . . . its increasing attractiveness to educated Nigerian youth."[16] Diamond argued that these were precisely the reasons for the federal intervention in the West. The NPC/NCNC intervention in the West was thus aimed to "prevent the Awolowo faction from taking power."[17] This was the attitude taken by many in the west despite Prime Minister Balewa's assurances that the Western crisis had reached a proportion in which the federal government must intervene to prevent a likely total breakdown of public order and peace.[18] The federal action was, nevertheless, perceived as an attempt to marginalize the Yoruba in Nigerian politics. Vaughan noted that "Balewa's declaration of an emergency thus created a feeling of vulnerability among Yorubas of diverse community and class backgrounds."[19]

Emergency rule in the west did not calm nerves but further entrenched the bitterness that had poisoned the region's politics. Cleavages within the political class in particular and in the civil society in general became the order of the day. Realignment of political forces pitched both political and traditional Yoruba leaders and sub-ethnic groups against one another. Deposed Akintola, now head of a new party, the Nigerian National Democratic Party (NNDP), was reinstated in 1963 as Western premier by the prime minister. The NNDP allied itself with the ruling NPC at the center. Meanwhile, Awolowo and some of his closest radical associates in the AG had been charged with a number of criminal offenses including treason. In June 1963, he was sentenced to 10 years in prison. The AG had also lost its position as the official opposition in the federal parliament. Accompanying the spate of political events in the West was sporadic violence throughout the region between the supporters of Akintola and Awolowo.

Political violence in the West came to a head during the October 1965 regional parliamentary elections, which produced disputed results. The bitterly contested election in the West was not only massively rigged, it was marred by open thuggery, arson, and politically motivated killings. The bloody riots continued until January 1966, when the armed forces staged a coup d'état, intervening for the first time in Nigerian politics. The Western political crisis and the failure to nip it in the bud had ultimately led to the collapse of democracy in Nigeria. The country would not see democratic rule for the next 13 years.

The Northern Pogroms (1966)

The January 1966 coup that terminated the First Republic did not resolve the ethnic/regional crisis in Nigeria. The military was highly politicized and divided along ethnic lines like the political class it had disposed. Under the succeeding military government of Maj. Gen. Johnson Aguiyi-Ironsi, a senior Igbo officer from the East, ethnic tensions, animosities, and wrangling continued to heighten. The uncontrolled ethnic rivalry and mutual suspicion eventually culminated in one of the most dastardly acts of violence in Nigerian history: the massacre of thousands of Igbo in northern Nigeria by the Hausa-Fulani in May, September, and October 1966.

The spate of the killing of the Igbo, the Northern Pogrom as it is often referred to, was initially an uncoordinated mob action, but it eventually acquired the official stamp of the northern military and political establishment and mass media encouragement. Its dress rehearsal occurred in late May in a spontaneous protest by students of Ahmadu Bello University in the northern town of Zaria, against the promulgation of the Unification Decree by the Ironsi government a few days earlier.[20] Perceived in the North as detrimental to its interest, the decree, designed to turn Nigeria from a federation into a unitary state, was highly resented in the region. The students' protest soon degenerated into a week of violent rioting in major northern cities including Kaduna, Kano, Jos, Katsina, and Sokoto. In these riots, the targets of attacks were southerners, particularly the Igbo. The casualty figure is staggering—about 3,000 according to Alexander Madiebo, commander of the Nigerian Army Artillery Regiment and a witness to the carnage.[21]

Anti-Southern sentiment had always been rife in the North. Northerners particularly harbored special animosity against the Igbo, who were numerous in the region. Many had migrated there even before independence and had established themselves as formidable traders, virtually dominating retail commerce in many northern cities. This was to the chagrin of many Northerners who felt that they were being economically marginalized in their own region of origin. The January coup and its aftermath, as will be seen later in this chapter, contributed to increased Northern suspicion of the Igbo. The latter was perceived as harboring intent to replace the Hausa-Fulani domination of the country with that of Igbo.

The "May Test Riots," as described by Madiebo, proved to be the precursor to the more organized and expanded massacres during

September and October. This renewed killing of the Igbo, mostly in the North, was conducted by mobs, but this time with involvement of Northern soldiers.[22] Later, as part of the Biafran wartime propaganda, Ojukwu described the massacres as "calculated and systematic acts of genocide and total extermination" of Biafrans.[23] In another wartime speech, of course, borne out of the Biafran propaganda, Ojukwu recalled the events in a rather graphic way:

By September 18 . . . riots had broken out in Makurdi, Minna, Gboko and Kaduna in Northern Nigeria. Our people—men, women and children—became the targets of well-organized and systematic mass murders. . . . By the third week of September, the reign of terror had spread to Lagos and Western Nigeria. Distinguished Biafrans in Ibadan and Oshogbo were abducted by Nigerians soldiers and killed. In Lagos, too, kidnapping of defenseless Biafran civilians by armed soldiers became the order of the day. The climax came with the massacres of September 29 and after. . . . On October 1, at Kano Airport alone, over 400 Biafrans awaiting airlifts home were surrounded by armed Northern Nigerian soldiers and civilians and massacred. . . . In the five months of massacres and atrocities, May–October, 1966, over 30,000 of our people were shot, hacked to death, burnt or buried alive; hundreds of women and children were ravished; unborn children were torn out of their mothers' wombs. Two million of our people deprived and dejected were forced to seek refuge in their homeland.[24]

The pogroms led to the mass exodus of the Igbo to their home region from all parts of Nigeria, most especially the North. The secession of the Eastern Region from Nigeria was to consequently follow, giving birth to the short-lived Republic of Biafra.

Genocide or War of Unity (1966–1970)

The destructive ethnic rivalry that had plagued the nation from independence and which was never resolved in the First Republic had eventually come to a head in the Biafran secession. The Nigerian military, an institution that had never evolved into an instrument of advancing national interest, also succumbed to the scourge of ethnic politics.[25] While the civil war had roots in colonial history, it was ultimately the culmination of the destructive political path the nation had towed since independence. Indeed, the war was the most profound expression of ethnic conflict in Nigeria. Although the war has been briefly discussed in Chapter 1, it might be useful here to take a look at the human dimension of its brutality.

The initial response of the Nigerian federal military government to Biafra's secession was a "police action," intended to bring a quick end to an unwarranted rebellion. This punitive action, however, proved to be inadequate to end the Igbo's determined resolve to establish a sovereign state—hence Nigeria's all-out war to crush Biafra. The war was to degenerate into one of the bloodiest conflicts in modern African history. It was characterized by devastating levels of death and destruction, particularly on the Biafran side. The number of war casualties is not certain, but it is believed that between one to three million Igbo perished during the war. Less than a year into the war, the *Times of London* was reporting the number of the dead as: "twice as much as the three year figure in Vietnam."[26]

The unimaginable scale of war casualty inside Biafra must not be explained solely in terms of the effect of combat. Beyond the victims of direct fighting, many more Biafrans perished as a result of Nigeria's strategy of mass starvation. When Nigeria declared total war on Biafra, it regarded mass starvation as a legitimate war weapon to be used against the rebels. In due course, pitiful pictures of starving Biafran children and women suffering from severe malnutrition (Kwashiokor) began to appear in newspapers and on television around the world. This was quickly exploited by Biafran propaganda to discredit Nigeria by tagging the war a genocidal one waged by the Hausa-Fulani to exterminate the Igbo.

Daily reports in Western mass media, in particular of the starving Biafran population, began to arouse global interest in the war.[27] As war casualties in Biafra mounted, calls for humanitarian intervention by human rights and religious organizations to alleviate the sufferings of the civil society became more vocal. For instance, in 1968, the noted American senator, Edward Kennedy, made the following appeal:

> The loss of life from starvation continues at more than 10,000 persons per day—over 1,000,000 lives in recent months. Without emergency measures now, the number will climb to 25,000 per day within a month—and some 2,000,000 deaths by the end of the year. The New Year will only bring greater disaster to a people caught in the passion of fratricidal war.[28]

The Biafran alleged genocidal intention by the federal government never translated into the expected worldwide support and recognition for the secessionist state. The Biafran propaganda machine was managed mainly by Markpress, a Geneva-based public relations firm, and by other organizations such as the U.S.-based Biafran Committee for Prevention of Genocide (BIAGEN). The failure of the Biafran propaganda campaign of Nigeria's genocidal intention was largely due to the federal government's effectiveness in counteracting it. The Biafran propaganda was discredited when in 1968, on invitation by the federal government to the war zone to observe firsthand the conduct of the federal troops, an international military observer team declared that there was "no evidence of any intent by the Federal troops to destroy the Ibo people or their property." The team made a firm determination that "the use of the term genocide is in no way justified."[29]

THE MILITARY IN POLITICS

Military intervention in politics is a familiar phenomenon in the developing world of Latin America, Asia, and Africa. In Africa, practically every state had at one time or the other experienced military rule. For most countries, the militarization of politics has exacerbated conflicts. In the first place, the instrument of military intervention, the coup d'état, is often a violent one. The failure of military rulers to bring about political stability and economic progress and development has engendered civil unrests. Except in very few places, a military government often replaced a previous one by way of a coup, hence a vicious circle of violence.[30]

Nigeria provides a good case study of the implications of military intervention in politics. In Nigeria's short history as an independent sovereign state, it has experienced seven military coups d'état, often very bloody. Military rule itself has lasted for almost 33 years (1966–1979 and 1983–1998). This section of the chapter looks at the ways in which military intervention in politics has made Nigeria a conflict hot spot.

Coups and Political Violence (1966–1997)

The forcible overthrow of government through military coups d'état is an expression of political violence. As an armed operation in which the military takes over a government through the barrel of the gun, a coup, by definition, is not a peaceful event. Coups in Nigeria, for the most part, have been violent, resulting in assassination of political and military leaders as well as causing the death of many more people.[31]

The first coup in Nigeria, which occurred on January 15, 1966, and which led to the usurpation of political power by the armed forces, was one of the bloodiest in the history of the nation. The coup not only overthrew the federal government, it led to the assassination of some of the most notable political bigwigs of the First Republic. Among the politician casualties were the prime minister, Balewa; the powerful Northern Region's premier, Sir Ahmadu Bello; the premier of the volatile Western Region, Chief Akintola; and the federal finance minister, Festus Okotie-Eboh. A number of top-ranking military officers were also casualties of the coup.[32]

Given the pronouncement of the authors of the January coup, the tragic killings that accompanied the attempt to terminate the rule of the discredited politicians were an inevitable price to pay to rescue the ship of the Nigerian state dangerously adrift and headed for disaster. Maj. Patrick Chukwuma Kaduna Nzeogwu, the coup's spokesperson, stated the nationalistic intention of his colleagues in a broadcast in northern Nigeria:

> Our enemies are the political profiteers, the swindlers, the men in the high and low places that seek bribes and demand ten percent; those that seek to keep the country divided permanently so that they can remain in office as ministers and VIPs of waste; the tribalists, the nepotists; those that make the country look big-for-nothing before international circles; those that have corrupted our society and put the Nigerian political calendar back by their words and deeds. . . . We promise that you will no more be ashamed to say you are a Nigerian.[33]

The accounts of the January coup by two of its major participants, Ben Gbulie and Adewale Ademoyega, have corroborated the altruistic motive of its planners.[34] It is doubtful, however, if these accounts have finally put to rest the controversy over whether the young army officers who staged the coup were really motivated by nationalistic impulse. Two prominent former high-ranking officers, Maj. Gen. David Ejoor and Maj. Gen. Chris Ali, have in more recent publications disputed the nationalistic inclination of the coup plotters, subscribing to the oft-repeated accusation that the coup was conceived to eliminate the Hausa-Fulani political domination of the country and replace it with that of the Igbo via military rule.[35]

A number of factors, indeed, lend credence to this belief. First, the ring leaders of the coup, the so-called "five majors," were all of eastern Nigerian origin except one.[36] Second, major casualties were predominantly Northerners, while no Igbo person was killed. Third, the military government that succeeded the deposed civilian regime was headed by an Igbo officer, Maj. Gen. Johnson Aguiyi-Ironsi. All these fuelled the interpretation of the coup, particularly in the North, as an "Igbo coup," executed to bring about Igbo hegemony. The policies of the new military government did not help to allay Northern fears of political marginalization and an alleged enthronement of Igbo dominance. What further aggrieved the North was the military government's promulgation of the indigenization decree, which, as mentioned earlier, triggered the May 1966 pogroms in the North.

The tense atmosphere that pervaded the post-January coup months exploded in another round of violence on July 29, 1966. In response to the so-called "Igbo coup," officers of Northern origin staged a counter-coup, overthrowing Ironsi's military government, and in so doing stamping out what they believed was a budding Igbo domination of the country. Like its January predecessor, the second coup was equally bloody. Among its important casualties were the head of state, Major General Ironsi, and the governor of the Western Region, Lt. Col. Adekunle Fajuyi. There was also random killing of Igbo soldiers.

The saga of coups continued to dominate the Nigerian political landscape. The administration of Lt. Col. (later General) Yakubu Gowon, which succeeded the Ironsi government, was toppled in a bloodless coup on July 25, 1975, after nine years. Nigerians, tired of the corrupt Gowon regime, hailed the coup and welcomed the new military administration of Brig. (later General) Murtala Ramat Mohammed. The new leader was very much loved by the populace because of his administration's dynamism and its intolerance of indiscipline and corruption that had characterized the previous administration. In the fourth Nigerian coup six months after taking office, on February 13, 1976, Mohammed was brutally assassinated.

The February coup had a more violent twist to it than previous ones. It was the first abortive coup in Nigeria, yet it was bloody, claiming the lives of a number of military officers. As planned by its leaders, a group of disgruntled junior and mid-level officers led by Lt. Col. Bukar Sukar Dimka, it was intended to be a bloodbath. Apart from Mohammed, the high echelon of his administration was targeted for assassination. Although the head of state was killed, the coup failed to topple the administration. The aftermath of the failed coup was mass arrest of its leaders and collaborators and their trial. Thirty-two of them were convicted by a special military tribunal for treason, and were executed by a firing squad. Mass execution of condemned coup plotters was, thereafter, to become a constant feature of Nigeria's military politics.

Nigeria's fifth coup occurred on December 31, 1983, which ended the country's second attempt at democratic rule. It terminated the discredited civilian administration of President Shehu Shagari, which had been democratically elected in 1979. It was a bloodless coup that installed the military junta of Maj. Gen. Muhammadu Buhari. The lackluster Buhari administration itself was overthrown in a bloodless coup on August 27, 1975, enthroning Gen. Ibrahim Babangida as military president.

The rounds of coups continued. During Babangida's brutal dictatorship, an alleged coup, still in the planning stage, was unearthed in December 1985. There was also an attempted bloodless coup on April 22, 1990, which failed to unseat the administration. Both coups were met with severe repercussions in that they led to the mass execution of officers convicted by a special military tribunal. The 1990 abortive coup was especially significant in that if it had succeeded as planned, it would have been the most bloody in the history of military coups in Nigeria.[37]

A palace coup, the last of the military political intrigues before the enthronement of democratic rule in 1999, occurred in November 1993. Chief Earnest Shonekan, whom Babangida had installed to head the so-called Interim National Government (ING) when he was literally forced to resign in August 1993, was edged out of power by army chief Gen. Sani Abacha. In December 1997, Abacha claimed that he had uncovered a coup in the making and rounded up some senior military officers who were tried and sentenced to death. Before the death sentences could be carried out, Abacha suddenly died on June 8, 1998, in mysterious circumstances, many believed from alleged poisoning. One of those sentenced to death was former head of state General Olusegun Obasanjo. It was widely believed that the phantom coup was a mere attempt by Abacha to eliminate those he perceived as a threat to his brutal regime.

Military Dictatorship

It was customary for every military government in Nigeria on overthrowing the previous regime to claim it had taken the action to correct every conceivable problem the nation was facing. When the military overthrew the Second Republic on December 31, 1983, its spokesperson, Brig. Sani Abacha, gave the following reasons for the coup: economic mismanagement, food shortages and high prices of commodities, collapsed health services, a deteriorating educational system, high unemployment, and massive corruption.[38] The military government of Maj. Gen. Muhammadu Buhari that took over the government promptly prided itself a "corrective regime." But military regimes' claim of messiahship was always a ploy to legitimize military rule—invariably, each successive military government ended up worse than the one it had overthrown.[39]

Military dictatorship in Nigeria was always intolerant, characterized by abuse of human rights and violation of civil liberties. In return, military government's draconian policies and arbitrary use of power often invited protests from the civil society, sometimes by way of violent riots. In the 1970s and 1980s, the booming economy tended to cushion the rough edges of military misrule. However, in the late 1980s and 1990s, the impact of the declining economy on the population introduced a new level of resistance to military rule. Also, during this period military despotism and violence against the populace assumed a proportion hitherto unknown in the nation's history. The attempt of the brutal regimes of Generals Babangida and Sani Abacha to crush every opposition pushed anti-military violence to an unprecedented height.

More than any previous regime, the Babangida administration institutionalized corruption in Nigeria in the face of a rapidly deteriorating
economy. To address the economic problems, the regime adopted in
1986 the Structural Adjustment Program (SAP), a prescription of the
International Monetary Fund (IMF). SAP proved to be a disastrous
approach to the ailing economy. The devaluation of the currency, the
naira, which was required by SAP, resulted in increased food prices,
house rents, transport fares, and other necessities. The resulting high
cost of living turned millions of working-class Nigerians into paupers
and nearly wiped out the middle class. Real wages, especially for the
working class, plummeted in the face of rising inflation. The unemployment rate skyrocketed as businesses closed down or downsized
and workers retrenched. Thus, rather than alleviate the sufferings of
the masses of the people, SAP, indeed, aggravated them.[40]

Growing opposition to the worsening economic condition and the
government's failed economic measures was manifested in widespread
civil unrest from 1987 through 1992. These protests and demonstrations, termed "SAP Riots," were championed by various interests
drawn from all sectors of the civil society, such as labor and trade
unions, student organizations, and professional bodies including those
of university teachers, lawyers, and journalists. Peasants were also
drawn into the protest movement as market women, cab drivers, private transporters, and other interest groups took to the streets.

Anti-SAP riots were initially organized by students of tertiary institutions throughout the country. In May 1986, students at Ahmadu Bello
University, Zaria, demonstrated against the imminent adoption of SAP
by the government. In the following years, student protests against the
government's discredited economic policies would crystallize. However,
the protest movement against SAP was largely coordinated by the
Nigeria Labor Congress (NLC), which, beginning in 1987, organized
nationwide public demonstrations and labor strikes.

Mass protests against SAP typically degenerated into violence in
many places causing destruction to life and property. Hundreds of people were killed during the rash of labor demonstrations and student
unrest, mostly because the government resorted to repressive measures.
The police and other security agencies were instruments of the junta's
repressive agenda. The use of the police during the riots is vividly
portrayed in the quote below:

> During the anti-SAP riots, the Nigerian Police used the best in their
> armory—armored cars, water spraying trucks, helicopters, different can-
> isters of tear gas, rifles, pistols, etc. In some parts of the country where
> the hostility was protracted and fierce, the police were assisted by the

army, which led to the death of many Nigerians—children, students, policemen and a number of pregnant women.[41]

Babangida's high-handedness and war on the Nigerian populace also found expression in arbitrary arrests, detention, and jailing of opposition elements without trial. Newspapers were closed at will, student organizations were abrogated, and a number of universities were shut down, some for long periods. A new phenomenon, political assassination, was introduced to the political dictionary of Nigeria during the Babangida era. In October 1986, a parcel bomb killed Dele Giwa, a newspaper editor critical of the government. The incident was widely believed to have been engineered by government agents.[42]

Perhaps Babangida's most dastardly act in power was the annulment of the June 12, 1993, presidential election won by the leading Yoruba politician, Chief Moshood K. Abiola, and which would have ushered in the Third Republic. Acknowledged by international observers as fair and free, the sudden declaration of the election null and void without justification triggered weeks of violent mass civil unrests in several parts of the country. The violent reaction was more prominent in the Yoruba states of Lagos, Oyo, Ogun, and Ondo. Many Yoruba had come to see the denial of Abiola's mandate as evidence of the Hausa-Fulani reluctance to relinquish power that it had held for much of Nigeria's history. In August, renewed mass civil unrest as a result of the election crisis paralyzed economic activities in the country. It was the continued protests that finally drove Babangida out of office. The military president resigned on August 26, 1993, installing the interim national government of Chief Shonekan, which never achieved legitimacy.

When in November 1993 General Abacha sacked the Shonekan government, Nigeria entered the most vicious period of military dictatorship. Abacha, whom Toyin Falola has described as the "worst dictator yet and the most brazenly corrupt and cruel"[43] led a diabolic regime whose reign of terror was unprecedented in Nigerian history. Apart from unrestrained persecution of perceived enemies of his dictatorship, "high profile serial killings," in the words of Afeaye Igbafe and O. J. Offiong, were a major feature of political violence during the Abacha years.[44] Patrick Igbinovia has recorded 16 unresolved politically motivated assassinations between 1993 and 1998, the years of Abacha's misrule.[45] One of the high-profile victims was Kudirat Abiola, the politically active wife of the detained winner of the annulled June 12 presidential election, Moshood Abiola.

The crisis of the June 12 election remained unresolved and continued to engender ethno-political tensions in the country. Abacha's clamping of Abiola into detention when the president-elect tried to claim his mandate by declaring himself president further convinced the Yoruba of the design of the North to perpetuate its political hegemony over Nigeria. Pro-democracy activists inside and outside of Nigeria mobilized in a number of organizations to challenge Abacha's blatant authoritarianism. The most prominent of these organizations was the National Democratic Coalition (NADECO), whose primary agenda was an end to military rule and the actualization of the June 12 presidential mandate.

Abacha's iron-fist rule and the reckless employment of the security forces to repress opposition brought about widespread civil unrest. A series of violent demonstrations occurred all over the country in protest against the junta's reign of terror. A spate of bomb attacks increasingly became a part of this protest movement. The sudden death of Abiola in detention on July 7, 1998, of a reported heart attack, triggered rioting in Lagos and other parts of the south, the bastion of the opposition to Abacha.[46] Resentment against the Abacha regime was particularly rife in the south as the Yoruba appeared to be the dictator's primary target for repression. It was not surprising that in some Yoruba circles, talks of Yoruba secession from the nation were openly expressed. Indeed, a Yoruba ethnic separatist group, the Oodua People's Congress (OPC), emerged.

MINORITY UPRISING AND COMMUNAL VIOLENCE

Mutual suspicion, for the most part, has defined the relationship between the three major Nigerian ethnic groups, the Hausa-Fulani, the Yoruba, and the Igbo. Many smaller ethnic groups, the so-called minorities, on their part deeply resented a perceived desire of the larger groups to stifle their interest and curtail their development. These smaller ethnic groups have on many occasions reacted violently to defend their own interests in the face of perceived threats from the larger groups. The Tiv riots in 1960 and 1964 were the first major minority uprising in Nigeria. The violent riots by the Tiv, a minority group in the North, were directed against an alleged domination and political control of the group by the Hausa-Fulani. The response of the federal government to the uprising was to brutally repress it, causing the death of hundreds of people.

Since the Tiv riots, minority discontentment and protests have continued to be an important part of ethnic and national politics in Nigeria. A new dimension to the expression of minority agitation was offered in April 1990, when some disgruntled elements in the armed forces executed an unsuccessful coup partly, by the admission of its planners, to defend minority interests. According to the coup's spokesperson, Maj. Gideon Gwaza Orkar, in his broadcast to the nation, the action was taken "on behalf of the patriotic and well-meaning peoples of the Middle Belt and the southern parts of this country." Orkar explained further that the coup was "a well conceived, planned and executed revolution for the marginalised, oppressed and enslaved peoples of the Middle Belt and the south," aimed at "freeing ourselves and children yet unborn from eternal slavery and colonization by a clique of this country." Orkar, a Tiv, also accused the "Northern aristocratic class" of "deliberate impoverishment of the peoples from the Middle Belt and the south."[47] One significant element of the abortive coup was that it went beyond the traditional aim of overthrowing an incumbent regime. Orkar decreed in his broadcast the temporary excision of the core northern states of Sokoto, Borno, Katsina, Kano, and Bauchi, from the Nigerian federation. The coup, as some observers have noted, could have triggered off another civil war in Nigeria.[48] The coup was put down and 69 of its conspirators executed.

Undoubtedly, the most volatile hot spot in contemporary Nigeria is the Niger Delta, a region that has seen unrelenting violence particularly since the early 1990s. The history of violent minority agitation in this turbulent region can be traced to Isaac Boro's revolt of 1966. Boro was a young revolutionary student leader, an Ijo from the Niger Delta who had organized a small band of revolutionaries called Delta Volunteer Service (DVS), with the aim of liberating the region from alleged oppression by the dominant ethnic groups. The DVS received paramilitary training in camps and launched a guerrilla campaign against the federal government in February 1966. The group's engagement with the police and the army was bloody. Although the insurgency failed, Boro did proclaim the region the "Niger Delta Peoples Republic." In a document titled "Declaration of Independence," Boro designated himself "General Officer Commanding the DVS and Leader of the Liberation Government." In the document he also ordered the following:

- Institution of a "State of Emergency . . . in the territory to give adequate protection to the Niger Delta people against aggressors."
- Invalidation of "all former agreements as regards the crude oil of the people undertaken by the now defunct Nigerian Government in the territory."
- Cessation of exploration in the region by "all oil companies . . . in their own interest," with the advice to "renew agreements with the new Republic."

- Installation of "the Niger Delta Volunteer Service," as "the law enforcing body and the standing armed force of the people."
- "Provisional Senate" of "84 members, six from each of the 14 clans" with the responsibility of advising "the Liberation Government on a new constitution for the People."[49]

Boro and his henchmen were tried for treason and sentenced to death after their defeat by the army. However, they were later pardoned, and Boro joined the army to fight on the Nigerian side during the Nigerian Civil War, where he was killed. His dream of liberating the Niger Delta from oppression and exploitation was to be taken up in a more violent way in the ensuing years.

Oil and Conflict in the Niger Delta

Oil is Nigeria's major export product and its main source of wealth. With enormous reserves, the nation is one of the leading producers of oil in the world. It is also a major supplier to the United States. Most of the country's oil is obtained in the Niger Delta, making the region potentially the richest part of the country.

Although the people of the oil-rich Niger Delta are literally sitting on wealth, they have remained some of the most impoverished in the country. Successive Nigerian governments have neglected to develop the region and to improve the abject condition of the people there. More importantly, the region has suffered gravely from years of environmental degradation as a result of oil exploration by multinational oil companies. The 1966 Boro-led uprising was essentially not just a rebellion against the federal government, it was as much a protest against the exploitation of the Niger Delta by the oil companies. This was evident during the uprising when the DVS insurgents attacked oil installations and inflicted damage to Shell-BP pipes. Boro's intention of a sovereign republic in the region was thus to preserve its wealth for its people.

A new level of violence commenced in the Niger Delta in the early 1990s as the local populations became increasingly aggressive in their demand for a fair share of the region's revenue. Protests were also aimed at government's failure to provide necessary amenities and to deal with widespread poverty. Also rife was opposition to the oil companies that had inflicted untold environmental damage on the region. Indeed, decades of exploration without regard to the well-being of the local communities by oil companies such as Mobil, Shell, Chevron, Texaco, and Agip had turned the Niger Delta into an environmental disaster. Its communities suffered greatly from health problems caused by massive environmental pollution. There were also economic repercussions from environmental damage. Polluted water and soil curtailed fishing and farming, the traditional occupations of many in the community. Oil-generated ecological damage caused by excessive oil drilling, oil spillage, and gas flaring also affected the livelihood of the people.

Umuechem, a small farming community in Rivers State, was one of the first in the Niger Delta to be brutalized by Nigerian armed forces. In response to a peaceful demonstration in 1990 against Shell's devastation of their land, and demand for the provision of basic necessities, units of the Nigerian mobile police invaded the community and killed scores of villagers and damaged homes.[50] In the following years, a number of other communities came under the violent sledgehammer of government's security forces.

The community hardest hit by the environmental degradation of the Niger Delta was Ogoniland. Karl Maier describes the plight of the Ogoni people thus:

> Over the years, 634 million barrels of oil worth approximately $30 billion had been pumped from Ogoniland alone. . . . In return, the Ogonis received much of the harm but few benefits the oil industry had to offer. Poverty is endemic in Ogoniland and the Niger Delta as a whole. Education and health facilities are primitive at best, and few Ogoni homes enjoy the most basic services, such as electricity and running water.[51]

The Ogoni, constituting about half a million people, began a well-organized protest movement in 1990. Under the auspices of the Movement for the Survival of the Ogoni People (MOSOP), an ethnic organization led by writer and environmentalist Ken Saro-Wiwa, the Ogoni protested the deplorable state of their homeland, demanded greater share of huge oil revenues, and political autonomy.[52]

A special military task force brought the full repressive power of the federal government on Ogoni activism. A series of military operations against defenseless local inhabitants led to hundreds of Ogoni deaths. Literally a war zone, the army destroyed Ogoni villages. The assault on the Ogoni assumed a new twist when MOSOP leader Saro-Wiwa and nine of his associates were arrested by Abacha's regime. They were accused of murder, tried, condemned to death in a kangaroo court, and summarily executed on November 10, 1995. The executions were carried out in spite of worldwide appeal, given the fishy nature of the accusation. More than anything else, Saro-Wiwa's execution turned the global searchlight on the massive violation of human rights in the Niger Delta and the environmental degradation of the region.[53]

The new democratic dispensation that began in 1999 has not been able to effectively deal with the Niger Delta conflicts. Since 2000, a spate of more violent insurgency has broken out in the region as other marginalized ethnic minorities became involved in the protest movement. A number of militant rebel groups including the Movement for the Emancipation of the Niger Delta (MEND), the Niger Delta People's Volunteer Force (NDPVF), and the Egbesu Boys emerged, dedicated to uncompromising violent opposition to state authority and foreign oil interests. Adopting guerrilla tactics, these groups have kidnapped and held foreign oil workers hostage and demanded ransom for their release. The militias have also attacked and vandalized oil installations and other infrastructure.[54] Their increasing campaign of terror and sabotage has led, on occasion, to the shutting down of major refineries such as those in Kaduna, Warri, and Port Harcourt. The deteriorating violence in the region has greatly disrupted oil production with adverse effect on the economy. In July 2008, Human Rights Watch reported that Nigeria's production plummeted "to its lowest level in 20 years, contributing to spiraling world oil prices."[55]

Nigeria is an oil-dependent economy. In order to ensure uninterrupted oil production, succeeding governments have found it necessary to protect the interests of the transnational oil companies against militant rebel activities. Since 2000, the government has escalated counterinsurgency military operations against local militias, the so-called oil-rebels. Such repressive military intervention has resulted in the killing of hundreds of people.

Apart from seeking the assistance of federal forces in dealing with rebel militias, some oil companies are themselves equipped with paramilitary forces. For instance, Shell had a military attachment, the "Supernumerary Police," with the responsibility to "guard the company's facilities . . . against crime."[56] Such paramilitary forces have been put to use to harass the local population. Allegations have been made of Shell's attempts or actual import of arms for the Nigerian police and its paramilitary force to be able to repress local opposition to its interest.

Oil, the main source of national wealth, has paradoxically become a key factor of conflict in Nigeria. The unending conflict has devastated the Niger Delta, turning the region into the most explosive part of the country since the civil war of 1967–1970. The long-running violent conflict has so far eluded solution, and this has continued to pose a major threat to national security.[57]

Ethnic Militias

In practically every region of Nigeria, conflicts between neighboring communities or small ethnic groups have occurred. Communal conflicts have become more deadly in recent years, aggravated by organized armed ethnic militias, or sometimes vigilante groups.[58]

The Niger Delta, perhaps, more than any other part of Nigeria, has seen violent communal conflicts such as between the Ogoni and their neighbors, Andoni, Okrika, and Ndoki (1993–1994), and between the Ijo and the Itsekiri (2003). Conflicts in this region have been intensified by armed militias. Although in most cases militias originated to protest foreign and federal governments' oil interests in the region, however, a number of them have increasingly perpetuated intercommunal conflicts. One of the major factors for intercommunal violence was the desire of respective ethnic militias to control the lucrative business of crude oil theft through "bunkering," a process of illegal tapping and extraction of oil that had become rampant in the region. This contest for access to oil wealth often resulted in violent attacks on one another by rival communities.

One of the most prominent armed ethnic militias in the Niger Delta was the NDPVF. Founded in 2004, it demanded more Ijo share of the region's oil wealth, an agenda that brought it into a violent collision course with the federal authorities and oil corporations. However, the NDPVF also was at loggerheads with neighboring ethnic groups, particularly the Itsekiri. In 2003 and 2004, it engaged another rival armed militia, the Niger Delta Vigilante (NDV) in destructive, deadly confrontations over the control of oil bunkering.

Ethnic militias have also been active in other parts of the country, however, with agendas different from those of the Niger Delta. In the Southwest, the most prominent militia was the OPC. It was formed in August 1994, originally as a nationalistic sociocultural organization to protect Yoruba interests in the wake of the annulled 1993 presidential election won by Abiola. A more radical, militant wing of the group soon transformed itself into a vigilante group, dedicated to combating crime. It was active in Yoruba states in the Southwest including Lagos, Oyo, Ogun, Osun, and Ekiti. In its attempt to stamp out crime, OPC vigilante forces made up of armed youths often terrorized other ethnic groups, principally the Hausa, resident in Yoruba cities. The July 1999 violent confrontation between the OPC and the Hausa community of Shagamu is worthy of mention. As reported by Pini Jason:

> the OPC hit Shagamu, near Lagos, in a big way. Shagamu has a large Hausa settler community. An Hausa lady who allegedly violated a Yoruba religious taboo was instantly killed by people suspected to be OPC members. By the time the police restored calm 48 hours later, over 200 people had been killed or wounded. Half of the houses in Shagamu had been razed. The Hausas loaded their dead and wounded in trucks

and headed back home to Kano. The gory sight provoked a backlash. The Hausas, in retaliation, attacked the Yoruba settlers in Kano.[59]

The OPC was also often in deadly violent clashes with the Nigerian police. Accused of human rights abuses, the organization was outlawed by the Obasanjo administration in 1999. Despite this, it continued to exist, engaging the police in sporadic violent confrontations.[60]

Religious Violence

Although Nigeria is officially a secular state, religion is a core element in its national life. Most Nigerians profess either Christianity or Islam, the nation's dominant religions. A few people adhere to a variety of traditional African religions, while there are pockets of believers in other religions such as the Rosicrucian (AMORC) Order, the Grail Movement, Judaism, and Hinduism.

Of significance in Nigeria's religious constitution is the Christian/ Muslim dichotomy along ethnic or regional lines. Christianity is strong in the South among the Igbo and the Yoruba and other southern groups, while Islam is predominant in the North, notably among the Hausa-Fulani. Religion thus intertwines with ethnicity, consequently making the line between ethnic and religious conflicts a rather thin one. Indeed, the incessant religious conflicts in the country have almost always had ethnic overtones. Occurring most often in the Islamic North, religious conflicts are primarily between fundamentalist northern Muslims and Christians mostly of southern origin.

Ethno-religious conflict has always dogged Nigeria's post-independence history.[61] However, since the end of the civil war in 1970, this has become even more commonplace and destructive. Indeed, from the 1980s until the present day, there has hardly been a year without violent clashes between Muslims and Christians.

One of the most violent and widespread religious disturbances in post–civil war Nigeria was the Maitatsine revolt, which occurred in December 1980 in the northern city of Kano and which subsequently spread to other northern cities such as Kaduna, Bauchi, and Maiduguri. Maitatsine was an Islamic fundamentalist sect that confronted the state in a series of bloody uprisings against the excesses and opulence of the political class. In the course of the disturbances, before the police finally repressed them, thousands of people had lost their lives.

Religious violence in Nigeria was not often against the state per se, but typically between Muslims and Christians. In the North, zealot Muslims have killed Christians, burned down their churches,

Table 3.1 Selected Religious Violence in Nigeria, 1980–2010

City (& State)	Region	Year	Type/Cause of Conflict
Kano (Kano)	North	1980	Maitatsine Uprising
Bulunkutu (Borno)	North	1981	Maitatsine Uprising
Kaduna (Kaduna)	North	1982	Maitatsine Uprising
Jimeta (Adamawa)	North	1984	Maitatsine Uprising
Gombe (Gombe)	North	1985	Maitatsine Uprising
Ilorin (Kwara)	South	1986	Muslim/Christian Clash
Ibadan (Oyo)	South	1986	University of Ibadan Muslim/ Christian Clash
Kaduna (Kaduna)	North	1986	Muslim/Christian Clash
Kafanchan	North	1987	College of Education Muslim/ Christian Clash
Kano (Kano)	North	1987	Muslim/Christian Clash
Sokoto (Sokoto)	North	1987	Muslim/Christian Clash
Jos (Plateau)	North	1987	Muslim/Christian Clash
Bauchi (Bauchi)	North	1991	Muslim/Christian Clash
Kano (Kano)	North	1991	Muslim riot over Reinhard Bonke (Christian) Crusade
Katsina (Katsina)	North	1991	Riot over newspaper comment on Islam
Kaduna (Kaduna)	North	2000	Clash over the introduction of *sharia'a*
Kano (Kano)	North	2001	Muslim protest over America's war in Afghanistan
Kaduna (Kaduna)	North	2002	Muslim protest over planned hosting of the Miss World beauty pageant in the city
Yelwa (Plateau)	North	2004	Christian attacks on Muslims
Kano (Kano)	North	2004	Muslim attacks on Christians as reprisal for the Yelwa violence
Maiduguri (Borno)	North	2006	Muslim riots in protest against Danish cartoons of the Prophet Mohammad
Jos (Plateau)	North	2008	Muslim/Christian Clash
Maiduguri (Borno)	North	2009	Violent campaign to extend *sharia'a* to the rest of the country by the Boko Haram Islamist movement
Jos (Plateau)	North	2010	Deadly Muslim/Christian Clash

and destroyed their homes and businesses. On occasion, these acts have led to revenge killing of Muslims in the South. The above table shows a selection of religious conflicts in Nigeria between 1980 and 2010.

Sharia'a and Violence

Ethno-religious tensions heightened in Nigeria when from October 1999 12 northern states of the federation with predominant Muslim populations began to adopt the Islamic legal code, the *sharia'a*. The introduction of *sharia'a* in the North immediately became a contentious issue as the nation debated its constitutionality. Opposition to *sharia'a*, mainly from the South and the Middle Belt, was on the grounds that it posed a threat to the secular nature of the Nigerian constitution. Christians particularly argued that *sharia'a* was a northern design to establish an Islamic theocracy in the country. Although under *sharia'a* some northern states have been able to manage relationships between its predominantly Muslim population and minority Christian elements, it has not been so everywhere. Religious tension over *sharia'a* has boiled into violent clashes between Christians and Muslims, claiming thousands of lives as happened in Kaduna in 2000.

Mutual Muslim/Christian animosities have continued to engender violent confrontations in virtually every state of northern Nigeria and many parts of the Middle Belt. In late November 2008, bloody religious riots ravaged the northern city of Jos, where over 400 people were reportedly killed as a result of a dispute over council elections.[62] Again, in January 2010, Jos, reputed for a history of religious violence, witnessed vicious Muslim/Christian clashes that left hundreds of people dead. Indeed, religious clashes in Nigeria have often recorded hundreds of deaths, massive destruction of property, and large-scale displacement of populations.

THE CRISIS OF GOVERNANCE

At least until the beginning of this century, Nigeria has been a nation of political instability. The crisis of democratic governance is clearly evident in the dismal failure of civilian rule and the entrenchment of military dictatorship. As shown in table 3.2 below, from independence to the end of the twentieth century, military, more than civilian leaders, ruled Nigeria.

Elections as War

Elections are a fundamental tenet of democratic governance. Democratic maturity is, to a large extent, measured by the ability of a nation to conduct free and fair elections and transfer power in a peaceful, orderly manner. For the most part, Nigeria has not demonstrated this ability. Apart from the 1993 presidential election, which was annulled by Babangida, every election in Nigeria since independence has been fraught with electoral irregularities, and sometimes by outright violence.

Indeed, the corrupt nature of politics and political life in Nigeria ensures that elections are bedeviled by violence. At one level, for politicians, elected

Table 3.2 Heads of State and Type of Government since Independence

Period	Head of State	Type of Government
1960–1966	Alhaji Abubakar Tafawa Balewa	Elected
1966	General Johnson Aguiyi-Ironsi	Military
1966–1975	Lt. Col. (later General) Yakubu Gowon	Military
1975–1976	Brigadier (later General) Murtala Mohammed	Military
1976–1979	Lt. Gen. (later General) Olusegun Obasanjo	Military
1979–1983	Alhaji Usman Shehu Shagari	Elected
1984–1985	Maj. Gen. Muhammadu Buhari	Military
1985–1993	Maj. Gen. Ibrahim Babangida	Military
1993	Chief Earnest Sonekan	Unelected (interim)
1993–1998	Gen. Sani Abacha	Military
1998–1999	Maj. Gen. Abdulsalami Abubakar	Military
1999–2007	Chief Olusegun Obasanjo	Elected
2007–2010	Alhaji Umaru Musa Yar'Adua	Elected
2010–Date	Dr. Goodluck Jonathan	Elected

position is an avenue to amass personal wealth—not an opportunity to serve. Thus, for a political aspirant, winning an election is a matter of do or die. It is a war in which all forms of dirty tactics must be employed to ensure victory. At another level, elections are a means to achieve sectional ethnic or regional interest, not national interest. There is often little hesitation to employ violence to achieve either personal or corporate interests.

The election crisis of December 1964 occasioned the first post-independence electoral political violence in Nigeria. In the bid for victory, political parties not only resorted to electoral malpractices, more than this, they took to the diabolic act of intimidating and harassing political opponents. In the Western Region, the extensive recruitment and use of thugs by political pundits to terrorize real and suspected opponents created an atmosphere of war. In the so-called "Operation Wetie,"[63] thugs committed atrocities such as arson and murder, an experience that would earn the region the unenviable epitaph of "Wild Wild West."

Subsequent elections in Nigeria have witnessed some level of violence before, during, or in the immediate aftermath of voting. The 1965 elections produced bloody rioting, thuggery, and destruction of life and property in the West following the disputed election results. The elections in 1983 were accompanied by violent riots in some parts of the federation, particularly in the South, notably in Ondo State. As indicated earlier on, the annulment of the credible presidential election of 1993 by Babangida triggered violent rioting in the states in the Southwest. When there was no outright display of violence, electoral fraud has been rampant, creating ethno-political tensions. The latest election, that of April 2007, the first to transfer power from one democratically elected government to another, was widely believed to be flawed as attested to by international observers. As a result of alleged electoral fraud, the legitimacy of the winner of the presidential election, Alhaji Umaru Yar'Adua of the People's Democratic Party (PDP), has been in question. The bitter aftermath of the election is seen in the long-drawn-out challenge to the election result by two of the defeated presidential candidates, Gen. Muhammadu Buhari, a former military head of state, and Alhaji Atiku Abubakar, a former vice president.

The conduct of the 2007 elections was not without its share of violence. Allegations of ballot stuffing and other irregularities triggered rioting in Daura, General Buhari's hometown, where some lives and property were allegedly destroyed. The elections in the Niger Delta were also marred by violence as gang-related terrorist activities compounded the already volatile situation in the region. Some unscrupulous politicians here have been accused of using the services of jobless young men and militia members to intimidate people in their election bids. Gangs in Rivers States have increasingly become more powerful and violent largely because of ties to influential politicians.[64]

Corruption and Violence

The Nigerian polity has always been very corrupt—right from the immediate post-independence period to the present. Corruption cuts across the type of government, whether democratic or military dictatorship. The political and military elite in politics have often seen political office as an opportunity to amass wealth through the looting of the national treasury. The 2009 corruption index released by Transparency International put Nigeria at number 130 out of 180 countries rated.[65] The institutionalization of corruption in Nigeria has greatly retarded economic development resulting in a progressive fall in the living standard of its people. The ranks of the ever-growing army of jobless people have found means of livelihood in violent crimes such as armed robbery, carjacking, and in recent times, kidnapping of individuals rich enough to pay ransom money. Where life and property are insecure, many Nigerians, especially in urban centers, virtually live in fear.

Drug Trafficking

Nigeria does not have a drug problem comparable to the drug wars in Latin American countries such as Colombia. However, in the general atmosphere of political ineptitude, illicit drug trafficking by unscrupulous

Nigerians has become more rampant. These drug barons have smuggled heroin, cocaine, and other illicit drugs to North and South America, Europe, and Southeast Asia. Although Nigeria does not produce these drugs, the country is widely known as a transit center in the global drug-trafficking trade. Despite stringent anti-narcotics laws, illicit drug trafficking has become a major problem in Nigeria.

***

To a large extent conflict is a defining dynamic in Nigeria's historical development. Political, economic, religious, and ethnic contradictions that the country inherited from pre-colonial and colonial periods have never been fully resolved in contemporary times. Compounding these are other factors such as crisis of governance, endemic political corruption, and economic mismanagement. These have continued to foment civil and often, violent, conflicts.

Notes

1. See "Population in Nigeria tops 140m," *BBC News Online*, December 29, 2006, retrieved on September 15, 2008, from: http://news.bbc.co.uk/2/hi/africa/6217719.stm.

2. See "Nigeria Overtakes Venezuela in Oil Exports to US," *International Business*, August 7, 2008, retrieved on September 15, 2008, from: http://economictimes.indiatimes.com/News/International_Business/%20Nigeria_overtakes_Venezuela_in_oil_exports_to_US/articleshow/3335211.cms.

3. Statements to this effect have been made by a number of high-ranking Nigerian government functionaries. See the following, for instance: Jaja Wachukwu (foreign minister) to the House of Representatives, *House of Representatives Debates* (January 1960: col. 54); and lecture by Ambassador Ibrahim Gambari to the Royal African Society, London, in *West Africa* (May 27–June 2, 1996: 822). Scholarly, more nuanced discourses on the perception of Nigeria as an African power are contained in Julius Ihonvbere, "Nigeria as Africa's Great Power: Constraints and Prospects for the 1990s," *International Journal*, Vol. 46 (Summer 1991: 510–535); and Stephen Wright and Julius Emeka Okolo, "Nigeria: Aspirations of Regional Power," in Stephen Wright (ed.), *Africa Foreign Policies* (Boulder, CO: Westview Press, 1999), 118–132.

4. There are numerous works on this theme. See the following, for instance, Abegunrin, *Nigeria and the Struggle for the Liberation of Zimbabwe: A Study of Foreign Policy Decision Making of an Emerging Nation* (Stockholm, Sweden: Bethany Books, 1992); Adekunle Ajala, "Nigeria and the Conflict in Southern Africa," in Gabriel O. Olusanya and R. A. Akindele (eds.), *Economic Development and Foreign Policy in Nigeria* (Lagos, Nigeria: Nigerian Institute of International Affairs, 1988); and Olajide Aluko, *Essays in Nigerian Foreign Policy* (London: George Allen and Unwin, 1981).

5. Abiodun Alao has identified about 20 international peacekeeping missions in which Nigeria was a part from 1960 and 2004. See his "Peacekeepers Abroad, Trouble-Makers at Home: The Nigerian Military, National Politics and Sub-Regional Policy in the 1990s," in Olayiwola Abegunrin and Olusoji Akomolafe (eds.), *Nigeria in Global Politics: Twentieth Century and Beyond* (New York: Nova Science Publishers, 2006), 67.

6. Authoritative works on this era of Yoruba history include S.A. Akintoye, *Revolution and Power Politics in Yorubaland, 1840–1893* (London: Longman, 1971), and J. F. Ade Ajayi and R. S. Smith, *Yoruba Warfare in the Nineteenth Century* (Cambridge, UK: Cambridge University Press, 1971).

7. A study of this subject is provided in G. O. Oguntomisin and Toyin Falola, "Refugees in Yorubaland in the Nineteenth Century," *Asian and African Studies*, Vol. 21 (1987).

8. More detailed analysis of the piecemeal conquest of Nigeria is provided in Toyin Falola, *The History of Nigeria* (Westport, CT: Greenwood Press, 1999), 52–65.

9. For general works on colonial Nigeria, see Adebayo Oyebade, *The Foundations of Nigeria: Essays in Honor of Toyin Falola* (Trenton, NJ: Africa World Press, 2003); Tekena Tamuno, *The Evolution of the Nigerian State: The Southern Phase, 1898–1914* (London: Longman, 1972); W. R. Crocker, *Nigeria: A Critique of British Colonial Administration* (London: Allen and Unwin, 1936).

10. See Adebayo Oyebade, "Colonial Political Systems," in Toyin Falola, *Africa, Vol. 4: Colonial Africa, 1885–1939* (Durham, NC: Carolina Academic Press, 2002), 71–86.

11. A concise study of ethnicity in Nigeria is provided in Marcellina U. Okechie-Offoha and Matthew N. O. Sadiku (eds.), *Ethnic and Cultural Diversity in Nigeria* (Trenton, NJ: Africa World Press, 1995).

12. The anthem was in use until 1978 when it was replaced with the current one, "Arise, O Compatriots."

13. The party was originally called National Council of Nigeria and Cameroon when Cameroon was administered as part of southern Nigeria.

14. Olufemi Vaughan, *Nigerian Chiefs: Traditional Power in Modern Politics, 1890s–1990s,"* (Rochester, NY: University of Rochester Press, 2000), 96. The background to this crisis is well articulated in Vaughan, 96–119. Several other important works have critically examined the crisis. See for instance, Larry Diamond, "Class, Ethnicity, and the Democratic State: Nigeria, 1950–1966," *Comparative Studies in Society and History,* Vol. 25, No. 3 (July 1983: 457–489); Mackintosh, "Politics in Nigeria: The Action Group Crisis of 1962," *Political Studies* (June 1963: 126–155); and Kenneth Post and Michael Vickers, *Structure and Conflict in Nigeria, 1960–1966* (London: Heinemann, 1973).

15. Cited in "The Crisis in Western Nigeria: May 1962, Speeches by Abubakar Tafawa Balewa," retrieved on October 3, 2008, from: http://www.dawodu.com/balewa2.htm.

16. Diamond, "Class, Ethnicity, and the Democratic State," 479.

17. Ibid.

18. Balewa cited the motivations for the federal intervention as lack of "properly constituted government" in western Nigeria, and "the desire to ensure that peace, order and tranquility is maintained throughout the parts of the federation" as. See "The Crisis in Western Nigeria."

19. Vaughan, *Nigerian Chiefs*, 105.

20. Falola, *The History of Nigeria*, 118.

21. Alexander Madiebo, *The Nigerian Revolution and the Biafran War* (Enugu: Fourth Dimension Publishers, 1980), 42. Madiebo later became the commander of the Biafran army during the Nigerian Civil War.

22. For a rather graphic account of the killings, see ibid., 84–86. For more balanced discourse, see John De St. Jorre, *The Nigerian Civil War* (London: Hodder and Stoughton, 1972), 84–86.

23. Odumegwu Ojukwu, "Address to Addis Ababa Peace Talks," August 5, 1968, cited in Kirk-Greene, *Crisis and Conflict*, II, 247.

24. Ibid., 255.

25. Ethnicity in the military is discussed in Pade Badru, *Imperialism and Ethnic Politics in Nigeria* (Trenton, NJ: Africa World Press, 1998), 65–78.

26. Cited in *West Africa*, March 30, 1968, 374.

27. For a discussion of the international ramifications of the war, see John J. Stremlau, *The International Politics of the Nigerian Civil War, 1967–1970* (Princeton, NJ: Princeton University Press, 1977).

28. "Senator Kennedy Appeals to America's Leaders for Greater Humanitarian aid to Nigeria-Biafra and Efforts to End the Civil War," Washington: Office of the Senator, November 17, 1968.

29. Cited in Kirk-Greene, *Crisis and Conflict*, II, 331.

30. For a thorough study of the African military and its intervention in African politics, see A. B. Assensoh and Yvette M. Alex-Assensoh, *African Military History and Politics: Coups and Ideological Incursions, 1900–Present* (New York: Palgrave, 2001).

31. For a study of coups in Nigeria, see Bernard-Thompson O. Ikegwuoha, *Nigeria, an Endless Cycle of Coup D'état: A Case with Coups, Power, Politics and Government, 1966–Nov. 1993* (Rome, Italy: Edizioni Progetto Gutenberg, 1994).

32. These officers included Brig. Samuel Adesoji Ademulegun, one of the most senior officers in the army and the 1st Brigade Commander; Brig. Zakariya Maimalari, the commanding officer of the 4th Battalion; Lt. Col. James Pam, the 3rd Battalion Commander; Lt. Col. Arthur Unegbe, the quartermaster-general, Army Headquarters, Lagos; Col. Ralph A. Shodeinde, the deputy commander, Nigerian Defense Academy; and Maj. Samuel Adekoge, deputy adjutant and quartermaster-general of the 1st Brigade, Kaduna; Col. Kur Mohammed, acting chief of staff, Army Headquarters, Lagos; and Lt. Col. Abogo Largema, commanding officer, the 4th Battalion, Ibadan.

33. Cited in M. O. Ené, "One Nation, One Destiny," a feature article on the Web site NigeriaWorld.com, retrieved on October 17, 2008, from: http://nigeriaworld.com/feature/publication/ene/100202.html.

34. The accounts are Ben Gbulie, *Nigeria's Five Majors: Coup D'etat of 15th January 1966, First Inside Account* (Onitsha, Nigeria: Africana

Educational Publishers, 1981); and Adewale Ademoyega, *Why We Struck: The Story of the First Nigerian Coup* (Ibadan, Nigeria: Evans Brothers, 1981).

35. See David Ejoor, *Reminiscences* (Lagos: Malthouse Press Limited, 1989); and Mohammed Chris Alli, *The Federal Republic of Nigerian Army: The Siege of a Nation* (Lagos, Nigeria: Malthouse Press Limited, 2001).

36. The five who were assigned command operations during the coup were Patrick Chukwuma Kaduna Nzeogwu, Emmanuel Ifeajuna, Don Okafor, Chris Anuforo, and Adewale Ademoyega. Ademoyega was the only non-Easterner. There were other officers who may have been part of the coup planning.

37. A critical discourse on this coup is provided in Julius Ihonvbere, "A Critical Evaluation of the Failed Coup in Nigeria," *Journal of Modern African Studies*, Vol. 294 (1991: 601–626).

38. Sani Abacha, Radio broadcast to the nation, December 31, 1983.

39. For general discussion of the military in Nigerian politics, see Toyin Falola, et al., *The Military Factor in Nigeria: 1966–1985* (Lewiston, NY: Edwin Mellen Press, 1994).

40. A brief discussion of Babangida's economic reforms with particular reference to SAP is provided in Adebayo Oyebade, "Reluctant Democracy: The State, the Opposition, and the Crisis of Political Transition, 1985–1993," in Adebayo Oyebade (ed.), *The Transformation of Nigeria: Essays in Honor of Toyin Falola* (Trenton, NJ: Africa World Press, 2002), 142–148. More detailed discourses on SAP in Nigeria are provided in Adebayo Olukoshi (ed.), *The Politics of Structural Adjustment in Nigeria* (London: James Currey, 1993); Eghosa E. Osaghae, *Structural Adjustment and Ethnicity in Nigeria* (Uppsala, Sweden: Nordiska Afrikainstitutet Research Report no. 98); and Julius Ihonvbere, "Structural Adjustment and Nigeria's Democratic Transition," *TransAfrica Forum* (Fall 1991: 61–81).

41. Cited in Rasheed Akinyemi, "Human Rights and Intervention in Africa," in Michael C. Davis, et al. (eds.), *International Intervention in the Post-Cold War World: Moral Responsibility and Power Politics* (Armonk, NY: M. E. Sharpe, 2003), 268.

42. Investigations on the murder never yielded anything. However, the Human Rights Violations Investigation Commission (also known as Oputa Panel) instituted by the former president, Olusegun Obasanjo, in its report submitted in May 2002, recommended that the "Federal Government should open up the case of Dele Giwa for proper investigation." The overview of conclusions and recommendations of the commission's report are provided in: http://www.dawodu.com/oputa1.pdf, retrieved on October 29, 2008. It should be noted that as yet, no one has been charged for Giwa's murder.

43. Falola, *The History of Nigeria*, 196. For critical evaluation of the Abacha regime, see Festus O. Egwaikhide and Victor Adefemi Isumonah, "Nigeria Paralysed: Socio-Political Life under General Sani Abacha," *Africa Development*, Vol. 26, Nos. 3 & 4 (2001: 219–224).

44. Afeaye Anthony Igbafe and O. J. Offiong, "Political Assassinations in Nigeria: An Exploratory Study, 1986–2005, *African Journal of Political Science and International Relations*, Vol. 1, No. 1 (May 2007: 6).

45. P. E. Igbinovia, "The Criminal in All of Us: Whose Ox Have We Not Taken," *University of Benin Inaugural Lecture Series* (Benin City, Nigeria: University of Benin Press, 2003), cited in Igbafe and Offiong, "Political Assassinations in Nigeria," 11.

46. See "Abiola's Death Sparks Unrest," British Broadcasting Corporation (BBC), July 8, 1998, retrieved November 13, 2008, from: http://news.bbc.co.uk/1/hi/world/africa/128410.stm.

47. Major Gideon Orkar's coup broadcast to the nation, April 22, 1990, Federal Radio Corporation of Nigeria (FRCN), Lagos. For the broadcast's transcript, see Nowa Omoigui, "The Orkar Coup of April 22, 1990," retrieved November 4, 2008, from: http://www.dawodu.com/omoigui8.htm. A critical analysis of the coup is provided in Ihonvbere, "A Critical Evaluation of the Failed 1990 Coup in Nigeria."

48. See, for instance, Olayemi Akinwumi, *Crisis and Conflicts in Nigeria: A Political History Since 1960* (Piscataway, NJ: Transaction Publishers, 2004), 102.

49. See Gani Fawehinmi, "The Murder of Dikibo: Another Lesson for Niger-Delta," in *The Nigerian Tribune*, February 14, 2004.

50. Human Rights Watch puts the number of those killed at about 80, and the houses damaged at 495. See Human Rights Watch, *The Price of Oil: Corporate Responsibility and Human Rights Violations in Nigeria's Oil Producing Communities* (New York: Human Rights Watch, 1999), 123. For more on the massacre, see Anyakwee Nsirimovu, *The Massacre of an Oil Producing Community: The Umuechem Tragedy Revisited* (Port Harcourt, Nigeria: Institute of Human Rights and Humanitarian Law, 1994); Jedrzej Georg Frynas, *Oil in Nigeria: Conflict and Litigation between Oil Companies and Village Communities* (New Brunswick, NJ: Transaction, 2000); and Rivers State Government, *Report of Judicial Commission of Inquiry into Umuechem Disturbances*, January 1991.

51. Karl Maier, *This House Has Fallen: Midnight in Nigeria* (New York: Public Affairs, 2000), 80.

52. See "Ogoni Bill of Rights," November 1990, retrieved November 18, 2008, from: http://www.waado.org/nigerdelta/RightsDeclaration/Ogoni.html.

53. Repression in Ogoniland is chronicled in Ken Saro-Wiwa, *Genocide in Nigeria: The Ogoni Tragedy* (Port Harcourt, Nigeria: Saros International Publishers, 1992); and Human Rights Watch/Africa, *Nigeria—The Ogoni Crisis: A Case Study of Military Repression in Southeastern Nigeria* (New York: Human Rights Watch, 1995).

54. See, for instance, Gilbert da Costa, "Nigerian Militants Destroy Oil Pipeline," Voice of America, September 17, 2008, retrieved September 18, 2008, from VOA online: http://www.voanews.com/english/2008-09-17-voa31.cfm.

55. Human Rights Watch, "Nigeria's Delta Blues," July 20, 2008, retrieved November 19, 2008, from: http://www.hrw.org/en/africa/nigeria.

56. Human Rights Watch, *The Price of Oil*, 174. On the subject, see also Nimi Wariboko, "State-Corporation Relationship: Impact on Management Practice," in Adebayo Oyebade (ed.), *The Transformation of Nigeria*, 308.

57. On this subject, see, for instance, Kenneth Omeje, *High Stakes and Stakeholders: Oil Conflict and Security in Nigeria* (Aldershot, UK: Ashgate

Publishing, Ltd., 2006); and Olayiwola Owolabi and Iwebunor Okwechime, "Oil and Security in Nigeria: The Niger Delta Crisis, *Africa Development*, Vol. 32, No. 1 (2007: 1–40).

58. Studies of ethnic militias and violence are provided in Ali Arazeem Abdullahi and L. Saka, "Ethno-Religious and Political Conflicts: Threat to Nigeria Nascent Democracy," *Journal of Sustainable Development in Africa*, Vol. 9, No. 3 (2007: 1–16); Funso Adesola, "National Security, Democratization and the Menace of "ethnic militias" in Nigeria, *West Africa Review*, Vol. 11 (2007); Amadu Sesay, et al. (eds.) *Ethnic Militias and the Future of Democracy in Nigeria* (Ile-Ife, Nigeria: Obafemi Awolowo University Press, 2003); and Tunde Babawale, "The Rise of Ethnic Militias, De-legitimisation of the State, and the Threat to Nigerian Federalism," *West Africa Review*, Vol. 3, No. 1 (2001).

59. Pini Jason, "What Does the OPC Want?" *New African*, March 2000, retrieved November 24, 2008, from: http://findarticles.com/p/articles/mi_qa5391/is_/ai_n21452657.

60. OPC is discussed in Yvan Guichaoua, "The Making of an Ethnic Militia: The Oodua People's Congress in Nigeria," CRISE Working Paper No. 26, (Oxford, UK: Center for Research on Inequality, Human Security and Ethnicity, 2006), 1-22, retrieved November 24, 2008, from http://www.crise.ox.ac.uk/pubs/workingpaper26.pdf; R. T. Akinyele, "Ethnic Militancy and National Stability in Nigeria: A Case Study of the Oodua People's Congress," *African Affairs*, Vol. 100, No. 401 (2001: 623–640); and Babawale, "The Rise of Ethnic Militias."

61. There are a number of works on religious conflicts in Nigeria. See, for example, Dennis Ityavyar and Zacharys Gundu, *Stakeholders in Peace and Conflicts: A Case of Ethno-Religious Conflicts in Plateau & Kaduna, Nigeria* (Jos, Nigeria: International Centre for Gender & Social Research, 2004); Toyin Falola, *Violence in Nigeria: The Crisis of Religious Politics and Secular Ideologies* (Rochester, NY: University of Rochester Press, 1998); F. U. Okafor (ed.), *New Strategies for Curbing Ethnic and Religious Conflicts in Nigeria* (Enugu, Nigeria: Fourth Dimension, 1997); S. O. Ilesanmi, *Religious Pluralism and the Nigerian State* (Athens: Ohio University Center for International Studies, 1997); and Matthew Hassan Kukah and Toyin Falola, *Religious Militancy and Self-Assertion: Islam and Politics in Nigeria* (Aldershot, UK: Ashgate, 1996).

62. "Nigeria: Jos Riots—Death Toll Hits 400," *Daily Independent* (Lagos), December 1, 2008, retrieved December 20, 2008, from: http://allafrica.com/stories/200812011158.html.

63. This meant literally to pour gasoline on and set someone on fire.

64. For a full report on this, see Human Rights Watch, "Politics as War: The Human Rights Impact and Causes of Post-Election Violence in Rivers State, Nigeria," Vol. 20, No. 3A (March 26, 2008), retrieved December 17, 2008, from: http://www.hrw.org/sites/default/files/reports/nigeria0308_1.pdf.

65. Transparency International's 2009 Corruption Perceptions Index (CPI), retrieved on November 24, 2009, from: http://spreadsheets.google.com/ccc?key=t8HR9iGR5s9Y6bZpxEZMx1A.

CHAPTER 4

Southern Africa

Units of Umkhonto we Sizwe today carried out planned attacks against government installations, particularly those connected with the policy of apartheid and race discrimination. . . . We . . . have always sought to achieve liberation without bloodshed and civil clash. We hope, even at this late hour, that our first actions will awaken everyone to a realization of the disastrous situation to which the Nationalist policy is leading. We hope that we will bring the Government and its supporters to their senses before it is too late, so that both the Government and its policies can be changed before matters reach the desperate state of civil war.

Command of Umkhonto we Sizwe, the military wing of the African National Congress (ANC), December 16, 1961.[1]

I have decided to dedicate the rest of my life to the liberation struggle until the independence of my country.

Eduardo Chivambo Mondlane, Mozambique's nationalist leader, 1962.[2]

There can be no solution to our racial problems while African nationalists believe that, provided they stirred up sufficient trouble, they will be able to blackmail the British Government into bringing about a miracle on their behalf by handing the country over to irresponsible rule.

Ian Smith, Rhodesia's prime minister, announcing the UDI, November 11, 1965.[3]

By most classifications, the countries of the Southern subregion of Africa are Angola, Botswana, Lesotho, Malawi, Mozambique, Namibia, South Africa, Swaziland, Zambia, and Zimbabwe. Included in the region are also the Indian Ocean island countries of Comoros, Madagascar, Mauritius, Réunion, and Seychelles. It is a region of diverse

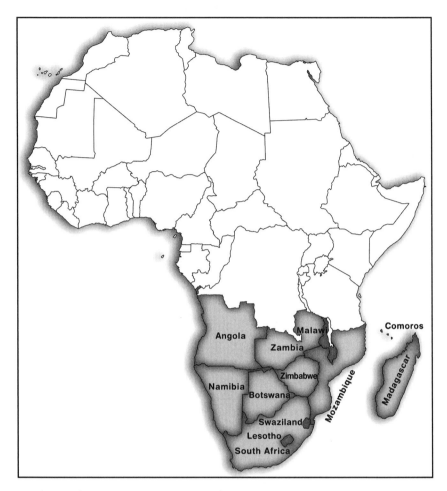

Southern African Region. (Courtesy of Sam Saverance.)

levels of economic and political development. South Africa has the biggest economy in Africa; by contrast, Swaziland, Lesotho, Malawi, and Comoros, are poor, and in-between, Botswana boasts of one the fastest growing economies in the developing world. While Zambia has maintained relative political stability, Zimbabwe has recently been bedeviled by crisis of governance. Both Angola and Mozambique are recovering from long and destructive civil wars.

Since the mid-1990s when white minority rule and the obnoxious apartheid system ended in South Africa, the subregion had been largely spared of violent conflicts. Historically, however, Southern Africa had been a region of conflicts witnessing, indeed, some of the most intense in Africa. During the pre-colonial period, the region, as in other parts of the continent, saw incessant and often violent conflicts. Ethnic groups and states clashed over conflicting political and economic interests. The arrival of Europeans in the region compounded local conflicts, just as it set into motion powerful forces in the form of population shifts and displacements with very destructive consequences for African societies.

Colonial Southern Africa, of course, was not free of intense conflicts. As in most parts of Africa, the conquest of African territories by European imperial powers preceding colonial rule was through violence. The colonial state, whether externally controlled or white settler–dominated, utilized violent means to subjugate the colonized people. Portuguese colonialism was virulently exploitative of Africa as it was politically oppressive. Even far worse was the case of internally colonized territories such as Rhodesia (now Zimbabwe), South West Africa (now Namibia), and South Africa, where the white minority population held exclusive political power legitimized by racist ideologies. In the end, in both instances of colonial states, black liberation struggle was violent.

Southern Africa did not cease to be a hot spot region after the wars of nationalism. Post-colonial Angola and Mozambique experienced long and devastating civil wars. The 25-year war in Angola was, perhaps, the most destructive in the modern history of Southern Africa. The Mozambican war, lasting 15 years, was no less brutal. Both wars not only had adverse repercussions in the entire region of Southern Africa, they also provided a platform for the infusion of superpower Cold War ideological power politics in the region.

Contemporary Southern Africa remains relatively free of serious conflicts, although the political turmoil in Zimbabwe generated by the relentless efforts of President Robert Mugabe to hold on to power has not fully been resolved and could threaten the political and economic stability of the region. Beginning with a review of historical perspective, this chapter examines the modern history of conflict in Southern Africa. It focuses on the complexities of African nationalist struggles that dominated much of the region's history, and it examines the role of external agencies in an era when the region's conflicts turned it into a theatre of Cold War ideological competition.[4]

SOUTHERN AFRICA AND CONFLICT IN HISTORICAL PERSPECTIVE

A dominant theme in the history of conflict in Southern Africa is incessant population displacement. This saga began early in the history of the region when waves of migrations to the region by the so-called

Bantu, a more culturally sophisticated people from West Africa, gradually displaced the indigenous Khoisan (the Khoikhoi and the San) who had lived around the Cape since the fifth century. Between the eighth and the fifteenth centuries, the process of state formation by the newcomers was in earnest, leading to the establishment of a number of kingdoms. The task of state building, however, brought about territorial wars among various groups. For example, the rise of the powerful, militaristic Zulu state partly orchestrated the nineteenth-century upheaval, the *Mfecane* or *difaqane*. Out of displacements and mass movements of people caused by the *Mfecane* emerged new kingdoms such Basotho and Ndebele, established by Moshoeshoe and Mzilikazi, respectively.

European incursion into Southern Africa increased the violent contestation for territories. Unlike most parts of the continent, Southern Africa became home to permanent European settlers. While the Portuguese who first set foot on the Cape in the fifteenth century as explorers failed to establish a stronghold on the Southern African tip, in 1652 the Dutch settled in the area and embarked on the task of building a colony. As other whites, particularly the British, joined the Dutch settlers, the expansion of the Cape Colony led to willful destruction of the Khoisan and their societies by the settlers in a manner described by Aran MacKinnon as "approaching the level of genocide."[5]

Conflicts among the Africans, the British, and the Boers characterized most of nineteenth century Southern Africa. The British design to expand their imperial authority into the eastern interior brought about a series of conflicts with African groups including the Xhosa and the Zulu. Although these groups mounted spirited resistance as seen in the Anglo-Xhosa War of 1834–1835 and the Anglo-Zulu War of 1879, this was often inadequate to forestall European expansion. In these conflicts, the hitherto independent African chiefdoms lost their sovereignty.

The struggle for territorial aggrandizement, however, did not only pit white settlers against African groups, but also Europeans against one another. Britain acquired the Cape Colony in 1814 and began to introduce some reform measures that threatened the economic and social dominance of the Dutch descendants, the Afrikaner Boers. In 1820, over 4,000 British settlers arrived in the colony, further altering its social and economic dynamics. Boers, unwilling to live under British control, chose to migrate north beyond the frontiers of the colony. The 1830s and 1840s saw their mass exodus in what was known as the "great trek," aimed at establishing new independent states in the north free from British control. This brought them into conflicts with African groups such as the Ndebele, who were displaced, and their lands encroached upon. In the Orange and Vaal River valleys, the Boers set up new states, the Orange Free State and Transvaal.[6]

By the late nineteenth century, colonial Southern Africa had already taken firm shape, born out of imperial competition. Both Angola and modern Mozambique had been colonies of Portugal since the late fifteenth century. The British annexed Basutoland (modern Lesotho) in 1868, Bechuanaland (modern Botswana) in 1885, and further north acquired the Rhodesias (modern Zambia and Zimbabwe). In 1903, the British extended protectorate status to Swaziland. Meanwhile, Germany had also occupied and colonized South West Africa by 1884.

The Anglo-Boer War of 1899–1902, a most brutal and bloody guerrilla war, marked the high point of British imperial penetration in Southern Africa. British imperial design on the Boer republics of Transvaal and the Orange Free State in the 1880s caused the bitter conflict in which they managed to subdue the Boer.[7] Following the war, a unified white state, the Union of South Africa comprising the Cape Colony, Natal, Orange Free State, and Transvaal, was created in 1910. Although existing within the British Empire, the union was self-governing under the control of the majority white population, the Afrikaner Boers, who proceeded to institute a white supremacist state in which Africans occupied a subordinate position.

For most of the colonial world, the post–World War II period began the dynamic age of decolonization. While it brought about the end of colonial rule in other regions of Africa by the 1960s, much of Southern Africa remained untouched by the winds of change blowing across the continent. Indeed, the last phase of African nationalism occurred in the region. Independence came late to Angola and Mozambique, obtained only in 1975. Zimbabwe followed suit in 1980, Namibia in 1990, and majority rule was attained in South Africa in 1995.

The nature of colonial dominance in Southern Africa necessarily made anti-colonial struggle more violent and prolonged. African nationalism was pitched against either recalcitrant external colonial authority unwilling to decolonize, or against determined internal power guided by an ideology of perpetual white dominance. As Britain and France dismantled their African colonial empires in the 1960s, Portuguese colonialism was hardly shaken by the prevailing pull of decolonization. Its two colonies in Southern Africa, Angola and Mozambique, remained firmly under its stranglehold. A relatively politically backward and economically weak imperial power, Portugal saw the continued exploitation of the wealth and resources of its colonial empire as vital to its own survival. Thus, the obdurate colonial power vehemently opposed nascent African nationalism, and throughout the decolonization period, remained impervious to legitimate African demands. The colonial intransigence toward African nationalism and its institution of repressive measures against nationalistic quests left nationalists in Lusophone

Africa with no other choice than armed struggle. The guerrilla wars fought against Portugal by Angola and Mozambique from the early 1960s to 1975 epitomized the devastating wars of independence in Africa.

Unlike Angola and Mozambique, the anti-colonial struggle in Rhodesia, South West Africa, and South Africa was against diabolic internal authorities, that is, white minority regimes that pursued a racist ideology of white supremacy that turned the African majority population into virtually colonized people. Unreceptive to any possibility of black majority rule, white minority regimes passed and implemented racist discriminatory laws and utilized, sometimes violently, repressive measures to ensure white dominance. In these white-ruled supremacist states, African nationalism had no other choice than to take a violent turn. Armed struggle began in Rhodesia and South West Africa in 1966, lasting 14 years in the former and over two decades in the later. In South Africa, the black liberation struggle was equally wrought with violent episodes in the face of settlers' consolidation of an oppressive white supremacist state.

The Portuguese and National Liberation Struggle: Angola and Mozambique

Anti-colonial war was one form of modern conflict in Southern Africa. Angola and Mozambique, for a long time part of the Portuguese colonial empire, fought protracted and devastating national liberation wars from the 1960s to the mid-1970s in order to achieve independence. Fought during the Cold War era, the wars were tainted by the prevailing East-West ideological competition.[8]

The nature of Portuguese colonialism provides a background to understanding the necessity of armed confrontation against Portugal by its African colonial possessions that include not only Angola and Mozambique, but also Portuguese Guinea (now Guinea Bissau) and Cape Verde, both in West Africa. In Angola, a colony with considerable white settler population particularly after 1950, black nationalism had to contend with this powerful sector of the society. Mozambique also had white settlers, though on a smaller scale. Although Portugal did not expressly practice racial segregation in its colonies as a matter of law or as state policy, in both Angola and Mozambique, European settlers held virtual monopoly of political and economic rights and privileges. Colonial laws, as in Angola, limited African land ownership as it expropriated lands for the settlers and instituted African forced labor on settler farms. Occupying a privileged position, settlers naturally preferred continued Portuguese colonial rule and viewed African nationalism with disfavor.

Further, Portuguese colonial rule was excessively politically repressive. Although the *assimilado*—that is, Africans who had been assimilated into the Portuguese culture by virtue of adoption of Western education, acceptance of Christianity, and demonstration of loyalty to Portugal—had some privileges, they lacked real political power and opportunities in the colonial bureaucracy. In any case, *assimilados* were comparatively few in number; the vast majority of Africans remained *indígenas* or subjects—poor, subject to forced labor, and denied basic political and civil rights. More importantly, apart from political oppression, Portuguese colonialism was characterized by massive economic exploitation of the people and the resources of the colonies. Portugal, indeed, saw its colonial possessions virtually in terms of a source for its own economic development and survival in a competitive capitalistic economy.[9] Angola, in particular, with its enormous resources including vast oil reserves, was a valued colony.

As decolonization shifted into gear in the 1950s, anti-colonial sentiment and protest against discriminatory and oppressive measures were increasingly met with violent opposition by Lisbon. The government employed every diabolical tactic at its disposal, including police action to harass nationalist leaders and discourage African resistance movements. Portugal's resort to repression in its colonies and refusal to allow nationalistic expression drove the anti-colonial movement underground.

War of Independence in Angola

Many political observers see the birth of the Angolan War of Independence in the peasant revolt of early January 1961 in the region of Baixa de Kassanje in Malanje Province, which was violently suppressed by the Portuguese military forces. In the Baixa de Kassanje revolt, workers of the multinational cotton plantation company, Cotonang, had led an armed uprising to demand improved work conditions, higher wages, and other rights. Portugal's brutal response ended in what some have described as a massacre—the killing of thousands of Angolan peasants by the Portuguese army.[10] The significance of the event was its electrifying effect on the nascent liberation struggle. As a contemporary commentator puts it, it "heightened awareness of freedom of Angolan patriots," and led to the decision "to start an armed struggle without truce against the Portuguese fascist regime . . ."[11]

Before the peasant uprising and the subsequent formal commencement of armed struggle against Portugal on February 4, 1961, revolutionary groups had been active since the early 1950s, albeit, mostly operating clandestinely. The Party of the United Struggle for Africans in Angola (*Partido da Luta Unida dos Africanos de Angola*; PLUA), emerged in 1953 and began to demand the country's independence. This organization later merged with the Angolan Communist Party (PCA) in December 1956 to become the Popular Movement for the Liberation of Angola (*Movimento Popular de Libertação de Angola*; MPLA), one of the three main nationalist organizations that would fight for Angola's independence. The MPLA was led by the poet, physician, and Marxist, Antonio Agostinho Neto. Based initially in Luanda, Angola's administrative capital, and popular among the Kimbundu, the movement adopted guerrilla war tactics against Portugal in February 1961 when insurgents launched a deadly attack against a police station and a prison in Luanda, with devastating retaliation by the Portuguese army. There were also violent reprisals from Luanda's whites as they killed hundreds of black residents of the city. The bloody incident of that February has often been seen as the official start of the liberation war.

Two other major revolutionary organizations fought the Portuguese in Angola's War of Independence. One was the National Front for the Liberation of Angola (*Frente Nacional de Libertação de Angola*; FNLA) founded in March 1962 by a Bakongo leader, Holden Alvaro Roberto. With a militia force of about 4,000 Bakongo, the FNLA immediately began bloody incursions into Angola from its operational base in Zaire (now Democratic Republic of Congo). The third group was the National Union for the Total Independence of Angola (*União Nacional para a Independência Total de Angola*; UNITA) formed in 1964 by Jonas Savimbi, a former lieutenant of Roberto who had broken from the FNLA. Based in the southeastern provinces among the Ovimbundu, UNITA launched its guerrilla war in late 1966.

The brutal liberation war lasted 14 years. On the battlefield, the Angolans were no match to Portugal's counterinsurgency forces, which were equipped with weapons supplied by Lisbon's NATO allies including the United States. Given the superior firepower of the Portuguese, the insurgents necessarily adopted guerrilla tactics, attacking Portuguese outposts. For the most part, however, the war did not go well for the nationalist fighters. Indeed, Portugal's counterinsurgency strategies including search-and-destroy operations forced the MPLA during the war to shift parts of its operational base to neighboring Zambia. However, despite heavy casualties, the guerilla fighters remained resolute in their mission to achieve independence for Angola.

Apart from Portugal's military superiority, the nationalists' war effort was also severely retarded by the seemingly irreconcilable contradictions inherent in the three major nationalist organizations involved in the struggle. Ideological differences and ethnicity prevented them from presenting a united front against the common enemy. The MPLA, leftist in orientation, was urban based and popular among the Mbundu. In contradistinction, the FNLA, rightist in political ideology, was rural based, and practically restricted to the Bakongo of the north. UNITA had its support deep in the south among the Ovimbundu. The great disparity among the three nationalist groups, each of which was also backed by different foreign interests, and the pursuit of personal agendas by their leaders created deep animosity and distrust among them that was never resolved during the war. Indeed, rather than fighting the Portuguese, on many occasions they engaged one another in military confrontations. The antagonism between the nationalist movements that characterized the wartime liberation movement would find further expression after independence when UNITA's opposition to the MPLA launched the country on a most vicious civil war.

War of Independence in Mozambique

Meanwhile, Mozambique was also engaged in a similar brutal war of independence against Portugal. In the early 1960s, Portuguese colonial repression and violent opposition to African nationalist expression persuaded several small anti-colonial revolutionary groups to merge in order to offer a more effective challenge to the colonial power. Out of this merger, in June 1962, Mozambique's main nationalist movement was born—the Front for the Liberation of Mozambique (*Frente de Libertação de Moçambique*; FRELIMO), which would lead the country to independence.[12]

FRELIMO was founded under the leadership of Eduardo Mondlane, who, before the revolution, had studied in the United States and subsequently became an instructor at a number of American universities.[13] On his return from the United States in 1962, he became one of Mozambique's leading revolutionary figures in the independence movement. Under Mondlane's tutelage, FRELIMO began to grow into a formidable nationalist organization. Its initial guerrilla fighters underwent military training in camps in Algeria and Tanzania.

In the face of Portugal's continued disinclination to negotiate political independence with the nationalists, FRELIMO began the liberation war in September 1964 when its guerrillas, employing hit-and-run tactics, launched military campaigns in the northern provinces of Cabo Delgado and Niassa. By 1968, the war had expanded to the central province of Tete. Mondlane was, however, assassinated on February 3, 1969, and the leadership baton passed on to Samora Machel, a FRELIMO military strategist.[14]

Under Machel's indefatigable military and political leadership, FRELIMO, with operational headquarters in Tanzania, intensified the armed struggle in the 1970s. Determined to create a popular uprising throughout Mozambique, its consequent populist ideology helped to aid the swelling of its rank and file, derived mainly from the peasantry. Although it largely failed to produce a widespread popular rebellion, its mass support posed a threat to the Portuguese colonial authority.

As in Angola, the Portuguese responded to the liberation war with devastating counterinsurgency campaigns. The Portuguese army launched *Operação Nó Górdio* (Gordian Knot Operation) in June 1970 under the command of Brig. Gen. Kaúlza de Arriaga. This was a seven-month military campaign fashioned along the lines of American military strategy in Vietnam. A massive and rather expensive offensive involving about three thousand additional Portuguese soldiers, the Portuguese army launched sustained ground assaults backed by intense aerial bombardment by the air force. The operation aimed at destroying the guerrillas' trails across the Tanzanian border and eliminating their bases and camps in Mozambique. Although the operation brought about devastating setbacks to the guerrillas, it did not lead to a decisive military victory for the Portuguese and the crushing of nationalist resistance. The violence that attended the operation and the increasing casualty rate on both sides of the conflict worried Lisbon. Realizing that it could not be continued indefinitely, the operation ended. Meanwhile, although weakened by the Gordian Knot Operation, FRELIMO fighters managed to recover sufficiently to continue a further thrust into the south.

End of Liberation Wars in Angola and Mozambique

For the most part, the liberation wars in Angola and Mozambique did not go well for the guerrilla fighters facing superior military might. By 1974, vast areas of the countries, particularly major urban centers, were still securely held by the Portuguese. However, the Portuguese colonial war effort, on many fronts at the same time, increasingly proved too costly financially and politically for Lisbon. Unable to score a decisive military victory against the nationalists in Angola, Mozambique, and Guinea Bissau (which was also fighting a liberation war), and in the face of mounting Portuguese casualties, discontentment set in within the war-weary Portuguese armed forces. But resentment against the colonial wars was not only manifest in the overburdened Portuguese military, it also became evident among the Portuguese citizenry at large. For the taxpayers in Portugal called upon to bear the financial brunt of the wars that many now considered not militarily winnable, the increasing running cost became an irritant. By the early 1970s, the rather unpopular colonial wars began to threaten the political standing of the *Estado Novo* regime. Ultimately, this was directly responsible for the Carnation Revolution of April 25, 1974, staged by elements of the Portuguese armed forces, the Movement of the Armed Forces (*Movimento das Forças Armadas*; MFA), which dethroned the dictatorship of Marcelo Caetano.

Although heroic nationalist resistance played a major role in the anti-colonial movement, the collapse of Portuguese colonialism in Africa could ultimately be found in the dethronement of the *Estado Novo* regime with its adamant notion that the Portuguese colonies were more like provinces of Portugal, rather than just colonies, and, by that fact, ineligible for independence. The post-revolution leftist regime, anti-colonial in posture and opposed to the official view of the colonies as provinces, promptly began to negotiate with the African nationalists toward bringing an end to the liberation wars. These negotiations led, in the case of Angola, to the signing of the Alvor Agreement on January 15, 1975, between the Portuguese authority and the leaders of the MPLA, UNITA, and FNLA. The agreement brought about the end of the war and, on November 11, 1975, Angola became independent.

Negotiation had moved faster in Mozambique where the nationalists were able to present a more united front. The negotiations between FRELIMO and the Portuguese authority led to the signing of the Lusaka Accord on September 8, 1974, which paved the way for Mozambique's independence on June 25, 1975.

WHITE MINORITY REGIMES AND LIBERATION STRUGGLE: RHODESIA AND SOUTH WEST AFRICA

Nationalists in Rhodesia and South West Africa faced a different adversary in their own wars of national liberation. Both were white-ruled supremacist colonies where, although blacks constituted the majority population, they were denied basic political, social, and economic rights. The struggle in Rhodesia and South West Africa was, therefore, against racist, white minority regimes, with the purpose of enthroning majority black rule. Just as the decolonization of the Portuguese colonial territories of Angola and Mozambique was achieved through armed confrontation of the colonial power, the liberation struggles in Rhodesia and South West Africa were violent in character. Here, African nationalists also took to guerilla warfare.

Rhodesia

Initially known as Southern Rhodesia, the British-ruled territory, which came to be called Rhodesia from 1963, had been self-governing and semi-sovereign since 1924 under the control of the white settlers. The already declining fortunes of Rhodesian blacks under white-settler rule further dovetailed in 1962 when the all-white electorate voted into power the Rhodesian Front (RF), a virulently racist party with a commitment to white supremacy and the subordination of Africans. On November 11, 1965, defying Britain's call for political reforms that would guarantee some rights to black Rhodesians, the RF took a significant step to further consolidate white dominance. In a political move known as the Unilateral Declaration of Independence (UDI), Ian Douglas Smith, RF's prime minister elected in 1964, announced the severance of the colony from Britain and the cutting of all ties with the mother country. Britain's response was to declare the illegality of the action of the RF and to refuse to recognize a Rhodesian state under white minority rule. However, London failed to take concrete action against the regime. The United Nations, under pressure from the Soviet Union and from a number of independent African states, imposed sanctions on the Rhodesian government. UN sanctions, ultimately, proved ineffective to deter the racist regime in its pursuit of its illegal course. The failure of sanctions was partly because some states, such as apartheid South Africa, the United States, and Portugal, refused to honor the sanctions.

The post-UDI saw the RF continued efforts to consolidate the racist political order in Rhodesia. Representing less than 5 percent of the population of the colony, Rhodesian white settlers held economic and political dominance. As in the Portuguese colonies, land appropriation laws delivered about half of the colony's lands to white settlers. Deprived of lands that had traditionally been theirs, Africans ended up as workers, forced to provide cheap labor on settler farms and to colonial mines. Though poorly paid, Africans were also often subjected to excessive taxation. At the same time, the settlers maintained absolute political power and occupied privileged positions as the government pursued a policy of racial discrimination. Racist laws disfranchised blacks, restricted their freedom of movement, and segregated them from whites. Thus, largely denied political, economic, and civil rights, Africans were effectively reduced to second-class status.

By the early 1960s, it was clear to Rhodesian African nationalists that only armed rebellion would bring about independence under black majority rule. The settlers were resolute in their political and economic domination of the colony, and were unwilling to yield any ground to nationalist agitations, even for moderate reforms. The challenge to white domination and political power was met by increased government repressive measures. Nationalist leaders were arrested and detained at will and their organizations proscribed. The denial of every civil avenue of political expression and organization forced nationalism underground and led to the emergence of sporadic guerilla activities against state establishments.

Armed struggle for independence under black majority rule began in earnest in 1966 championed by two main revolutionary political movements that had hitherto operated clandestinely because of their proscription by the settler government. One was the Zimbabwe African People's Union (ZAPU), which had been established in December 1961 under the leadership of a prominent nationalist and trade union leader, Joshua Nkomo. ZAPU sought to attract and mobilize urban workers, and formed a military wing, Zimbabwe People's Revolutionary Army (ZIPRA).

The Zimbabwe African National Union (ZANU), which emerged in August 1963 as a breakaway faction of ZAPU, was the other major nationalist movement involved in the Rhodesian armed liberation struggle. It was formed by a more radical element of ZAPU led by the Rev. Ndabaningi Sithole and other associates, including Robert Mugabe, who felt that the movement was not radical enough in its opposition to the racist government and therefore yearned for a more militant strategy. ZANU took to Marxist ideology and espoused the strategy of mobilizing the rural population. Its military wing was the Zimbabwe African National Liberation Army (ZANLA). ZAPU and ZANU's shared goal of independence under black majority rule remained paramount despite their differences. Indeed, in 1976, in order to provide a stronger challenge to the minority regime, the two movements combined their armed wings into what was called the Patriotic Front (PF).

The initial guerrilla efforts achieved very little success at the beginning of the armed struggle. However, by the early 1970s, the nationalists had significantly intensified their military campaigns with increasing success, controlling significant parts of Rhodesia by 1978. But the success of the liberation movement was by no means achieved solely by the military power of the revolutionary organizations. Indeed, international isolation of the illegal minority-ruled Rhodesian state and pressure on the racist RF regime significantly aided the success of the armed struggle. The UN and most states, including the Soviet Union, never recognized the UDI, isolating Rhodesia in the international community.[15] With the end of colonial rule in Angola and Mozambique, and the consequent expulsion of Portugal from Southern Africa in 1975, Rhodesia became even more isolated in the region. This development was a severe blow to the Rhodesian regime as newly independent Mozambique (and also Zambia) offered the guerrillas operational bases. Meanwhile, the United States and Britain exerted pressure on the RF to negotiate with the nationalists. In a weak diplomatic standing in the world, and as a result of Anglo-American pressure, the RF was forced to introduce in 1979 the so-called "internal settlement," which was essentially a compromise political arrangement in which moderate African leaders would share power with the RF. However, this arrangement did not include mainstream nationalist leaders such as Nkomo and Mugabe, ZAPU and ZANU leaders, respectively. Indeed, "internal arrangement," while it produced an African prime minister, Bishop Abel Muzorewa, whose United African National Council (UANC) formed a coalition government with the RF, in reality this political experiment instituted limited black rule and still retained political and economic dominance of whites. ZAPU and ZANU leaders flatly rejected the compromise and the UANC/RF coalition government as did many African states. ZAPU/ZANU-PF thus continued the armed struggle. Faced with the intensification of the guerrilla war, continued isolation in the international community, and the biting effect on the economy of economic embargo, the Rhodesian government finally accepted the principle of black majority rule.

The Lancaster House negotiations between the nationalist leaders and the Rhodesian government held at Lancaster House in late 1979 in London under the auspices of the British government paved the way for the end of the Rhodesian conflict. Out of the negotiations came an agreement on December 21, 1979, which among other stipulations, proposed independence for Rhodesia the following year, with the country, thereafter, to be known as Zimbabwe. Independence was declared on April 18, 1980, after 14 years of armed struggle.[16]

Namibia

South West Africa was a German colony from the early nineteenth century until World War I.[17] After its defeat during the war, the colonial power lost all of its African territories including South West Africa, which was occupied by apartheid South Africa in 1915. In 1920, the colony, officially tagged "mandated' territory of the League of Nations, came under South Africa's control, which was expected to hold the territory in trust for the League. However, attracted by its enormous agricultural and mineral resources, it became, in reality, its de facto colony and was transformed into a province. South Africa soon extended its apartheid policies and racist laws to the colony. Under the apartheid system, the South African authority favored the minority white population of the colony, which it granted special privileges. Segregation along the South African lines was imposed and reserves were introduced. Racial discrimination against the black majority denied them political and economic rights. The colonial economy was extremely exploitative in a system where blacks were reduced to providers of labor.[18]

An organized anti-colonial protest movement began to gain grounds in the post–World War II period. Initially, early organizations such as the South West Africa National Union (SWANU), formed in 1959, demanded moderate changes. South Africa was not willing to give in to even moderate changes and, therefore, took to repression of nascent nationalism. An incident, "the Windhoek Shootings" in 1959, clearly indicated South Africa's intolerance of the African protest movement. In this incident, which occurred at Windhoek, the colony's capital, police shot and killed about 11 black demonstrators and wounded another 50 more as they protested against the authorities' policy to forcibly remove them from their homes and relocate them. Repressive measures by South Africa and its recalcitrant attitude to demands for change led to the emergence of more radical protest movements. The South West Africa People's Organization (SWAPO), formed in April 1960 from the merger of a number of organizations, began to call for the end of South African rule and for independence for the colony. The nationalists' approach was essentially peaceful, working through the UN to terminate South African rule. In 1966, the General Assembly voted to end South Africa's League mandate over South West Africa and requested that the territory's administration be transferred to the UN Council for South West Africa. However, the apartheid regime remained unresponsive to the UN order. Its response to African nationalism was to turn its repressive machine against the movement in an attempt to stifle it. Nationalist leaders were arrested, some herded to political detention, while others, to avoid incarceration, fled to exile. One of the most prominent victims of South Africa's violent repression was Sam Nujoma, who had in 1958 cofounded the Ovamboland People's Organization (OPO) and would later head SWAPO. He was arrested a number of times and jailed, and also spent a considerable long time in exile in Dar-es-Salaam, Tanzania. Faced with the reality that the apartheid regime would never accede to their demand for independence, nationalists turned to armed struggle.

The war of independence in South West Africa commenced in 1966 when SWAPO guerrillas began attacks on the occupying South African forces. As it occurred in other Southern Africa settler states, the war was bitter and long. SWAPO's military operations were conducted under its armed wing, the People's Liberation Army of Namibia (PLAN). From a slow, weak start, PLAN progressively gained momentum. SWAPO's war effort was enhanced by mass support for the nationalist cause. The opposition from various civil organizations helped to increase the pressure on the South African government. Meanwhile, in 1968, SWAPO renamed the country "Namibia," a name that was formalized after independence.

The attainment of independence in 1975 by Angola, Namibia's northern neighbor, introduced a new dynamic to the war. Angola began to provide military bases to SWAPO guerrillas, a boost to the armed struggle and a significant setback to South Africa. Apart from Angola, Zambia also offered military bases to the guerrillas.

Also critical in the liberation struggle was the sustained international pressure on South Africa by the UN and the OAU. Both organizations threw their full diplomatic weight behind the nationalist cause, recognizing SWAPO as the legitimate nationalist organization representing the will of the Namibian people. Indeed, within the UN, African states cooperated in support of the liberation struggle. Their concerted effort was instrumental to the formation by the General Assembly, of the UN Council for South West Africa, in May 1967. The UN declared South Africa's rule illegal and mandated the council to assume the responsibility of administering the territory until independence. In 1971, the International Court of Justice (ICJ) also declared South Africa's continued occupation of the territory illegal, and consequently called for its withdrawal.

However, South Africa continued to flagrantly defy the UN order to end its illegal occupation of Namibia until 1988, when its forces were roundly defeated inside Angola by Angolan/Cuban troops. The Cuban troops were in Angola to back the ruling MPLA forces fighting against UNITA rebels in a most violent post-independence civil war. Primarily to retaliate against Angola's support for SWAPO guerrillas, South Africa had in turn supported UNITA and also intermittently invaded Angola. However, the South African defeat proved a turning point in its recalcitrant attitude toward Namibian independence.

In the face of a declining economy combined with international pressure and the realization that it could not win the guerrilla war against SWAPO, South Africa entered into negotiations that would lead to Namibia's independence on March 21, 1990. Twenty-four years after it had commenced, the war of independence finally ended. In the UN supervised pre-independence elections held in November 1989, SWAPO won, and its leader, Nujoma, became the first president of independent Namibia.[19]

RACIAL OPPRESSION AND VIOLENT RESISTANCE IN SOUTH AFRICA

Black resistance against a most diabolically racist sociopolitical and economic order in the Republic of South Africa installed by its white-supremacist government is a classic case of the struggle against an internal colonial system characteristic of the subregion of Southern Africa. It was a struggle that was long, bitter, and sometimes violent and bloody.

The Union of South Africa, comprising the four colonies of Cape, Natal, Orange Free State, and Transvaal, became independent of Britain in 1910. Ruled by white settlers, a white supremacist state emerged, where the whites held political and economic privileges and blacks, who constituted the majority population, were systematically denied civil and economic rights. The racist order intensified significantly in 1948 when the Afrikaner National Party (ANP) assumed control of power after winning the all-white election. The ANP, the party of the extremely racist Afrikaans-speaking whites, began to install a much more oppressive system as it introduced apartheid as state political philosophy. Apartheid not only racially segregated blacks from whites, it became the basis of South Africa's political, administrative, economic, and social system. It was a doctrine of racial subordination at the extreme, which relegated blacks to a subservient position in all facets of life. In practice, it was oppressive to blacks as an array of racist laws designed to keep them as second-class citizens denied basic rights, reduced to providers of cheap labor, were strictly enforced. The debasing quality of apartheid to the black population is succinctly articulated by MacKinnon:

> Blacks (African, Indian, and Coloured people) were exiled within their own country and forced to live in a twilight world which intersected with the white-dominated nation only through subordination and oppression. Apartheid, moreover, rendered the people visible only through roles based on race and class.[20]

By the 1960s, the apartheid system had been well established. The power of the racist state was further enhanced by a robust economy, now hinged on growing industrial capitalism, and no longer on a dependent colonial economy. Also, South Africa now boasted of a powerful military. Indeed, the South African Defense Force (SADF) would become the most powerful military on the continent. As an economic and military power in Africa, South Africa was in a good stead, not only to consolidate its racist system at home, but also to pose a significant threat to its independent neighbors that sided with the anti-apartheid movement.[21]

The African protest movement predated the introduction of apartheid in 1948. The South African Native National Congress (SANNC) had been established in 1912 by the black-educated elite to serve as an African mouthpiece in the union. In the post 1940s, the black protest movement became more radicalized as apartheid laws further oppressed Africans and eroded more of their rights. In 1952, the African National Congress (ANC), the preeminent nationalist organization, began the Defiance Campaign to oppose the racist and unjust pass laws that were used to segregate blacks and deny them free movement. The pass laws had also become the state's principal instrument of suppressing the nationalist movement. The campaign, which included not only Africans, but also Indians and Coloreds, was met with the repression of the South African authority. Thousands of the protesters were arrested; several were sent to prison, including Walter Sisulu, ANC's secretary-general, and Nelson Mandela, who would become the icon of the struggle.

Armed Resistance and State Repression

The mass mobilization of black South Africans against pass laws provided the needed momentum to sustain the resistance movement. In the 1960s, a new generation of black leaders began to adopt a more militant anti-apartheid campaign with the failure of peaceful protests to bring about change to the oppressive and racist South African system. One of the most violent acts perpetrated by the apartheid government against blacks, which was to tilt the struggle in favor of armed confrontation, was the Sharpeville Massacre of March 21, 1960. This was the killing by the South African police of 69 of the thousands of unarmed anti-pass law protesters in the township of Sharpeville, south of Johannesburg. Although originally planned by the ANC, the campaign was preemptively launched by the Pan Africanist Congress (PAC), believing that it was best suited for making it effective. In any case, the killings were nothing less than a barbarous act. Most of the protesters killed were actually shot in the back as they fled the police carnage. As many as two hundred other protesters were wounded.[22]

The aftermath of the killings brought about mass demonstrations and marches throughout the country in protest. The police arrested and detained hundreds of thousands of protesters. An outpouring of condemnation of the massacre flowed from across the world including the UN Security Council. In the face of the crisis, the government was compelled to declare a state of emergency and, thereupon, instituted martial law in the country. Undeterred by the worldwide protest against the massacre, the South African government stepped up its repression of black political leaders; many were sentenced to prison terms for their anti-apartheid political activities, while others fled into exile. In April 1960, the government banned both the ANC and the PAC, thus making them illegal organizations. In effect, the liberation struggle was driven underground as it continued to operate from exile, principally in Tanzania. The most significant repercussion of the Sharpeville Massacre was that it revealed the futility of passive resistance to the apartheid system. At the clandestine executive meeting of the ANC in Durban in June 1961, Mandela argued the raison d'être of armed struggle: "the state had given us no alternative to violence."[23] Reversing nonviolence as the "inviolate principle" of the ANC, Mandela was mandated to establish an armed wing for the ANC. Mandela recalled the significance of this momentous decision:

> This was a faithful step. For fifty years, the ANC had treated non-violence as a core principle, beyond question or debate. We were embarking on a new and more dangerous path, a path of organized violence, the results of which we did not and could not know. I, who had never been a soldier, who had never fought in battle, had been given the task of starting an army. The name of this new organization was Umkhonto we Sizwe (The Spear of the Nation).[24]

Operating underground, Umkhonto we Sizwe commenced the armed resistance in December 1961 with bomb attacks in Johannesburg, Port Elizabeth, and Durban, on government facilities, including jails and post offices, as well as on electricity power stations. In its armed campaign, the ANC, an organization that had consistently eschewed violence, made stringent efforts to avoid civilian casualties. This philosophy was not respected by the PAC, whose armed wing, Poqo, was also involved in the armed struggle. More militant than Umkhonto we Sizwe, and virulently anti-white, Poqo pursued a deliberate policy of violent attacks against government interests without regard to sanctity of life. Indeed, Poqo was involved in violent murders of opponents, not just whites, but blacks considered traitors.

The apartheid state stepped up its repressive policy in the wake of the armed responses to the apartheid system. Determined to destroy the movement, the government stepped up police action against the nationalists and also took to massive arrests of ANC and PAC members and the incarceration of their leaders. Mandela was arrested in 1962 and was subsequently tried and sentenced to life imprisonment along with a number of his compatriots. The crackdown on the anti-apartheid movement almost drove the PAC out of existence.

The brutal policies of the government and the incarceration of anti-apartheid leaders did not stem the tide of opposition to the racist regime. The ANC and the PAC continued to organize in exile and operate clandestinely internally. By the beginning of the 1970s, the movement had been further broadened when various black civil organizations joined the struggle. Particularly, unions of urban black workers, whose members had always been severely exploited and subjected to low wages and harsh work conditions, organized strikes, not only in demand of their immediate rights, but also in the quest for greater social, economic, and political equality. The massive strikes in Durban in January 1973 are a case in point. Organized by workers and supported by political leaders and other opponents of the apartheid system, the strikes initially began with about 2,000 workers of the Coronation Brick and Tile Works. Before the end of the month, the strike had attracted over 30,000 workers from various industries in Durban. The wave of strikes was a major development in the black struggle against apartheid. Workers became a more politically conscious class with a stake in black liberation. Previously stifled by apartheid laws, workers' organizations defiantly grew; and the spate of strikes in subsequent years confirmed the expansion of labor unionism and its crystallization as an important force in South Africa's political dynamics, and also as a formidable segment of the black liberation movement.

Just as urban black workers helped to redefine the anti-apartheid struggle in South Africa in the early 1970s, radical student activism and unionism played a similar role. The students' movement embraced the political philosophy of "black consciousness," whose main proponent was a radical, activist medical student, Steve Biko, who organized the South African Students' Organization (SASO), a union of black university students. Akin to the "Black Power" movement of the 1960s in the United States, black consciousness raised political awareness among young South African blacks and became an instrument for fighting the unjust racist South African system.[25]

Youth activism was not restricted to university students; students in post-primary institutions also became increasingly radicalized by the ideology of black consciousness. For a long time, South African black students had endured substandard education and inadequate or poor facilities under apartheid policies. Unwilling to continue to accept third-rate education, the students organized to build a powerful protest movement. In March 1972, they formed the South African Students' Movement (SASM) to champion their cause. Mass demonstrations were organized, the most dramatic occurring in Soweto.[26] On June 16, 1976, about ten thousand secondary school students protesting against the Bantu Education Act, which compelled black students to receive instruction in Afrikaans, the language of the racist political overlords, were met by police bullets. This was the most brutal act of violence against blacks in modern South African history. As the police, notorious for unrestrained use of force, opened fire on the unarmed and defenseless students, over six hundred of them were murdered. Thousands more were arrested and jailed.

Perhaps more than any other event in South Africa, the bloody attempt to suppress the Soweto Uprising brought the anti-apartheid struggle to the attention of the world. Western countries, particularly the United States, that had hitherto sat on the fence in condemning apartheid, now began to impose economic sanctions on South Africa. Internally, in the wake of the uprising, further violent acts of unrest by students and other activists exploded throughout the country. Students not merely boycotted schools, they resorted to acts of vandalism by destroying school facilities. In the face of widespread black militancy, the apartheid regime employed more brutal repressive measures. One of the most prominent victims of these measures was the black consciousness proponent Steve Biko, who was arrested on August 21, 1977 and died the next month in police custody in mysterious circumstances. Although the police reported his death as resulting from a "hunger strike," later investigations revealed that he had died from severe beatings and injuries to his head received at the hands of South African security forces.[27]

By the 1980s, violence had become a common feature in South Africa. Although the ANC, the leading opposition movement, and the PAC had been outlawed and could not operate openly, nevertheless, they continued to function—underground within the country, and effectively from exile. Thousands of black South Africans had volunteered for training as guerrilla fighters in ANC military camps in Tanzania and other neighboring states. Many were able to infiltrate back into the country and conduct sabotage attacks on government interests. The South African authority, in turn, turned up the heat on the anti-apartheid movement in determination to nip it in the bud. South Africa became notorious for the use of its police and other security forces to indiscriminately brutalize its black population. By the end of the decade, to placate that segment of its society, the South African government introduced some half-hearted reforms that did not meet African demands. Indeed, the basic structure of apartheid remained.

End of Apartheid

The demise of apartheid in South Africa in the early 1990s could be attributed to internal and external factors. The increased violence attending the anti-apartheid order inside the country had rendered governance virtually impossible and threatened to destabilize the country. In combination with the political instability in South Africa engendered by heightening violence was international pressure exerted on the apartheid regime. First, pressure came from the OAU and its member states, particularly the Frontline States (FLS), that is, neighboring African states such as Angola, Botswana, Mozambique, Tanzania, Zambia, Zimbabwe (and Nigeria, outside the region), which provided support for the anti-apartheid movement.

Second, intense pressure on the apartheid regime to end its racist policies came from Western countries, notably the United States and Britain. Cold War politics had initially prevented the West from strongly condemning apartheid and supporting the liberation struggle. However, the Cold War détente of the mid-1980s removed this impediment, and there was greater call for the termination of apartheid and institution of real democracy. In the United States, the African American constituency played an important role in raising public awareness of the oppression of the black population of South Africa, and in championing the anti-apartheid cause. Notable African Americans—such as civil rights leader Rev. Jesse Jackson of the Rainbow Coalition, and black civil and political organizations such as the National Association for the Advancement of Colored People (NAACP) and the Congressional Black Caucus—had consistently denounced the South African racist government. In 1984, Randal Robinson, executive director of TransAfrica Forum, an anti-apartheid lobby group; Eleanor Holmes Norton, civil rights advocate and Georgia University law professor; and Mary Frances Berry, also a civil rights advocate, staged a protest at the South African embassy in Washington, DC, aimed at mobilizing support for the anti-apartheid movement in America and at opposing America's support, under President Ronald Reagan, for the racist South African regime. The trio helped to organize a campaign to free South Africa from apartheid, which drew massive support nationwide. Widespread protests and demonstrations in many American cities and consistent pressure on Washington to withdraw support from the South African supremacist government from many African American leaders and from various segments of American society eventually culminated in the passage in 1986 of an important Congressional legislation, the comprehensive Anti-Apartheid Act. Sponsored by congressman Ronald Dellums of California, and passed despite President Ronald Reagan's veto, for the first time, the United States Congress called for an end to South Africa's apartheid policy. The act imposed economic sanctions on the racist state, outlawed new American trade and investment in the country, and demanded the release of political prisoners including Mandela. This step was copied by a number of European states and by Japan, pushing Pretoria further into isolation.

A more concerted economic sanctions regime against South Africa and the drastic reduction in foreign trade and investment sent the country's economy into deep recession. The new Afrikaner leadership of F. W. de Klerk that took over the reigns of government in the early 1990s saw the writing on the wall. De Klerk, who became South Africa's president in 1989, realized the futility of continued resistance to the anti-colonial struggle and took the pragmatic approach of dismantling the oppressive system. De Klerk began to repeal apartheid laws, revoked the proscription of the ANC and the PAC, and in 1990 released Mandela from prison after 27 years of incarceration.

Mandela was one of the most influential political figures of the twentieth century. His role in the anti-apartheid struggle to end South Africa's racist and ruthlessly oppressive policy cannot be overemphasized. He was the embodiment of the long, arduous struggle for "the ideal of a democratic and free society in which all persons live together in harmony and with equal opportunities," as he pointed out. This was an ideal, according to him, for which he was prepared to die, if necessary.[28] The successful and peaceful end to the armed resistance, in a most profound way, had a lot to do with Mandela's leadership of the movement, in and out of prison. Upon his release from prison, Mandela led the negotiations with the authorities in Pretoria that culminated in the first multiethnic elections in the history of South Africa, held in 1994. The election of Mandela as president and the ANC as the ruling party provided the final nail on the coffin of apartheid.

CIVIL WARS IN ANGOLA AND MOZAMBIQUE

Long, bloody, and devastating civil wars characterized post-independence Angola and Mozambique. The Angolan war began on the heels of independence in 1975 as the MPLA took over the reins of government from the Portuguese colonial authorities. Based in Luanda, the nation's capital, the MPLA government under Agostinho Neto as president proclaimed the country a Marxist state, the Peoples Republic of Angola. The refusal of the two other major liberation groups, the FNLA and UNITA, to accept MPLA's rule precipitated the civil war that was to last for two-and-a-half decades.

Even before the end of the anti-colonial war, both the FNLA and UNITA had begun to engage the MPLA, the most powerful of the nationalist organizations, in serious confrontations. In a bid for power, the FNLA commenced a march on Luanda from the north in March 1975, with the aim of dislodging the MPLA from the city. However, the FNLA was roundly defeated by MPLA forces aided by major arms supply from the Soviet Union and through the military backing of Cuban forces that Castro had sent to aid it. Following this routing, the FNLA rapidly lost steam, soon collapsed and eventually disappeared from the Angola scene. Also, its main backer, the United States, had abandoned it after its failure to wrest Luanda from the hands of the MPLA.

Meanwhile, in southern Angola, UNITA, allied with apartheid South Africa, launched its own vicious war against the MPLA government. South Africa's agenda in the Angolan Civil War was to prevent the emergence of a Marxist state across its frontiers, especially one that was vehemently opposed to its apartheid policy. The Cuban-backed Angolan forces were, however, able to halt the late 1975 UNITA-SADF's drive toward Luanda. Nevertheless, UNITA proved to be a more formidable and determined foe than the FNLA.

The driving force behind UNITA was its leader, Jonas Savimbi, perhaps the most notorious warlord in Southern Africa. Before he became the darling of Washington, the warlord had initially turned to China for support. With arms shipment from the United States to UNITA, and incessant SADF military incursions into Angola on behalf of the rebel movement, Savimbi was able to maintain control of a considerable part of southern Angola, establishing his base at Huambo. Meanwhile, the MPLA continued to enjoy Soviet, East European, and Cuban military aid, as well as diplomatic support from the OAU. Indeed, the MPLA government was the only Angolan authority recognized by the OAU as legitimately representing the Angolan people.

UNITA–South Africa's alliance was met with a severe blow in 1987 when the SADF suffered a major and decisive military defeat at the hands of MPLA forces and their Cuban allies. The defeat compelled South Africa to reconsider its role in the Angolan crisis. With the cost of its war efforts, which had begun to deal a blow to its economy, and the growing number of casualties among white soldiers, South Africa was ready to negotiate. Angola's willingness to negotiate as well led to a cease-fire in March 1991 between all the warring factions. The Bicesse Accords of May that came out of the negotiations stipulated, among other things, the holding of multiparty elections that would be the first in Angola since independence in 1975. The stage seemed set for the cessation of hostilities and the return of peace to Angola.

The Angolan elections of 1992 expected to return Angola to multiparty democracy were contested by all the political factions in the country including UNITA, which had transformed itself into a political party. The prospect of peace that the Bicesse Accords were designed to achieve, however, proved illusory. José Eduardo dos Santos of the MPLA, incumbent president who had succeeded Agonstinho Neto following his death in September 1979, won the presidential election. MPLA also won a majority in the parliament. The elections, unfortunately, did not bring peace back to Angola. Savimbi, who lost the presidential vote, refused to accept the result under a rather frivolous excuse that it was neither free nor fair. Refusing to accept his loss at the polls, Savimbi resumed the war. The Angolan Civil War had entered its second phase.

The renewed fighting between UNITA and the MPLA government was as vicious as the first phase of the war. In 1994, another attempt was made to end the war when both sides signed the Lusaka Protocol in Zambia, which stipulated, among other provisions, disarming UNITA and integrating its senior officers into the Angolan military and police. This latest peace plan, however, soon floundered as its objectives, particularly UNITA's demobilization and integration, did not go well. Its failure was largely due to Savimbi's hard-line and uncooperative attitude. Indeed, the government, thereafter, refused to deal with him, preferring instead to talk with the leadership of a breakaway group, UNITA-Renovada. The cease-fire achieved by the Lusaka Protocol collapsed in 1998

UNITA's fortunes declined in the late 1990s. It lost considerable external support as the Cold War began to wane. A new international arms embargo on sales of conflict diamonds dealt a severe blow to its source of revenue, which was the mainstay of its ability to prosecute the war. Internally, the movement lost thousands of its war-weary officers and soldiers to desertion. The decline of UNITA as a fighting force enabled the government to assume the upper hand in the civil war. In 2002, the long and vicious Angolan fratricidal conflict finally came to an end 27 years after it had started. What precipitated the conclusion of the war was Savimbi's death; he was killed in combat by government forces on February 22. With its recalcitrant leader out of the picture, the UNITA leadership signed a cease-fire agreement with the government in April. Unlike the earlier peace agreements, the post-Savimbi one endured.

Mozambique followed the same destructive path as post-colonial Angola. A declared Marxist state, independent Mozambique under the presidency of Samora Machel and the ruling FRELIMO faced a tumultuous post-independence period. The FRELIMO government's intolerance of political pluralism did not help the post-colonial task of nation building. Politically, FRELIMO instituted a one-party system, banning any opposition party from taking part in the new nation's political process. However, a dissident movement, *Resistência Nacional Moçambicana* (RENAMO; or as sometimes referred to, the Mozambican National Resistance; MNR), emerged in 1977 to violently oppose the FRELIMO government.

RENAMO was by no means a movement with any progressive political ideology or clearly defined goals other than opposition to the FRELIMO government and a desire to overthrow it. Essentially, it served as proxy for Rhodesia and South Africa in their pursuit of a campaign of destabilization of Southern African states opposed to their diabolic, oppressive, and racist system. The bloody civil war that would last 17 years began only two years after independence when RENAMO insurgents commenced terror campaigns against civilian populations and the nation's fledgling infrastructures. RENAMO fighters indiscriminately killed people perceived to favor FRELIMO, and destroyed government and economic infrastructure such as hospitals, schools, factories, seaports, roads, bridges, and railroads.

Thanks to South African tutelage, RENAMO grew from a small force of a few hundred fighters to an army of guerrillas numbering about 8,000, recruited mainly from the ranks of Mozambique's economically dissatisfied population. Initially, RENAMO found an ally in the white minority-ruled Rhodesia, eager to punish Mozambique for offering sanctuary to Zimbabwe's nationalist organizations fighting a war of liberation against the white-supremacist state. Rhodesia's interest in offering support for RENAMO was to use the rebel movement to counter FRELIMO's Marxist government, destabilize the state, and disrupt its support for Zimbabwe's guerrillas. Rhodesia's sponsorship of RENAMO, however, ended in 1980 when the state became independent and political authority was transferred to its black majority.

RENAMO's growing power in Mozambique was actually a product of apartheid South Africa's support for it. Indeed, the South Africans literally financed the rebel movement, hoping, as Rhodesia, to use it to destabilize Mozambique, which was equally aiding the ANC and other nationalist groups in their anti-apartheid struggle. With South Africa's military backing, RENAMO's ruthless guerrilla campaign began to take a heavy toll on Mozambique's economy and national security by the early 1980s. RENAMO effectively controlled vast territories, especially rural areas, and the SADF incessantly raided Mozambique's border areas. South Africa's impact was such that FRELIMO was driven to sue for peace in 1984 when on March 16 it signed a non-aggression pact with Mozambique, the Nkomati Accord. By this agreement, South Africa was required to cease support for RENAMO, while the government of Mozambique was to end providing the ANC bases of operation against South Africa. Although South Africa's military assistance to RENAMO diminished thereafter, evidence suggests that it did not cease altogether.

Meanwhile, the Mozambican president, Samora Machel, began to pursue a policy of political liberalization and rapprochement with the West. This was possible as the Cold War had begun to wane in the late 1980s. However, the president was killed in a plane crash in October 1986, which South Africa was widely suspected of masterminding. His successor, Joaquim Chissano, continued the former president's policy. A new constitution was drawn in 1990, which provided for a multi-party system and a free market economy. Chissano also began to initiate talks with RENAMO toward ending the bloody conflict. The government's resources to continue to prosecute the war were severely limited. RENAMO, which was also losing South Africa's vital military backing as the apartheid state transitioned to democracy, was equally amenable to peace talks. War weary, the two Mozambican sides were driven to the peace table. The result was the General Peace Agreement often referred to as the Rome Agreement, signed on October 4, 1992. Under this agreement, both FRELIMO and RENAMO accepted the cease-fire, to be followed by demobilization of RENAMO forces and the integration of some of its soldiers into the regular Mozambican army. A national election was also to be held. The cease-fire and demobilization of forces were accomplished under the supervision of a UN peacekeeping force, the United Nations Operation in Mozambique (ONUMOZ). The multiparty election in which RENAMO participated as a legitimate political party was held in late October 1994 under the auspices of a team of international observers. The election, won by Chissano and the ruling party, FRELIMO, was the first in Mozambique since independence. The success of the implementation of the Rome Agreement and the subsequent election marked the effective end of the civil war.

The civil wars in Angola and Mozambique, commencing soon after independence, threatened to destroy the young states. Protracted and destructive, the wars claimed millions of lives, turned several million others into refugees or internally displaced persons, destroyed much-needed infrastructure, destabilized the nations for several years, and nearly ruined their economies. The brutality of the wars is reflected in atrocities committed by all the guerrilla movements and South African forces. RENAMO in Mozambique was widely known for its indiscriminate killing of civilians. Like in other conflict regions of Africa, the use of child soldiers was prevalent. UNITA and RENAMO, for instance, widely used children in combat.

Peculiar to these wars, particularly that of Angola, was widespread use of mines by all sides to the conflict. Indeed, mines constituted one of the most potent weapons employed by the belligerents. Mine explosions were responsible for the deaths of millions, particularly civilians. The devastating result of the use of mines in conflict situations is evident in post-war Angola where mines buried during the war continued to kill or maim people for many years after the conflict. Angola has the unenviable distinction of being the country with the world's highest number of amputees—victims of mines.[29]

THE COLD WAR, SOUTH AFRICA, AND REGIONAL CONFLICT

The post-colonial period coincided with the advent of the Cold War in Africa. The period saw the determination of the United States and the erstwhile Soviet Union to expand and maintain their ideological, economic, and military power in the continent. In the early 1960s, the Congo crisis provided for the superpowers an operational theatre for Cold War competition. However, by the 1970s, Southern Africa, with its many conflicts, had turned into the center stage of Soviet-American Cold War rivalry.[30]

The expansion of Soviet influence in Africa was more pronounced in Southern Africa where, in Angola and Mozambique, the post-independence ruling parties, the MPLA and FRELIMO, respectively, proclaimed Marxist states. Soviet influence increased as the two countries became embroiled in post-independence bloody civil wars. In Angola, the MPLA was armed by the Soviet Union and a number of East European states. Significant military support also came from Fidel Castro's Cuba, a Moscow client state. In late 1975, Cuba began sending combat troops, technicians, and military advisers to help the Angolans to contain UNITA rebels and their South African allies. In Mozambique, FRELIMO also enjoyed extensive Soviet military and technical support. Arms transfer from other Soviet-bloc states, including East Germany, also supported its war effort. Soviet military aid to MPLA, in particular, and to FRELIMO as well, was not limited to light weapons such as rifles; it included heavy hardware such as anti-aircraft guns, rockets, tanks, armored vehicles, and MIG jet fighters.

The liberation wars in Rhodesia and South West Africa also provided the Soviets the opportunity to expand their influence in Southern Africa. The Kremlin backed ZAPU and supplied it with much of its arms in its guerrilla war against the white minority regime. Meanwhile, rival communist China, seeking also to make an inroad into Africa, threw its support behind Mugabe's ZANU. During the liberation war in Namibia, SWAPO had links with the East; its guerrillas were trained in the Soviet Union and other communist countries.

The 1970s and 1980s saw the United States' attempt to contain the growing Soviet power in Southern Africa. Washington's strategy was to back the rebel groups in Angola and Mozambique fighting against the Marxist governments of both states. In Angola, the United States initially supported FNLA, the group it saw as most likely to promote its interest in the post-independence period. Indeed, its leader, Holden Roberto, was said to have been on the payroll of the National Security Council (NSC) in the 1950s and 1960s.[31] However, the United States soon realized that UNITA, under the notorious warlord Savimbi, was more suited to counter the Soviet-backed MPLA. The United States' support subsequently shifted to this rebel group, which began to receive significant American covert military aid from 1976, which Congress subsequently sanctioned. Less blatant, but equally significant, was America's covert support for RENAMO. The United States' support for the Mozambican rebel movement was mainly through South Africa, used as proxy.

The United States' Cold War strategic alliance with South Africa had its rationale in Washington's historic political ties with, and extensive investment in, the racist state. Pretoria became, for the United States, an instrument for American containment policy in Southern Africa. Although America's rhetoric condemned South Africa's apartheid policy that oppressed its black population, Cold War consideration prevented Washington from backing its anti-apartheid pronouncements with concrete action.

South Africa managed to exploit its perceived ideological importance to the West and project itself as a bulwark against communism. Its propaganda consistently portrayed the ANC as a Moscow-driven communist organization that must be curtailed. While the ANC certainly had links with communist states such as the Soviet Union and East Germany, it was by no means communist in ideological commitment. However, the South African propaganda swayed the United States, which in the 1980s covertly backed the apartheid state in its attempt to destroy the ANC. President Ronald Reagan's policy of "constructive engagement" of the early 1980s demonstrated American intransigence toward the anti-apartheid struggle. The administration refused to impose sanctions on South Africa in the face of growing international and UN demand. Instead, the administration sought to engage the racist white supremacist regime constructively in the wrong-headed belief that apartheid could be reformed.

From the late 1970s and before the collapse of its apartheid policy, South Africa was a destabilizing force in the region. Its campaign of destabilization was directed, in particular, against the Frontline States—Angola, Botswana, Mozambique, Tanzania, and Zambia, and Zimbabwe—which provided succor to the anti-apartheid movement.

Military and economic power conferred upon the apartheid state the power to pursue its destabilization agenda. Pretoria became involved in many of the modern conflicts in the region with a view to using them to cripple the states in conflict. This was true of the civil wars in Angola and Mozambique where South Africa aided both militarily and economically their respective rebel movements. As part of its destabilization campaign, South Africa also violated the national sovereignty of neighboring states through military incursions and, on occasion, occupation of foreign territories. For example, the SADF invaded Zimbabwe and Lesotho in August and December 1982, respectively, and in 1981 occupied parts of southern Angola. Cross-border raids, aerial bombardment, political assassinations, and other forms of aggression on neighbors were justified as necessary to dislodge ANC guerrillas and leaders, and to stamp out the movement's operational bases.[32]

There was also the economic dimension of South Africa's destabilization campaign in Southern Africa. Relatively economically weak, most of the neighboring states depended, one way or the other, on South Africa for economic survival. Particularly, they depended on South Africa's transport and communications systems. With this reality, South Africa pursued a deliberate policy of economic manipulation designed to engender neighboring states' economic dependence on Pretoria. Landlocked Lesotho provided a good example of economic dependence on South Africa. Unwilling to commit economic suicide, Lesotho bowed to South Africa's military and economic pressure and refused to grant safe haven to the ANC. In Mozambique, South Africa's exploitation of its civil war through its sponsorship of RENAMO severely damaged the country's already fragile economy. It was the near economic collapse that compelled FRELIMO to sign the Nkomati Accord in 1984.

South Africa's destabilization strategy in Southern Africa, in the end, did not endure. However, it severely retarded political and economic progress of its neighbors and helped to prolong the destructive regional conflicts. According to a report by the United Nations' Economic Commission for Africa (ECA), by 1988, South Africa's destabilization campaign in Southern Africa had caused $60 billion worth of damages.[33]

***

Historically, Southern Africa had been a hot spot. The pre-colonial history of the region was dotted with ethnic clashes. The advent of Europeans in the region added a racial dimension to the conflicts. In Angola and Mozambique, African nationalists had to fight brutal guerrilla wars against the occupying colonial power, Portugal. Also, African nationalists in Rhodesia, South West Africa, and South Africa had to wage equally long and brutal wars against internal colonialism instituted by white supremacist regimes that had reduced their black populations to second-class citizens.

An important element of modern Southern African conflicts is the injection of Cold War politics. The liberation struggle essentially served as proxy for superpower competition. The United States and the Soviet Union and their respective allies backed one nationalist group or the other depending on their ideological leaning. External interference through proxies prolonged and exacerbated the conflicts. Apartheid South Africa was a major force in the region. Its destabilization campaign toward its neighbors through direct military intervention and economic pressure contributed to the region's instability.

The collapse of apartheid in South Africa has brought major conflicts in Southern Africa to an end. Low-intensity conflicts, however, remain.

This is notable in Zimbabwe where severe economic downturn and a crisis of governance have resulted in violence.

Notes

1. Cited in http://www.anc.org.za/ancdocs/history/manifesto-mk.html, retrieved July 5, 2009.

2. "Biography: Eduardo Chivambo Mondlane (1920–1969)," Oberlin College Archives, RG 30/307, retrieved June 10, 2009, from: http://www.oberlin.edu/archive/holdings/finding/RG30/SG307/biography2.html.

3. See complete text in "Prime Minister Ian Smith: Announcement of Unilateral Declaration of Independence, November 11, 1965," retrieved June 17, 2009, from: http://www.fordham.edu/halsall/mod/1965Rhodesia-UDI.html#Ian%20Smith.

4. This chapter focuses on Southern African states where intense conflicts have occurred, namely Angola, Mozambique, Zimbabwe, Namibia, and South Africa. For an overview of political developments in the states of Botswana, Swaziland, Lesotho, Comoros, Seychelles, and Mauritius, see Funso Afolayan, "Southern African States, 1939 to Independence," in Toyin Falola (ed.), *The End of Colonial Rule: Nationalism and Decolonization, Africa Vol. 4* (Durham, NC: Carolina Academic Press, 2002), 399–426.

5. Aran S. MacKinnon, *The Making of South Africa: Culture and Politics* (Upper Saddle River, NJ: Pearson Prentice Hall, 2003), 31.

6. A comprehensive work on this subject is Norman Etherington, *The Great Treks: The Transformation of Southern Africa, 1815–1854* (London: Longman, 2001).

7. Important sources on the war include: Bill Nasson, *The South African War, 1899–1902* (New York: Oxford University Press, 1999); Thomas Pakenham, *The Boer War* (New York: Random House, 1979); and Peter Warwick, *Black People and the South African War, 1899–1902* (Cambridge, UK: Cambridge University Press, 1983).

8. For an overview of the anti-colonial wars, see Adebayo Oyebade, "Radical Nationalism and Wars of Liberation," in Falola (ed.), *The End of Colonial Rule*, 63–87.

9. Portuguese colonialism in Southern Africa is discussed in Gerald Bender, *Angola under the Portuguese: The Myth and the Reality* (Berkeley: University of California Press, 1978).

10. The event is commemorated and celebrated in Angola annually on January 4, which is now a national holiday designated "Colonial Repression Martyrs Day." See Manuel Jerónimo, "Angola: 'Baixa De Kassanje' Massacre Turns 47 Years," ANGOP: *Agência* Angola Press, January 3, 2008. Retrieved June 4, 2009, from: http://www.portalangop.co.ao/motix/en_us/noticias/politica/Baixa-Kassanje-Massacre-Turns-Years,87938cd9-93ae-43f9-ad77-da9c238146f8.html.

11. Jerónimo, "Angola: 'Baixa De Kassanje' Massacre."

12. The formation of FRELIMO is discussed in Eduardo Mondlane, *The Struggle for Mozambique* (Harmondsworth, UK: Penguin, 1969).

13. See Eduardo Mondlane, "The Development of Nationalism in Mozambique," in Aquino de Braganca and Immanuel Wallerstein (eds.), *The African Liberation Reader: The National Liberation Movements, Vol. 2* (London: Zed Books, 1982), 15–20.

14. For more on Mondlane, see Herbert Shore, "Eduardo Chivambo Mondlane," in Harvey Glickman (ed.), *Political Leaders of Contemporary Africa South of the Sahara: A Biographical Dictionary* (Westport, CT: Greenwood Press, 1992).

15. For further discussion on this subject, see Robert Good, *UDI: The International Politics of the Rhodesian Rebellion* (London: Faber and Faber, 1973).

16. For discussions on the liberation struggle in Zimbabwe, see N. Bhebe and T. Ranger (eds.), *Society in Zimbabwe's Liberation War* (Portsmouth, NH: Heinemann, 1993); M. Tamarkin, *The Making of Zimbabwe: Decolonization in Regional and International Politics* (London: Frank Cass, 1990); Lewis H. Gann and Thomas H. Henriksen, *The Struggle for Zimbabwe: Battle in the Bush* (New York: Praeger, 1981); E. H. Morris-Jones (ed.), *From Rhodesia to Zimbabwe* (London: Frank Cass, 1980); and Elaine Windrich, *Britain and the Politics of Rhodesian Independence* (London: Croom Helm, 1978).

17. On German colonization, see Helmut Bley, *Namibia under German Rule* (Hamburg, Germany: Lit, 1996).

18. For South Africa's rule until the end of World War II, see Patricia Hayes, et al. (eds.), *Namibia under South African Rule: Mobility and Containment, 1915–46* (Athens: Ohio University Press, 1998).

19. On the Namibian liberation struggle, see Denis Herbstein and John Evenson, *The Devils Are among Us: The War for Namibia* (London: Zed Books, 1990); Peter Katjavivi, *A History of Resistance in Namibia* (London: James Currey, 1987); and Alfred T. Moleah, *Namibia: The Struggle for Liberation* (Wilmington, DE: Disa Press, 1983).

20. MacKinnon, *The Making of South Africa*, 211. An important discussion of apartheid is provided on pages 210–245.

21. For an important scholarly analysis of the apartheid state, see Dan O'Meara, *Forty Lost Years: The Apartheid State and the Politics of the National Party, 1948–94* (Johannesburg: Ravan, 1996).

22. Useful analysis of the massacre is provided in Philip H. Frankel, *An Ordinary Atrocity: Sharpeville and Its Massacre* (New Haven, CT: Yale University Press, 2001).

23. Nelson Mandela, *Mandela: An Illustrated Autobiography* (Boston: Little, Brown and Company, 1996), 88.

24. Ibid., 89.

25. Biko's contribution to the subject is provided in Millard Arnold (ed.), *Steve Biko: Black Consciousness in South Africa* (New York: Random House, 1978).

26. Soweto stands for South Western Townships (of Johannesburg).

27. For more on Biko, see Andile Mngxitama, Amanda Alexander, and Nigel C. Gibson (eds.), *Biko Lives: Contesting the Legacies of Steve Biko* (New York: Palgrave, 2008).

28. Cited in "I Am Prepared to Die," Nelson Mandela's statement from the dock at the opening of the defense case in the Rivonia Trial, Pretoria Supreme Court, April 20, 1964, retrieved on July 10, 2009, from: http://www.anc.org.za/ancdocs/history/mandela/1960s/rivonia.html.

29. A number of works provide good synthesis of the civil wars in Angola and Mozambique. See, for instance, John Prendergast, *Angola's Deadly War: Dealing with Savimbi's Hell on Earth* (Washington, DC: United States Institute of Peace, 1999); Human Rights Watch, *Angola Unravels: The Rise and Fall of the Lusaka Peace Process* (New York: Human Rights Watch, 1999); Fernando Andresen Guimarães, *The Origins of the Angolan Civil War: Foreign Intervention and Domestic Political Conflict* (New York: St. Martin's Press, 1998); Stephen Chan and Moisés Venâncio, *War and Peace in Mozambique* (New York: St. Martin's Press, 1998); Margaret Hall and Tom Young, *Confronting Leviathan: Mozambique since Independence* (Athens: Ohio University Press, 1997); James Ciment, *Angola and Mozambique: Postcolonial Wars in Southern Africa* (New York: Facts on File, 1997); Alex Vines, *RENAMO: From Terrorism to Democracy in Mozambique* (London: James Currey, 1996); Rachel Waterhouse, *Mozambique: Rising from the Ashes* (Oxford, UK: OXFAM, 1996); and M. F. Chingono, *Conspicuous Destruction: War, Famine and the Reform Process in Mozambique, 1975–1992* (New York: Human Rights Watch, 1992).

30. The literature on Cold War politics in Southern Africa is rich. See, for instance, the following: Edward George, *The Cuban Intervention in Angola, 1965–1991: From Che Guevara to Cuito Cuanavale* (New York: Frank Cass, 2005); Mark T. Berger, "The Cold War and National Liberation in Southern Africa: The United States and the Emergence of Zimbabwe," *Intelligence and National Security: An Inter-Disciplinary Journal*, Vol. 18, No. 1 (2003: 171–179); G. Wright, *Destruction of a Nation: United States Policy towards Angola since 1945* (London: Pluto Press, 1997); D. Spikes, *Angola and the Politics of Intervention* (Jefferson, NC: McFarland Publishers, 1993); M. Anstee, *Orphan of the Cold War: The Inside Story of the Collapse of the Angola Peace Process* (New York: St. Martin's Press, 1996); and Thomas J. Noer, *Cold War and Black Liberation: The United States and White Rule in Africa, 1948–1968* (Columbia: University of Missouri Press, 1985).

31. See John Frederick Walker, *A Certain Curve of Horn: The Hundred-Year Quest for the Giant Sable Antelope of Angola* (New York: Atlantic Monthly Press, 2004), 146–148.

32. Despite any credible evidence, many believed that the death of the Mozambican president, Samora Machel, in a plane crash in October 1986, was a political assassination masterminded by South Africa.

33. See United Nations, *South African Destabilization: The Economic Cost of Frontline Resistance to Apartheid* (New York: Economic Commission for Africa, 1989), 8. For other studies of apartheid South Africa in Southern Africa, see William Minter, *Apartheid's Contras: An Inquiry into the Roots of War in Angola and Mozambique* (London: Zed, 1994); Joseph Hanlon, *Beggar Your Neighbours: Apartheid Power in Southern Africa* (London: James Currey, 1986); and Sam C. Nolutshungu, *South Africa in Africa: A Study of Ideology and Foreign Policy* (Manchester, UK: Manchester University Press, 1975).

CHAPTER 5

East Africa and the Great Lakes Region

While the world looks elsewhere a tiny country in Central Africa has been eliminating the opposition elite by "selective genocide."
Roger M. Williams, on the 1972 Hutu-Tutsi conflict in Burundi.[1]

The Somali coast is currently the world's most dangerous area as far as piracy is concerned.
BBC News, Africa[2]

. . . the conflict in the Sudan is the longest running conflict in Africa . . .
Machakos Protocol, July 20, 2002[3]

The humanitarian situation in northern Uganda is worse than in Iraq, or anywhere else in the world.
Jan Egeland, United Nations Under-Secretary-General for Humanitarian Affairs.[4]

The rape capital of the world is eastern Congo.
Nicholas D. Kristof,
New York Times columnist, 2008.[5]

East Africa is a vast region extending from Sudan in the north to Tanzania in the south. A broad region of great diversity culturally and geographically, East Africa can be divided further into two subregions. There is the northern segment of the region in the proximity of the

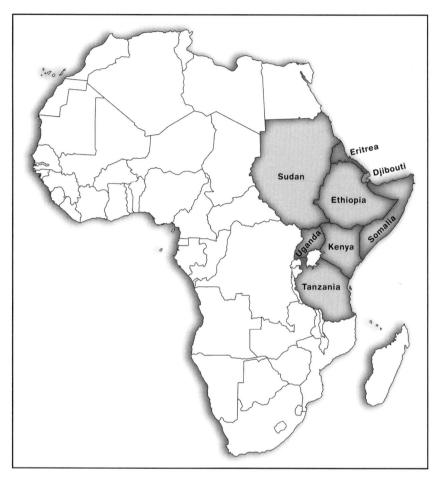

Countries of East Africa. (Courtesy of Sam Saverance.)

Red Sea, often referred to as the Horn of Africa. This subregion is comprised of Djibouti, Eritrea, and Somalia, as well as Sudan and Ethiopia farther west. Constituting the rest of East Africa are the more southerly states of Kenya, Tanzania, and Uganda.

Historical and archaeological evidence suggests that East Africa is the oldest region of Africa in terms of human habitation. Archaeological excavation in Ethiopia, Kenya, and Tanzania has yielded fossilized remains of early human species. Historians believe that it was from East Africa that humans fanned out to other parts of the continent and to the rest of the world.

The history of East Africa is partly shaped by two major external influences. First, Arab Islamic culture became a major force in the region as a result of incursions by Muslim traders from the Arabian Peninsula, beginning in the tenth century CE. In the Horn, except for Ethiopia, Southern Sudan, and Eritrea, Arab influence is significantly strong. Islamic expansion from Arabia through the Red Sea has had a major impact on the culture of the adjacent states of Djibouti, Somalia, and Sudan. Southward, beyond Mogadishu in Somalia, Islamic influence also came to bear on the coastal stretch down to Mozambique, the area often referred to as the Swahili Coast. The Indian Ocean trading system connecting Arabia to this region of East Africa led to the establishment there of coastal and island trading outposts including Malindi and Mombasa in Kenya and Zanzibar in Tanzania. The Islamization and Arabization of significant parts of East Africa has been an important factor for conflict in the region as demonstrated in the Sudan where recurring civil wars have raged between the Arab-dominated north and the non-Arab peoples of the south.

The second major external influence that has defined East African history is European imperial intrusion from the mid-nineteenth century. With the construction of the Suez Canal in 1869 by Britain, the Horn assumed a strategic importance to European powers as the Red Sea became a major international passageway to Asian markets. Britain, France, and Italy were the dominant colonial powers in East Africa. As in other parts of Africa, European colonization of the region left an enduring legacy of ethnic division that has contributed to post-colonial conflicts. Irredentism in the Horn stems from colonial division of the Somali people, separated into British Somaliland, French Somaliland, Italian Somaliland, Ethiopia, and Kenya.

This chapter examines East Africa as a hot spot region, with particular attention to its major conflicts. Indeed, the region has always been one of intense conflicts. The Horn, in particular, has historically and in modern times been a very volatile subregion. Conflicts of various types and intensity have occurred here and continue to occur. For instance, Sudan was embroiled in complex civil wars even before its attainment of independence in 1956. In 2004, the Sudanese deadly conflict reached a genocidal proportion and has so far defied resolution. Violent inter-state conflicts involving other states of the Horn such as Somalia, Ethiopia, and Eritrea have long threatened the stability of the entire subregion. In recent times, the failed state of Somalia, which has witnessed years of warlord power struggle, banditry, and lawlessness, has turned into a hot spot of international piracy.

While innumerable serious conflicts have dotted the political landscape of the Horn, the more southerly states of Kenya and Tanzania have largely been spared from major debilitating conflicts. However, they have not altogether escaped low-level conflicts and civil strife arising from brutal dictatorship, ethnic animosity, economic underdevelopment, and political weakness. In Kenya, the façade of ethnic harmony and political stability was shattered by the bloody civil unrest that attended the presidential election of December 27, 2007, which threatened to destabilize the state. Uganda, on the other hand, has seen a more devastating conflict. Although, largely ignored by the international community, the state has for decades been embroiled in a protracted and deadly civil war in its northern region. This conflict has also spilled to Sudan and the DRC.

During the Cold War, East Africa, particularly the Horn, was a theatre of big power strategic interest. Ethiopia provides a classic case of superpower power play in the subregion. Initially, Ethiopia under its famous monarch, Emperor Haile Selassie, was staunchly pro-West, with military assistance agreement with Washington. However, with the demise of the emperor's imperial government in 1974, Ethiopia made a 360-degrees ideological turnaround, adopting Marxism, and virtually becoming a Soviet client state. In any case, the subregion's plethora of conflicts bore the imprint of superpower meddling. The massive infusion of weapons, particularly small arms, into the subregion by the Cold War adversaries, complicated local conflicts and undermined their prospects of resolution. Although the end of the Cold War in the late 1980s has significantly lessened external powers' influence in the Horn, the subregion is not totally divested of external interests. Since the terrorist attacks on the United States on September 11, 2001, American and Western attention has been focused on the Horn to prevent the subregion from being a haven for Al-Qaeda terrorists. Also, escalating piracy off the coast of Somalia involving international shipping has heightened external interest in the region.

The major conflicts in the Great Lakes region of Central and Eastern Africa are also examined in this chapter. This is a region that encompasses the cluster of states around lakes Tanganyika, Victoria, Kivu, Edward, and Albert. Since the 1990s, the region has experienced violent conflicts, most especially in Burundi, Rwanda, and the DRC.

A recurring theme in this region's conflicts is genocide. While genocide has been reportedly committed in Burundi's ethnic conflict, which has led to the deaths of over 200,000 people since 1993, the killings in Rwanda in 1994 in which thousands of ethnic Tutsi were slaughtered clearly constituted genocide. Although not tagged as genocide, the ongoing conflict in eastern DRC has been very devastating, claiming more casualties than any contemporary African conflict. Given years of political turbulence and violent armed conflicts, the Great Lakes region is noted for massive population displacements that have turned the area into a humanitarian disaster.

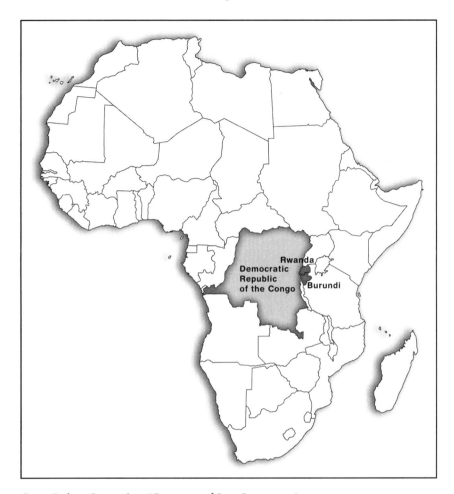

Great Lakes Countries. (Courtesy of Sam Saverance.)

ETHIOPIA'S WARS AND RED TERROR

A landlocked country, Ethiopia shares borders with all the states in the Horn of Africa, and also with Kenya. It is bordered in the north by Eritrea, in the northeast by Djibouti, in the east and southeast by Somalia, in the south by Kenya, and in the west and northwest by Sudan. Often considered Africa's oldest nation, Ethiopia (formerly known as Abyssinia) has an ancient history with historical records dating to 3000 BCE. The prominent ancient kingdom of Aksum (or Axum) established about 500 BCE, and which had attained prominence at least by the first century CE, was located in the northern part of the modern Ethiopian state. Noted for developing a Christian civilization,

Aksum's influence at the height of its power reached beyond present-day Ethiopia to the Islamic world of Yemen and Arabia. Although by the eighth century Islamic expansion beyond the Arabian Peninsula had significantly diminished Ethiopia's influence across the Red Sea, the state was still a formidable entity in the region.[6]

Wars of Colonial Resistance

The modern history of Ethiopia is rather distinct from that of other African countries in one important respect.[7] While the rest of Africa (with the exception of Liberia) succumbed to European imperial rule, Ethiopia successfully resisted colonial subjugation. As the European scramble for Africa got underway in the late nineteenth century, Italy, a latecomer to the colonial enterprise, sought to expand its African possessions, namely Eritrea and Somalia, by acquiring Ethiopia. Italy's attempt to conquer Ethiopia brought about the first Italo-Ethiopian War, in which the Ethiopians roundly defeated the Italians at the famous Battle of Adwa (or Adowa) in 1896. Following its defeat, Italy signed a peace treaty with Ethiopia on October 26, 1896, in which it recognized the independence of the African state. For the moment, Italy's dream of acquiring a vast empire in the Horn was on hold.

Ethiopia's successful colonial resistance, and particularly its triumph at Adwa over the Italians, represented great pride for the African world. Ethiopia became a symbol of Africa's political independence, and would serve as inspiration for black nationalism, not only on the African continent, but also in the Diaspora. Conversely, for the Italians, the humiliating Adwa defeat was a painful injury to national pride. The consequent Italian desire for *revanche* partly precipitated the second Italo-Ethiopian War of 1935–1936.

In reality, the Italians had never abandoned a dream of colonial expansion in the Horn. Benito Mussolini's well-known expression of the desire of Italy to have "a place in the sun" vividly supports this. Italy used the pretext of a border skirmish, the so-called "Wal-wal Incident" in December 1934 between Ethiopia and Italian Somaliland, to orchestrate hostilities against Ethiopia. Rejecting arbitration of the border dispute as demanded by Ethiopia's emperor, Haile Selassie, Mussolini ordered Italian forces to invade Ethiopia in October 1935. During the seven-month campaign, the Italians employed massive air attacks accompanied by the use of mustard gas to defeat Ethiopia. Italian military occupation of Ethiopia followed the war, and its annexation with the two Italian colonies of Eritrea and Italian Somaliland formed Italian East Africa. Despite this development, the Ethiopians never surrendered their sovereignty to Italy. Indeed, Italy encountered nationwide resistance during this brief period of occupation. During World War II, Anglo-Ethiopian forces liberated Ethiopia from the Italian occupation.[8]

The Derg Revolution and Civil War

Haile Selassie, the long-reigning Ethiopian imperial ruler (1930–1974) was easily the most notable personality in modern Ethiopian history. His long official title, "His Imperial Majesty, King of Kings, Lord of Lords, Conquering Lion of the Tribe of Judah, and Elect of God," indicated this. Beyond his native Ethiopia where he was revered by many, in the rest of Africa he commanded immense respect. He had presided over the establishment, in 1963, of the pan-African organization, the OAU, at his capital, Addis Ababa. In the African Diaspora, he was an icon; Jamaican Rastafarians believed he was *Jah* (God).[9]

Despite his international stature, Selassie's political fortunes had actually begun to wane by the 1960s as growing demand for political reforms in Ethiopia gained ground. Imperial rule had been so entrenched in Ethiopia that the emperor was unresponsive to calls for change. Corruption and the failure to bring about political reform to the archaic governmental system instigated a growing sense of discontentment particularly among students and the elite. An attempted overthrow of the emperor in an unsuccessful coup in December 1960 was a signal of the impending demise of the monarch. Further complicating the political situation, however, was the Eritrean War of Independence. Eritrea had been formally annexed by Ethiopia in 1962 when the emperor unilaterally abrogated a UN resolution that had federated the former Italian colony with it. Ethiopia was forced to expend a great deal of its resources on the conflict, which further aggravated the already faltering economy. To make matters worse, a severe famine from 1972 to 1974 ravaged the country, in which about 200,000 people perished. It was the combination of these factors that brought about the termination of the monarchy. Selassie was deposed in September 1974 by the Coordinating Committee of the Armed Forces, Police, and Territorial Army (otherwise known as the *Derg*), made up of elements of the military and the police.

The Derg had been in the making by 1973 as a Marxist, revolutionary organization, and had steadily gained power. In a power struggle within the organization after the overthrow of Selassie, Mengistu Haile Mariam emerged chief of state, succeeding the emperor. The Derg declared Ethiopia a socialist state, effectively turning it into a Soviet client state and reversing its pro-West stance under Selassie. Massive Soviet military aid began to flow into Ethiopia, complemented by support from other Eastern-bloc states.

Under the Derg revolution that lasted from 1974 to 1991, Ethiopia was virtually a totalitarian state characterized by bloody repression of opponents of its ideological leanings. In what was known as the Red Terror, between 1977 and 1987, the revolution exterminated thousands of dissenters. Hundreds were tortured and imprisoned without trial, while several thousands more fled the country into exile. The regime's authoritarianism and policies created economic misery for many people. In addition, another devastating famine caused by drought hit Ethiopia in 1984–1985, weakened the economy, and adversely affected millions; it also claimed several thousand lives.

Meanwhile, by the late 1970s, Ethiopia was already in a state of civil war as the regime was confronted with insurrections by separatist groups, chiefly in the regions of Eritrea and Tigray. In Eritrea the guerrillas of the Eritrean People's Liberation Front (EPLF) continued to fight the Mengistu's regime for the independence of the region. The opposition to the Derg in Tigray province was led by a rebel group known as the Tigray People's Liberation Front (TPLF). The civil war also involved a number of opposition rebel groups including the Ethiopian Democratic Union (EDU) and the Ethiopian People's Revolutionary Party (EPRP).

In the midst of the civil war, in 1977, the regime had to contend with Somalia's invasion of the Ogaden region in its irredentist claim against Ethiopia. Although Mengistu was able to contain the crisis through Soviet and Cuban military support, this and the other conflicts were a great drain on the state's dwindling resources. The civil war had also been a brutal one where a lot of atrocities were committed by both sides of the conflict. The general state of war, economic misery brought about by failed policies, and political repression forced thousands of Ethiopians to seek succor in other countries both inside and outside Africa. In May 1991, Mengistu's reign of terror ended when the brutal dictator fled into exile in Zimbabwe as advancing forces of the Ethiopian People's Revolutionary Democratic Front (EPRDF), a coalition of rebel movements, were poised to take Addis Ababa.[10]

ERITREA

Northeast of Ethiopia, and formerly its northern province, is the independent state of Eritrea. During the colonial era in Africa, Eritrea was a colony of Italy until 1941, when the British occupied the territory and took over its administration.[11] Britain ruled the colony as a UN trust territory until 1952 when, by a resolution of the General Assembly, it was federated with Ethiopia as an autonomous province. Eritrean history took a dramatic turn when, in 1962, Emperor Haile

Selassie unilaterally annexed the hitherto autonomous state. This development immediately brought to the fore the simmering nationalist sentiment among the Eritreans and set the stage for the Eritrean War of Independence.

War of Independence

Eritrean nationalist impulse in the immediate post–World War II period lacked mass support and was fragmented by cultural and ethno-religious differences. It found initial expression among the Muslim population, which opposed Ethiopia's overlordship and feared possible abrogation of the province's autonomy and its eventual annexation by Ethiopia, ruled by a deep-rooted Christian monarchy. On the other hand, Eritrean Christians, influenced by the Orthodox Church, which favored Eritrean union with Ethiopia, were slow to imbibe nationalist ideals. They were also suspicious of Muslim domination in an independent Eritrea. However, nationalist sentiment gradually gained mass acceptance, propelled by Ethiopia's annexation of Eritrea in 1962.

Ethiopia's imperial rule over Eritrea from the beginning was characterized by repression of democratic ideals in the former Italian colony, which had enjoyed a relatively higher degree of civic and democratic liberties than Ethiopia. The monarchy, absolute in orientation and irreconcilable to democratic tenets, systematically chipped away at the civil liberties of Eritreans. It curtailed Eritrea's press freedom, suppressed its political parties and associations, and outlawed its labor unions. Also, the imperial authority abolished the use of Eritrea's two major languages, Arabic and Tigrinya, as official languages of instruction and administration, and replaced them with Amharic, Ethiopia's lingua franca.

Eritrean nationalist initiative initially centered on seeking international pressure to bear on Ethiopia to end its repressive rule in the province. However, the recalcitrance of the Ethiopian authority led to the advocacy of armed opposition. This new course was initially championed by the Eritrean Liberation Front (ELF) under the leadership of Idris Muhammad Adam, with its following mainly among Eritrean Muslims, a particular target of imperial oppression. By September 1961, ELF's armed wing, the Eritrean Liberation Army (ELA), had begun a guerrilla war against Ethiopia's forces, supported by a number of Islamic states such as Sudan, Iran, and Syria. Ethiopia, blessed with massive American aid, was able to respond effectively to the ELF insurgency.

Meanwhile, the ELF became fragmented as a result of internal struggles. Splinter groups emerged including the Eritrean Peoples Liberation Front (EPLF), formed in the mid-1970s.[12] Although both the EFL and

EPLF had a common goal of Eritrean independence, a bitter civil war for national supremacy ensued between them. By the late 1970s, the EPLF had taken the initiative in the war of independence.

Under the Derg rule, the guerrilla war intensified and Eritrean armed groups, particularly the EFL and the EPLF, continued to conduct guerrilla operations against Ethiopian forces. Mengistu's policy was particularly repressive toward Eritrea. His counterinsurgency strategy included massive deployment of forces to destroy the Eritrean military machine. Despite a series of offensives by the Ethiopian Army against Eritrean guerrillas from the late 1970s to the mid-1980s, the insurgency remained undefeated.

The tide of the war turned in the late 1980s as the Eastern Communist bloc collapsed and the Cold War began to wind to a halt. Mengistu became increasingly isolated, and the much needed military support from the Soviet Union, which itself was facing disintegration, was no longer forthcoming. Faced with cessation of Soviet assistance and a civil war at home, Ethiopia's fighting forces lost steam. The EPLF seized the precarious position in which the Derg had found itself to step up its campaign for independence. EPLF's military campaigns, by March 1988, had led to its capture of strategic regions of Eritrea including the major cities of Afabet and Keren. By early 1991, virtually the whole of Eritrea was under the EPLF control. The coalition of anti-Derg forces that finally forced Mengistu out of power in May 1991 made Eritrea's independence a fait accompli.

The Eritrean War of Independence was a long and brutal one that lasted 30 solid years. Over 60,000 people died from the conflict and several thousand others, including children, became refugees in Sudan and other neighboring countries. Eritrea formally declared independence on May 24, 1993, after a UN-moderated independence referendum held in April confirmed the wish of Eritreans for self-rule.[13]

Eritrean-Ethiopian Border Conflict

Despite the long and bitter Eritrean War of Independence, its immediate postwar relations with Ethiopia were cordial. However, a devastating two-year border war between the two states soon destroyed this mutual cordial relationship.

The border conflict broke out on May 6, 1998, when contingents of the Eritrean armed forces occupied the village of Badme along the border with Ethiopia. This disputed territory had previously been administered by Ethiopia. Indeed, Eritrea had not claimed the territory at independence in 1993; its inhabitants had also regarded themselves as Ethiopians, under Ethiopia's authority.[14]

Although Ethiopian-Eritrean relations were cordial until the outbreak of this conflict, areas of likely border tensions were never addressed in 1993. The failure to clearly delineate the border in disputed areas posed a threat to peaceful coexistence between the two states. A boundary commission established by the two states with the responsibility of dealing with unresolved border issues had not achieved its purpose when the conflict began in May 1998. Apart from boundary tensions, other contentious issues between Ethiopia and Eritrea contributed to the atmosphere that triggered the conflict in 1998. For example, there was disagreement over Eritrean creation of its own currency and problems over bilateral trade.

The crisis over Eritrea's occupation of Badme further escalated as Eritrean forces attacked other places in the attempt to expand their control around the border area. Ethiopia responded by launching a full-scale offensive on Eritrea to take back occupied territories. The vicious ground war of tanks and artilleries intensified with the introduction of aerial attacks by the countries' respective air forces.

The war came to an end when the two sides agreed on June 18, 2000, to a cease-fire and accepted arbitration of their border dispute. To facilitate the cease-fire agreement, the UN subsequently authorized and deployed to the region a 4,000-strong peacekeeping force, the United Nations Mission in Ethiopia and Eritrea (UNMEE). In December, at Algiers, the Algerian capital, both parties signed a comprehensive peace agreement. By the Algiers agreement, an independent commission, the Eritrea-Ethiopia Boundary Commission (EEBC) was subsequently created on April 13, 2002, to deal with the border dispute.

The two-year conflict had been a very violent one, causing heavy causalities. Many estimates put the number of the dead on both sides at 70,000, although higher figures exist.[15] Apart from war casualties, the conflict displaced millions of people; the respective governments expelled several thousand people from their territories, all creating a massive refugee problem in the region. The conflict also proved very costly for both parties in material and financial terms. Infrastructural destruction was enormous, particularly for Eritrea, and the cost of weapons used in the war further depleted the already exhausted resources of the states.

Lasting peace has not yet materialized between Ethiopia and Eritrea, and border tensions have persisted despite the peace treaty. In 2005, the UN warned of possible renewal of hostilities as a result of military buildup along their borders. In 2007, tensions heightened again and threatened renewed conflict.[16]

SOMALIA: A FAILED STATE

At independence in 1960, the Somali government under President Mohammed Siad Barre adopted as state policy the incorporation into Somalia of all Somali people living in different parts of the Horn. This irredentist "Greater Somalia" policy thus meant that ethnic Somali in Ethiopia, Djibouti, and Kenya would be united under the political authority of Somalia. The pursuit of this pan-Somali policy with tenacity, at least until the 1990s, brought Somalia into small-scale conflicts, particularly with Ethiopia, but also with Kenya and Djibouti. In 1964, for example, Somalia had border skirmishes with Ethiopia and Kenya.[17]

The Ogaden War

One manifestation of Somalia's irredentist claim in the Horn was the Ogaden War of 1977–1978. The Ogaden region of Ethiopia had always been a target of Somalia because it was home to numerous ethnic Somali. In the pursuit of its irredentist policy, Somalia invaded the region in July 1997 with several thousand troops of the Somali National Army (SNA) manning tanks, artilleries, and armored vehicles supported by air power. In alliance with the invading Somali forces was the Western Somali Liberation Front (WSLF), a separatist movement in the Ogaden that had traditionally opposed the Ethiopian government. By late July, the Somalis had captured a number of key Ogaden cities.

Ethiopia's counteroffensive was buoyed by massive Communist bloc military assistance. The Soviet Union, Cuba, North Korea, and East Germany provided various types of military assistance to Ethiopia. Soviet intervention was especially crucial to the outcome of the conflict in favor of Ethiopia. The Soviets not only provided the Ethiopians sophisticated military equipment, they also airlifted Cuban combat troops to join the fighting against the SNA. By the end of February 1978, there were up to 17,000 Cuban troops and technicians in Ethiopia. The joint Ethiopian-Cuban counteroffensive brought about Somalia's defeat by mid-March. Somali forces withdrew and Ethiopia regained all the lost territories. At least until mid-1980, WSLF insurgents allied with remnants of the SNA continued sporadic guerrilla attacks in the Ogaden. However, another major Ethiopian-Somali border war was to occur in 1982.

The Ogaden conflict provides a classic case study of superpower Cold War rivalry in Africa and the manipulation of vulnerable African states. The Horn was an obvious strategic prize to the superpowers given its proximity to the Red Sea, a gateway to the Indian Ocean and

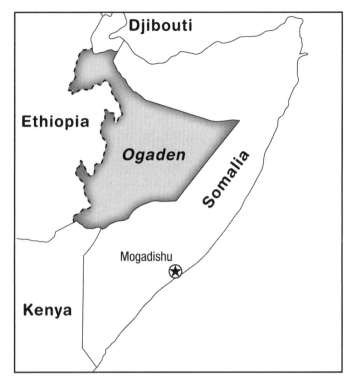

Ogaden. (Courtesy of Sam Saverance.)

the Persian Gulf. The United States had established a footing in the region during Haile Selassie's imperial era, by turning Ethiopia into a client state. Until Selassie's overthrow in 1974, Washington provided Ethiopia with military assistance and helped it to build a sophisticated arsenal. Washington's Cold War adversary, the Soviet Union, on the other hand, maintained a strong presence in neighboring Somalia, using the state as a counterforce to American influence in the region. As a Soviet client state, Somalia received massive military aid from the Kremlin. The Somali arms buildup was essentially a product of Soviet military assistance.

The demise of Haile Selassie in 1974 brought about a dramatic repositioning of the superpowers in their pursuit of Cold War interests. With a Marxist government, the Derg, now in Addis Ababa and hostile to Washington, the Soviet Union shifted support to the erstwhile American ally, Ethiopia. The Soviet friendship with Ethiopia, however, cost the Kremlin the clientele of Somalia. Siad Barre turned to Washington, which gladly replaced Soviet patronage. In the late 1970s, the United States began to provide Somalia military and economic assistance. In exchange, the United States eyed military bases in the country, particularly the strategic port of Berbera on the Gulf of Aden. America unflinchingly supported the dictator despite his appalling human rights record. The 1982 border conflict with Ethiopia provided the United States the justification to further escalate its military assistance to Somalia.

State Collapse and Civil War

For much of its post-independence history, Somalia was virtually a pawn in the chessboard of superpower Cold War rivalry. In the 1990s, the state entered a new phase in its recent history when the central authority collapsed and it turned into a failed state. Somalia would remain in this political state for much of the first decade of the twenty-first century.

The Ogaden War was an element in Somalia's tortuous road to collapse as a state. The disastrous war weakened the state politically and economically, and dealt a severe blow to the military, which lost a significant portion of its personnel as well as resources. Both in the military and in the civil society, the humiliating defeat brought to the fore discontentment with the autocratic rule of Siad Barre. The abortive coup of April 1978, occurring at the heels of the crushing defeat in the Ogaden War, was indicative of the discontentment that had been brewing in the Somali society for sometime.

Siad Barre came to power in a military coup in 1969 and soon instituted a dictatorship that was not only brutal, but also discriminatory against Somali clans other than his own. Members of his clan, the Darod, were favored in every level of government, while other clans such as the Mijertyn and the Issaq were denied positions and promotions in the government and in the armed forces, and, indeed, bore the brunt of the president's repressive measures. His politics of nepotism laid the foundation for the clan warfare that later bedeviled the nation.

Opposition to Barre crystallized in the 1980s as armed groups and militias representing opposing clans began to engage the government in armed confrontation with the goal of overthrowing it. Among the most prominent of these opposition groups were the Somali Salvation Front (SSF), later called the Somali Salvation Democratic Front (SSDF); and the Somali National Movement (SNM), some of which were provided operational bases by Ethiopia. Barre responded to the growing insurgency by brutally repressing political dissent and recklessly using military power to crush rebel forces. However, Barre's strategy only escalated resistance to his iron rule. His abandonment of the unsuccessful pan-Somali policy after the Ogaden War brought him more enemies—the Ogaden in Somalia, as well as their kin across the border in Ethiopia. Indeed, a dissident group, the Somali Patriotic Movement (SPM), formed in 1985 as a result of a split in the SSDF and consisted of large numbers of Ogaden officers. What had essentially become a civil war intensified by 1988 as opposition guerrillas increased offensives in every region of the country and succeeded in wresting from the government the control of many parts of the country.[18] By early 1990, Barre's control of Somalia had practically been reduced to the capital, Mogadishu. The political situation became more precarious as a result of prevailing drought, which caused the deaths of thousands of Somalis.

Although the various strands of the insurgency movement failed to provide a concerted opposition to Barre, increased antagonism from more of the population because of his repressive policies severely weakened his grip on power. In January 1991, Barre was overthrown. However, his exile, first to Kenya and later to Nigeria, did not end the civil war. A provisional government in Mogadishu set up in February 1991 was unable to exercise control over the whole country. Talks regarding a power-sharing arrangement failed, and clan warlords engaged themselves in violent power struggles that threw Somalia further into chaos. Mogadishu, the capital, became a major battleground between rival clan militias. Somalia virtually became ungovernable, and, indeed, lacked a viable central government. It had effectively become a failed state characterized by lawlessness and anarchy.[19]

Operation Restore Hope

By 1992, the situation in Somalia was so grave that it begged for international intervention. The clan warfare had claimed hundreds of thousands of lives; starvation from famine had added thousands more. Attempts by the United Nations to deliver relief to the suffering and starving population were not wholly successful because of the infighting and sabotage by the warring clans, particularly the faction led by warlord Mohammed Farah Aideed. The continued deterioration of the human conditions prompted the United States' intervention in December 1992.

The road to American intervention in Somalia began in late 1992 when President George H. W. Bush announced the decision of his administration to send nearly 30,000 American troops to the Somali capital on humanitarian grounds.[20] The American mission objective in Somalia, Bush emphasized, was to be limited and swift. Its aim was "to open the supply routes, to get the food moving, and to prepare the way for a UN peace-keeping force to keep it moving."[21] Bush assured Americans that U.S. troops "will not stay longer than is absolutely necessary."[22] Despite the assurance by the president that the mission, code named "Operation Restore Hope," had a limited objective, opposition to it was rife in many quarters, even within the Bush administration itself.[23] The general sentiment in the foreign policy community, in particular, was that Washington should have no business in a place like Somalia where United States strategic and security interests no longer existed given that the Cold War had ended.[24]

"Operation Restore Hope" proved to be a costly foreign policy adventure. The expected short-run and limited-scope mission proved to be illusory. With the order to capture Aideed, the primarily humanitarian mission took on the character of a counterinsurgency operation. This extension of the original mandate to help feed the impoverished and starving population of Somalia led to a tragic course of events for the American soldiers. While on a mission to capture Aideed in October 1993, a contingent of the American forces was ambushed by armed Somalis. In the encounter, two American helicopters were shot down and 18 American soldiers lost their lives.[25]

The killing of American soldiers in Somalia was particularly made more shocking by the spectacle of the near-mutilated body of one of the dead soldiers being dragged along the streets of Mogadishu by Somalis. The tragic and humiliating incident, beamed into American homes in a dramatic way by major news networks, caused intense official and public questioning of the wisdom of America's presence in a conflict region where its interest was not at stake. The mounting opposition to the American intervention was the reason for President Bill Clinton's announcement within days of the killings that American troops would be withdrawn from the crisis-ridden country early the following year. "Operation Restore Hope" had left a legacy on post–Cold War United States foreign policy in Africa. Washington was fully persuaded of the futility of any deep involvement in African crises. The "Somalia syndrome," a term defined by Herbert Howe as "the U.S. fear of prolonged commitments of prestige, time, money, and troops in largely unknown areas for ill-defined (or largely nonexistent) national interests,"[26] was, henceforth, to haunt American response to African crises. It was precisely this "syndrome" that informed President Clinton's Presidential Decision Directive 25 (PDD-25) of May 6, 1994, which was a comprehensive policy review establishing a new framework for decision making regarding American participation in peacekeeping around the globe.[27]

The American mission in Somalia failed largely because it lacked a clear mandate. It deviated from humanitarian intervention to identification and pursuit of Aideed as a wanted person. PDD-25, as a response to the Somali fiasco, outlined new policy guidelines under which United States participation in international peacekeeping missions could be sanctioned. Among the new set of guidelines is that the objectives of the mission must be clearly defined and an endpoint to American participation be identified. Further, the mission must advance American interests, and the risks to American forces must be weighed and determined acceptable.[28]

Intensified Clan Warfare

Since the deposition of Siad Barre in 1991, Somalia has never recovered from political instability and has continued to limp on as a failed state. Warlord antagonism, clan insurgency, and radical Islamism have not allowed the return of peace. A number of attempts to establish a workable government did not yield fruitful results. In 2006, militias loyal to Islamic leaders waged a running battle with Somalia's interim government, the Transitional Federal Government (TFG), backed by Ethiopia's military presence. By June, the Islamic Courts Union (ICU), a coalition of *Sharia* courts, was in control of Mogadishu and major parts of Southern Somalia. Although favored by many Somalis as a harbinger of law and order and essential social services, the ICU was routed out of Mogadishu in January 2007 by Somali government forces with the help of Ethiopian troops. However, violence continued as succeeding Islamist groups, including Al-Shabab and Hizbul Islam, continued their guerrilla war against the government. The withdrawal of Ethiopian forces from Somalia in January 2009 provided the insurgents the opportunity to escalate their activities. The fragile government of Somalia, supported by a weakened military and African Union (AU) forces, was unable to prevent the Islamist incursions that led to their establishment of control over large portions of the south. Indeed, in May, the Islamist rebels launched a successful attack on Mogadishu, which put most of the city under their control and severely restricted government jurisdiction to a small portion. Radical Islamic militants have continued to launch devastating attacks on Mogadishu, seeking complete control of the city and the overthrow of the government.

One significant effect of the continued rounds of violence in Somalia is the steady stream of migrants and refugees to neighboring countries, particularly Yemen. Hundreds of fleeing Somalis have died of suffocation and drowning in desperate attempts to cross the Gulf of Aden in overcrowded unseaworthy vessels.

PIRACY IN THE HORN

On April 8, 2009, Somali pirates attacked an American-flagged commercial vessel, MV *Maersk Alabama*, about 350 miles off the coast of

Somalia. Well reported in U.S. media, the attack, particularly the seizure of the vessel's captain as hostage by the pirates, brought to the fore the magnitude of the serious problem of piracy that had plagued the seas off the Horn of Africa for years.[29]

The pirates' attack on the American vessel was a trend in what had become a common occurrence in the strategic waters of the Horn since the collapse of Somalia as a state.[30] In recent years, piracy in the region had escalated, reaching a proportion that called for concerted international response. According to recent reports issued by the International Maritime Bureau (IMB), there were 111 piracy attacks off the coast of Somalia and the Gulf of Aden in 2008, an increase of nearly 200 percent from 2007. By the first half of 2009, 130 incidents had been recorded.[31] Somali piracy has thus become a major threat to international maritime traffic.

Somalia, a lawless, failed state characterized by years of clan conflict, is particularly amenable to piracy activities. Its central government lacks authority over vast sections of the state, and is unable to control its territorial waters. Unable to maintain law and order, and to provide necessary social and welfare services to its people, many Somalis have been driven to piracy as a means of survival in an environment of hardship and prolonged, devastating war. Piracy has gradually become a lucrative business, netting millions of dollars in ransom money paid for the release of kidnapped crews of hijacked vessels. In 2008, Somali pirates and their supporters were said to have collected over $30 million from ransom.[32] Apart from personal gains, ransom money has also been a source of funding for warlords, and thus, the protracted clan warfare.

The Somali piracy operation has targeted international shipping without discrimination. While it has disproportionately affected Western commercial shipping, vessels of other nations have been seized as well. The upsurge of piracy off the Somali coast prompted the UN to pass a series of resolutions in 2008 (Res. 1814, 1816, and 1838) to curtail the epidemic. Resolution 1838, for instance, called on all states interested in the security of maritime activities to take part actively in the fight against the Somali piracy by deploying naval vessels and military aircraft in accordance with international law.[33]

Nations such as Canada, Denmark, France, India, the Netherlands, Russia, Spain, the United Kingdom, and the United States have taken initiatives toward this goal.[34] International anti-piracy efforts have also included initiatives by the North Atlantic Treaty Organization (NATO), European Union (EU), and AU. However, in the face of continuing absence of a viable government in Somalia able to maintain security, it remains to be seen how effective international efforts would be in combating piracy in the region.

CIVIL WARS IN SUDAN

The long, complex, and devastating Sudanese conflict has its beginnings predating independence in 1956.[35] The conflict occurred in two phases, often identified as the First and Second Sudanese Civil Wars. The first phase of the civil war occurred from 1955 to 1972, while the second phase, essentially a continuation of the first, occurred from 1983 to 2005. Fundamental to this rather prolonged civil war is the racial/ethno-religious and cultural division within the Sudanese state. Northern Sudan is predominantly made up of people who identify themselves as Arabs, and who are generally Muslims. The South, on the other hand, consists of ethnic groups of black African origins, and a population largely made up of Christians. This racial and religious divide has pervaded Sudanese society for much of its modern history and has been the source of the nation's persistent conflict.

The post-colonial state of Sudan was dominated by the Muslim Arabs of the North whose control of political power became an instrument for oppressing the Christian, black Africans of the South. In particular, Southerners opposed the Sudanese government's policy of spreading Islamic influence into their region. The initial Southern protest was a nonviolent one, but the government's increased repression in which thousands of Southern Sudanese separatists were arrested and their leaders assassinated or summarily executed turned the resistance movement into a violent one.

The Sudanese conflict escalated in 1963 with the formation of the Anya-Nya Liberation Movement, which proclaimed an autonomous state in the South and embarked on a guerrilla war against the government. The Anya-Nya rebellion lasted until 1972, when a peace agreement, the Addis Ababa Accord, was signed in March by the Sudanese dictator, General Jafar el-Nimeiri, and the Southern rebels. The agreement, among other provisions, granted Southern autonomy within the Sudanese state. The Anya-Nya guerrillas, thereafter, laid down their guns and, thus, ended the first phase of the civil war that had lasted 17 years.

The Addis Ababa peace agreement failed to bring about lasting peace; ultimately, it had merely introduced an 11-year interregnum into the civil war. Southerners accused Nimeiri of violating the terms of the accord, notably his imposition of the Islamic legal system, the *sharia'a*, on the South in his drive to Islamize the entire country.

Southern resistance to Nimeiri began in 1983, and thus, the commencement of the second Sudanese Civil War, or more accurately, the continuation of the first. Much of the renewed fighting occurred in the South where separatist groups, principally the Sudan People's Liberation Movement (SPLM) with its military wing and the Sudan People's Liberation Army (SPLA), which led the Southern war effort. From 1983 to 2005, the SPLA fought the governments of President Nimeiri, Prime Minister Sadiq al-Mahdi, and President Omar al-Bashir in the struggle to establish Southern autonomy. The war particularly devastated the South as basic educational and health care services were disrupted or destroyed. An already weak Southern economy became weaker in the wake of lack of investment and gainful employment. The generality of the populace became more impoverished.

Infighting among the Southern-based dissident rebel groups further complicated the war. However, the early 1990s saw a number of attempts by African states and the international community to mediate the entrenched conflict toward a peaceful resolution. Although sporadic fighting continued in the South, there had been some progress toward peace agreement by 2003. The war ended in January 2005 when the SPLA/SPLM and the government signed the Comprehensive Peace Agreement (CPA) in Nairobi, Kenya, which recognized the autonomy of the South for six years and scheduled a referendum for 2011 to decide the question of independence for the region. In accordance with the CPA, SPLM joined the government as a political party with its leader, John Garang, assuming the vice presidency in a power-sharing arrangement.

The Sudanese conflict had been the longest-fought war in modern Africa, and one of its bloodiest. At the end of the first phase of the conflict, over half a million Sudanese had died. The entire war caused the deaths of about 2 million people, a massive proportion of which was civilian. Millions of people, especially in the South, were uprooted and displaced from their homes, many becoming refugees in surrounding states such as Egypt, Ethiopia, Kenya, Uganda, and others. The economy steadily deteriorated during the war years; agricultural production was curtailed, ensuring widespread famine in the 1980s and 1990s, and consequently, the deaths of hundreds of thousands of people as a result of starvation.

The brutal conflict was not without atrocities committed by either side. The civilian death toll in the South was staggering, and the SPLA accused the government of waging a genocidal war against the Southern people. Indeed, the United States Congress affirmed in December 2004 that since 1989, the Sudanese government had conducted against the civilian populations of Southern Sudan, "a coordinated policy of ethnic cleansing and genocide that has cost the lives of more than 2,000,000 people and displaced more than 4,000,000 people."[36] The government allegedly prevented free access of international humanitarian relief and medical aid agencies to famine- and war-devastated areas in need of the services. This further caused the deaths of many people from starvation.

Accusations also surfaced during the war of the sale by government-sponsored militias of captured Southern Sudanese children and women to wealthy Arabs who used them as domestic servants, farm hands, and sex slaves. There were reports of the purchase of many of these enslaved people by international aid workers in order to free them.

The implementation of the CPA has met some challenges. Soon after taking office as vice president, former SPLM leader John Garang died in an air crash on July 31, 2005. His death, which some believed was suspicious, caused deadly unrest in the Sudanese capital. Garang was a major party in the evolution of the peace plan, and many observers felt that he was critical to its implementation. However, the plan to build a government of national unity in Sudan as stipulated in the agreement, moved forward even as it continued to meet challenges. In October 2007, the SPLM threatened to withdraw its participation in the national government, accusing the government of violating the CPA. Although, the CPA is still on track, the outbreak of another bloody civil war in the western province of Darfur, yet unresolved, has been an unwelcome diversion in its implementation.

The Darfur Crisis

The Second Sudanese Civil War, which had lasted 21 years, was barely concluded when the bloody conflict in Darfur broke out. The Darfur war began in February 2003 when two rebel groups, the Sudan Liberation Movement (SLM) and Justice and Equality Movement (JEM), began an insurgency against the Sudanese government. The rebels had accused the government of oppressing the non-Arab, black African population of the region. Indeed, Darfur had been a neglected province in Sudan, economically and socially marginalized and under-developed, with its people politically oppressed. Further, Darfur had been severely affected by famine. President al-Bashir's brutal response to the rebellion in the region was to earn the Sudanese government the accusation of genocide against the people. The allegation of genocidal intent by the government and atrocities being committed against Darfuris drew unparalleled international attention to the war, more than any conflict in contemporary Africa. It triggered a worldwide movement dedicated to promoting human rights in the region and stopping the violence. Perhaps the most vocal of these movements is Save Darfur Coalition, a human rights organization based in the United States but campaigning globally to raise awareness about the Darfur atrocities with a commitment to ending them. Its goals are:

- Ending the violence against civilians;
- Facilitating adequate and unhindered humanitarian aid;
- Establishing conditions for the safe and voluntary return of displaced people to their homes;
- Promoting the long-term sustainable development of Darfur; and
- Holding the perpetrators accountable.[37]

Allegation of genocide against the Sudanese government of al-Bashir was, in fact, not new. During the second civil war, the SPLM accused the government of waging a war of genocide against the South, an allegation Khartoum denied and dubbed propaganda. However, in Darfur, renewed allegation of genocide was more forceful and came largely from independent quarters such as human rights advocacy groups and non-governmental organizations (NGOs).[38] The most powerful pronouncement of the war in Darfur as genocide was the one made by the United States in September 2004 by Secretary of State Colin Powell. Powell had declared in a testimony before the United States Senate Foreign Relations Committee that "genocide has been committed in Darfur, and that the government of Sudan and the Janjaweed bear responsibility," and that "genocide may still be occurring."[39]

The war in Darfur has deservedly attracted notoriety due to its brutal conduct by the Sudanese military. In its very destructive counterinsurgency offensives, government forces attacked and destroyed Darfur villages, killing hundreds of thousands of civilians of African descent and displacing millions from their homes. Apart from the violence from the war, hundreds more perished from famine-induced starvation and diseases. Further atrocities were committed in Darfur by Arab militias, allegedly with the Sudanese government's complicity. Indeed, the government was widely believed to have provided financial resources to these militias, arming them to fight civilians believed to side with the rebel movements. There have also been reports of joint attacks launched by regular government troops and militias. The Janjaweed, in particular, which has been described as "the infamous horse and camel-mounted militiamen,"[40] was responsible for destructive campaigns against civilians, pillaging villages, indiscriminately killing people, raping women, kidnapping and enslaving children, and stealing or destroying livestock and crops.

Darfur. (Courtesy of Sam Saverance.)

The Sudanese government's deliberate efforts to prevent much needed relief reaching Darfur created further crisis in the region. The refugee population swelled massively, and many fled the region to seek solace in neighboring Chad and the Central African Republic. The spillover of the war into Chad has created tensions between N'Djamena and Khartoum. The Janjaweed militia regularly launched cross-border raids into eastern Chad in which villages and towns were pillaged, homes destroyed, people killed, and cattle stolen. The Sudanese militia's incursion into Chad has further complicated Chad's own civil war which erupted in 2005.

While the war in Darfur attracted wide interest, international engagement there seemed to be inadequate as the carnage persisted. The AU peacekeeping force, the African Union Mission in Sudan (AMIS), introduced to the region in 2004, proved ill-equipped to fulfill its mandate. Although the UN stopped short of labeling the Sudanese government's campaign in Darfur genocide, it vehemently condemned the atrocities and gross human rights violation being committed there. As the conflict escalated and the killing of civilians, sexual violation of women, and torture of people intensified, the UN Security Council established in July 2007 a peacekeeping force to bolster the AU force. This joint hybrid force, known as the African Union-United Nations Mission in Darfur (UNAMID), began operations on December 31, 2007.

Despite international efforts to end the Darfur conflict and a number of peace agreements by the warring parties, such as the Darfur Peace Agreement (DPA) of May 5, 2006, the region is yet to see peace and stability. Violence has continued, resulting in more deaths and displacements. According to UN estimates, by August 2009, about 4.2 million people had been affected by the war, 2.2 million of whom were internally displaced persons (IDPs), and another 236,000 living in refugee camps in eastern Chad.[41]

Meanwhile, accused of war crimes against humanity in Darfur, the Sudanese president, al-Bashir, had charges brought against him by the International Criminal Court (ICC) in The Hague in July 2008. An arrest warrant for the president followed on March 4, 2009, making him the first incumbent head of state to be ordered arrested by the ICC. The Sudanese government denied the charges against al-Bashir, and so far the Sudanese president has not been arrested.

TERRORISM

The devastating al-Qaeda terrorist attacks on the United States on September 11, 2001, which claimed the lives of almost 3,000 people, orchestrated a global war on terrorism. The worldwide search to destroy Islamic terrorist networks inevitably incorporated Africa.

To be sure, Africa had always featured in some ways in Western anti-terrorist campaigns. In the 1980s, Washington believed that the eccentric Libyan leader Muammar Gaddafi was a sponsor of terrorist acts. This was precisely the motivation for the United States' bombing of Tripoli, Libya's capital, in April 1986. President Ronald Reagan's order of preemptive air strikes against military targets in Libya was, according to the White House, to obliterate "terrorist centers" in the country and destroy Gaddafi's ability to sponsor terror acts.[42]

Since the late 1990s, however, terrorism has increasingly been associated with a number of East African countries including Sudan, Somalia, Eritrea, Ethiopia, and Uganda, where the United States has either identified or suspected the existence of al-Qaeda cells. But the first terrorist act of great magnitude in the region was the simultaneous bombing of the American embassies in Dar-es-Salam, Tanzania, and Nairobi, Kenya, in August 1998. Islamic jihadists with links to Osama bin Laden's al-Qaeda organizations were implicated in these attacks that killed over two hundred Africans and a dozen Americans in both countries.

In its war on terrorism, the focus of American interest in Africa has been on Sudan and Somalia. Before the September 11 terrorist attacks, the al-Qaeda chieftain had found refuge in Sudan, from 1991 to 1996, after his expulsion from his native Saudi Arabia. Indeed, in the early 1990s, Sudan was a haven for Islamic extremists and Mujahidin (guerrilla fighters), such that in 1993, the United States placed the declared Islamic state on its list of countries sponsoring terrorism.

Sudan offered Osama bin Laden a working environment to further consolidate his al-Qaeda organization. Sudan's provision of a haven to militant Islamists caused the United States, in August 1998, to launch cruise missiles on a pharmaceutical factory believed to be a chemical weapons plant linked to bin Laden.

Somalia was even more of a security concern to the United States in its post–September 11 anti-terrorism campaign. There was justified fear in Washington that Somalia, lacking a viable central government, would provide sanctuary for terrorists dislodged from Afghanistan after the overthrow of the Taliban. Indeed, there were claims of an al-Qaeda presence in this lawless state.

Since the late 1980s, Somalia had harbored fundamentalist Islamic groups that the United States feared could be exploited by an influx of al-Qaeda terrorists. One such radical Islamic group was al-Itihaad al-Islamiya (Islamic Union), which had an agenda of establishing an Islamic State in Somalia. This organization was believed to have established ties with bin Laden in the 1990s, and been involved in the American embassy bombings in Kenya and Tanzania, and in other terrorist attacks in Ethiopia in 1996 and 1997. Although operating predominantly in Somalia, its cells also existed in Ethiopia and Kenya. Hounded by Ethiopia's military in the late 1990s, intelligence reports indicate that the organization has lost its power and influence and is now operating as a small group.

Hizbul al-Shabaab is another Islamic fundamentalist group currently active in Somalia and believed by the United States to have links to al-Qaeda. The organization has waged consistent guerrilla war against the Somali government, which it wished to overthrow, and its backers, Ethiopian and AU forces.

In its war on terrorism, the United States in early 2003 established a military base in neighboring Djibouti from where counterterrorist operations in the Horn could be coordinated. From this African "front on the war on terror," the United States conducted air strikes against militant Islamists with supposed links to al-Qaeda.[43] Another prong in the American counterterrorist policy in Africa has been the provision of financial support, training, and equipment to the militaries of African states willing to be allies of the United States in the global war on terrorism.[44]

UGANDA

Political repression, ethnic violence, and civil war characterized much of Uganda's post-independence history. President Milton Obote, who ruled Uganda from 1962 to 1971, established a one-party dictatorship characterized by corruption and brutal repression of opposition. Obote was deposed in 1971 by the army chief, General Idi Amin, who, upon taking power, took Uganda to a new level of macabre political repression. Until he was overthrown in 1979, Amin's bloody reign of terror resulted in the deaths of an estimated 300,000 Ugandans, victims of the regime's extrajudicial killings. Many more Ugandans were forced into exile to escape his murderous rule. Amin came to epitomize the worst in the endemic leadership misrule in Africa. In 1979, the brutal dictator ordered his army to invade neighboring Tanzania, which triggered a war between the two states. Tanzania was not only victorious against Amin's 45,000-strong invasion force, the Tanzanians, allied with Ugandan opposition elements in exile, succeeded in driving the dictator out of power. Amin fled into exile in Saudi Arabia, leaving behind a devastated, bankrupt state. The Amin period had claimed the lives of many people, some of whom were eliminated by direct orders of the dictator.

The post-Amin Uganda was not any better for the East African country. Milton Obote returned to power in a flawed election in 1980, purportedly won by his Uganda People's Congress (UPC). His second administration was equally despotic, characterized by political witch hunt murder of opponents, and persecution of ethnic groups which did not favor his rule. Opposition to his regime soon crystallized in antigovernment guerrilla war by militant groups among which was the National Resistance Movement (NRM) under the leadership of Yoweri Museveni. For the second time, Obote was deposed from power in 1985. Meanwhile, an estimated 100,000 people had died during the guerrilla war against Obote's Uganda National Liberation Army (UNLA). In 1986, Museveni's MRN took control of power.[45]

War in Northern Uganda

Following decades of brutal dictatorship, economic mismanagement, and interethnic conflict, the administration of President Museveni that took over the reins of power in 1986 faced enormous challenges of nation building, particularly ethnic reconciliation. Most observers of contemporary Uganda would agree that the nation has made tremendous progress in nation building under Museveni. This progress, however, has been hampered by residual ethnic animosity that has manifested in a vicious war in the northern part of the country.

The war that began in 1987 was orchestrated by an armed group that christened itself the Lord's Resistance Army (LRA) led by a self-professed spirit medium, Joseph Kony, arguably the most brutal of the warlords produced by African conflicts. His violent movement, once described as "Africa's longest-lived insurgent group,"[46] and consisting mainly of abducted child soldiers, emerged from remnants of a number of rebel groups among the Acholi of northern Uganda that had failed in their resistance to the Museveni government when it took over power. The most popular of these groups was another professed spiritualist movement known as the Holy Spirit Movement (HSM), also led by a spirit medium, Alice Lakwena.[47] Like the earlier groups, the LRA was opposed to the Museveni's southern-based NRM government, which had deposed the Acholi and broken its dominance of political power in Uganda.

However, LRA's declared aim was the spiritual cleansing of the state in which the Biblical Ten Commandments would be the premise of governance in Uganda. But the guerrilla war against the government could rationally be explained as motivated by Northern loss of political power and the deep-rooted ethnic divide in Ugandan politics. Although opposition to the Museveni regime was rife in the North, the LRA failed to attract mass support of the Acholi, whom it later turned against and terrorized. Given its unpopularity, the rebel movement resorted to impressments in order to swell its ranks, and looting to obtain supplies. The LRA became noted for the abduction of thousands of children from their homes and their removal to military bases. Boys were used as combatants, while girls were turned into sex slaves. The rebels also adopted the practice of mutilating their victims and committing other acts of gross violation of human rights.

The LRA received a boost in 1994 when the government of Sudan began to support it with supplies and arm its fighters. Khartoum also provided the movement with territories whereby the insurgents shifted their base to Southern Sudan. The Sudanese government's support for LRA was retaliation against Museveni's backing of the SPLM in the civil war in Sudan. Before the war ended in 2005, the Sudanese government had used the LRA to fight the SPLM.

For the most part, despite its brutality, the LRA war has attracted little international attention. It has not only destabilized northern Uganda for long, it has also stunted its development. The spillover of the war into southern Sudan has also had a devastating effect on that war-torn region. In line with its operational tactics, the rebels have raided villages, looted properties, abducted children, and generally terrorized people. The rebel activities in Sudan have caused thousands of civilian casualties and millions of displaced people.

In 2006, peace negotiations, the Juba talks, between the Ugandan government and the rebels had begun designed to bring an end to the war. The result was a permanent cease-fire agreement signed in February 2008. A final peace agreement expected to follow, to be signed by the two parties in March 2008. However, this never happened, as the LRA leader, Joseph Kony, refused to sign the peace agreement unless the ICC arrest warrant on him was rescinded. Thus, the prospect of a final end to the two-decade-old war frizzled. Kony has so far eluded capture, despite the United States' assistance to the Ugandan government to apprehend or kill him. For instance, on December 14, 2008, the United States military backed and financed Operation Lightning Thunder, an unsuccessful Ugandan military bombardment of a LRC camp in Uganda in the hope of killing Kony.[48]

The LRA has renewed its attacks in southern Sudan, causing thousands of Sudanese to flee their homes. LRA disturbances have also created tensions in the northeastern part of the Democratic Republic of Congo (DRC) and eastern part of the Central African Republic (CAR). In the DRC, thousands of people have been forced to flee their homes.[49]

CONFLICTS IN THE GREAT LAKES: RWANDA, BURUNDI, AND DEMOCRATIC REPUBLIC OF CONGO

The Great Lakes region of Africa has, since the 1990s, been arguably the most violent hot spot in Africa. A myriad of crises define the region—political violence, civil wars and insurgencies, cross-border conflicts, genocide, and complex multistate conflicts. This section of the chapter takes a look at the more destructive of the region's conflicts, the Rwandan genocide, the Burundian Civil War, and the vicious crisis in eastern DRC.

Genocide in Rwanda

The Great Lakes region saw its most gruesome conflict in the Rwandan genocide of 1994. The genocide began when Rwanda's president, Juvenal Habyariamana, a Hutu, and his Burundian counterpart, Cyprien Ntarya-mira, died in a plane crash at Kigali Airport on April 6, 1994. Following this accident, extremist Hutus and the Hutu militia, the Interahawe, began a month-long slaughter of Tutsis and moderate Hutus. By the time the carnage ended, at least 800,000 Rwandans had been hacked to death, many with machetes.[50]

International response to the carnage has been a major issue in the Rwandan genocide. The crisis suffered from needed timely international intervention that could, perhaps, have minimized or even averted it. This is true since the international community was aware of the volatile nature of the ethno-political dispensation in Rwanda that had always threatened to explode into a major conflagration. Indeed, long before the genocide, Rwanda had been under considerable international observation on account of the constant bloody feuds between the Hutus and the Tutsi. In 1990, Tutsi exiles in Uganda had formed the Rwandan Patriotic Front (RPF) to oppose the Kigali government, commencing a two-year guerrilla war against it. However, in July 1992, peace initiatives by the OAU produced a cease-fire accord, the Arusha Peace Agreement, between the Hutu-led Rwandan government and the RPF. To monitor the cease-fire, the OAU established in July an observer mission, the Neutral Military Observer Group (NMOG), made up of contingents from African states. The mission was later expanded to become NMOG II. The UN took over the task of peace monitoring when in June 1993, the Security Council established the United Nations Observer Mission Uganda-Rwanda (UNOMUR).[51] This observer mission was later replaced by the United Nations Assistance Mission for Rwanda (UNAMIR) in October 1993.[52] Thus, prior to the genocide, it was very well known that Rwanda was a keg of gunpowder waiting to explode. Indeed, months before the killings started, the United States may have received intelligence reports that Rwanda was headed for ethnic cleansing of a monumental proportion. A Department of Defense statement in early April 1994 predicted that "unless both sides can be convinced to return to the peace process . . . a massive (hundreds of thousands of deaths) bloodbath will ensue that would likely spill over into Burundi."[53]

Despite the warning signs of an impending catastrophe in Rwanda, the UN was unable to put in place a peacekeeping force adequate to prevent or contain it. When the genocide began, the ill-equipped UNAMIR, with no clear mandate, was helpless in maintaining order and security. In the presence of the mission, the massacre proceeded without any effective challenge to it. In 1999, UN Secretary-General Kofi Annan acknowledged that UNAMIR "was neither mandated nor equipped for the kind of forceful action which would have been needed to prevent or halt the genocide."[54]

Western inclination to minimize commitment to Africa contributed to the inability of UNAMIR to contain the genocide. As a result of pressure from the power brokers in the Security Council, the UN vacillated in the face of genocide when immediate action was required. UNAMIR was left to disintegrate when it should have been strengthened to deal with the situation. Belgium withdrew its contingent from the mission when a number of its soldiers were killed in the massacre, and Bangladesh soon followed suit. While the massacre lasted, instead of beefing up the mission by adequately reinforcing it and expanding its mandate to allow it to effect a cease-fire, the UN chose to drastically reduce it. On April 21, 1994, a Security Council vote significantly reduced UNAMIR's strength.[55]

Pressure from the United States was partly responsible for the UN's momentous April decision to cut down the UNAMIR force. In the Security Council, the United States opposed moves to strengthen the mission, even arguing for its complete withdrawal.[56] In May, in the face of deteriorating security and humanitarian conditions in Kigali, the Rwandan capital, a fresh proposal to expand UNAMIR to 5,500 troops was debated in the Security Council.[57] Even this move to strengthen the force was opposed by the United States.

In his meticulous examination of the United States' intelligence resources relating to the Rwandan crisis, William Ferroggiaro concluded that American officials "knew so much, but still decided against taking action or leading other nations to prevent or stop the genocide."[58] The reason for Washington's position was the fear that if the UN intervened in Rwanda militarily, American troops would be called upon to bear the brunt of peacekeeping operations there.[59] The top echelon of the Clinton administration, including the president himself, did not favor any commitment of American troops to peacekeeping abroad, especially in Africa. The Pentagon also shared this view of a limited American role in peacekeeping.[60] The Republican-controlled Congress had also always made clear its opposition to United States military peacekeeping operations in conflict situations outside the realm of American national security. The United States' policy in Rwanda was, in the final analysis, never a large one. Washington's direct intervention did not take place until well after the massacres had ended, when President Clinton sent a humanitarian mission to the country to assist in the refugee crisis. During his 1998 African trip,

Clinton publicly acknowledged America's unwillingness to play a major role in the crisis.[61]

Although genocide in Rwanda was not prevented or nipped in the bud in a timely fashion, in the aftermath of the crisis, the international community made an important statement—that perpetrators of genocide would be prosecuted. In November 1994, the UN recognized that "serious violations of humanitarian law were committed in Rwanda." By a Security Council resolution, the organization created the International Criminal Tribunal for Rwanda (ICTR) based in Arusha, Tanzania. Its mandate was to prosecute "persons responsible for genocide and other serious violations of international humanitarian law committed" in Rwanda during the crisis, and, also, possibly the "prosecution of Rwandan citizens responsible for genocide and other such violations of international law committed in the territory of neighboring States."[62] The tribunal, however, has been greatly criticized for inaction. Indeed, it was not until 1997 that it began its first trial.

Meanwhile, given the overwhelmed national justice system and the delay in ICTR trials in the face of pressure to bring to justice thousands of genocide perpetrators who had clogged the jails, the Rwandan government was compelled to search for an alternative justice system. In 2002, a conflict resolution apparatus called *gacaca* was established, fashioned after traditional communal practice. The modernized *gacaca* was designed to speed the pace of genocide trials, bring about restorative justice, ascertain the truth about the genocide, and facilitate healing and reconciliation among Rwandans. An important feature of *gacaca*, therefore, was community involvement in the process of conflict resolution.[63]

Civil War in Burundi

As in Rwanda, colonial history of divide-and-rule and ethnic polarization in Burundi left a legacy of post-independence tension between the two dominant groups, the Hutu and the Tutsi. Since independence from Belgium in 1962, Burundi had been locked in a vicious cycle of ethno-political strife that had nearly destroyed the fragile state.

It is generally believed that genocide occurred first in Burundi, although the violent conflicts in the country did not attract international awareness. In 1972, feeling marginalized in Burundian politics and particularly deprived of fair representation in the national army, the Hutu started an uprising that caused the deaths of two thousand Tutsi. The government, under Tutsi control, met this rebellion with massive retaliation. It unleashed the Tutsi-dominated army on the Hutu in a massacre that brought about the deaths of between 100,000 and 150,000 Hutu. The Tutsi killed any Hutu they could lay their hands on, but Hutu elites were particularly marked for extermination. The massacre cemented the animosity that had plagued interethnic relations in Burundi. In a report on this catastrophic tragedy, titled "The Burundi Affair," the International Commission of Jurists and the International League for the Rights of Man, accused the government of acts of genocide against the Hutu.[64]

Burundi continued to experience ethnic tensions that culminated in intermittent violent conflicts. In 1988, for example, mutual killings claimed the lives of about 25,000 Hutu and Tutsi. In 1993, a civil war broke out following the Tutsi-engineered assassination of Melchoir Ndadaye, Burundi's first Hutu president. The Hutu responded to the president's death by killing thousands of Tutsi civilians. The circle of violence continued with a Tutsi orchestrated massacre of 30,000 Hutu. Hundreds more fled to neighboring states as refugees. At the end of the day, the interethnic killings had claimed the lives of about 50,000 Burundians.

The killing of President Ntaryamira on April 6, 1994, in the plane crash that also killed the Rwandan president, threatened the precarious security situation in Burundi. Indeed, as acknowledged by Washington, there was genuine fear of a replica of the Rwandan genocide in Burundi.[65] UN Secretary-General Boutros Boutros-Ghali also warned the Security Council in December 1995 that "there is a real danger of the situation in Burundi degenerating to the point where it might explode into ethnic violence on a massive scale."[66] Conscious of the failure of the international community in Rwanda a year earlier, Boutros-Ghali was anxious for an early UN intervention in Burundi to prevent "a repetition of the tragic events in Rwanda."[67] The Secretary-General, therefore, proposed a Security Council–mandated multinational humanitarian mission composed of forces from willing nations to intervene in Burundi.[68] Although the United States offered to support the proposed mission with military supplies, it would not commit itself to contributing troops. In the end, although Ntaryamira's death aggravated the prevailing violence, no large-scale killings in the proportion of a massacre occurred.

However, the civil war escalated in 1999 as the Tutsi-controlled government responded with repression to increased Hutu guerrilla attacks. Thousands of Hutus were herded into camps where many lived in abject conditions and were ravaged by diseases. Meanwhile, the influx into Burundi of as many as 200,000 Hutu refugees from Rwanda who had fled the genocide there exacerbated the Burundian conflict. Attempts at resolving the conflict through cease-fire talks including the one held in 2000 in Tanzania, under the auspices of the former South African president, Nelson Mandela, failed to bring about peace.

However, Burundi managed to make developments in the peace process. In mid-2005, democratic elections were held, which brought the 12-year interethnic war to an end. In its post-independence history, Burundi had endured years of ethnic strife that not only produced enormous loss of lives, but also massive destruction to the country's infrastructure.[69]

Civil Wars and Violence in the Democratic Republic of Congo

The Democratic Republic of Congo (DRC), originally known as the Congo, had always been a troubled state. Following its independence in 1960, a major political crisis broke out in the country, which, exacerbated by foreign powers' intervention, nearly destroyed the new state. Over the next three decades, Zaire, as the country was subsequently called, suffered political and economic strangulation under the dictatorship of President Mobutu Sésé Seko. With the backing of some Western powers, principally the United States, Mobutu presided over one of the most repressive and corrupt regimes in Africa. However, by the late 1990s, Mobutu was struggling to hold on to power amidst escalating opposition to his ruthless regime. He had reduced Zaire, a potentially rich state with enormous resources, to an economically prostrated one characterized by widespread inflation, rampant unemployment, and poverty. Politically, Zaire was drifting toward collapse as Mobutu, faced initially with popular unrest, subsequently had to contend with a guerrilla war.

Meanwhile, Zaire suffered form the fallout of the Rwandan genocide. The genocide created an intense refugee crisis in the eastern part of Zaire as a result of the million Hutu refugees that fled Rwanda, fearing reprisal by the new Tutsi government in Kigali. The Hutu militias operating in Zaire's eastern border soon became Mobutu's willing instrument used to fight the Congolese rebels combating his government.

A full-scale civil war had begun in November 1996 when Laurent-Désiré Kabila, long-time adversary of Mobutu, led his Alliance of Democratic Forces for the Liberation of Congo-Zaire (ADFLC) in a guerrilla insurgency aimed at overthrowing the president. Kabila's war effort was principally aided by Rwandan and Ugandan forces. Kabila's Rwandan Tutsi-dominated army rapidly ploughed its way toward Kinshasa, Zaire's capital, murdering in the process thousands of Rwandan Hutu exiles in the Congo. By May 1997, Kabila's rebel army had fought its way into the capital. Mobutu's ruthless regime thereafter fell and the dictator fled into exile in Morocco. Following Mobutu's demise, Kabila proclaimed himself president and renamed the country the Democratic Republic of Congo, the original name of the country.

The civil war did not end with Kabila's takeover of power. Foreign interests continued to play a destabilizing role in the DRC, which not only further complicated the war, but also regionalized it. From the late 1990s, not less than half-a-dozen neighboring states were involved in the war. Rwanda, which had helped Kabila to overthrow Mobutu, wished to maintain a continued presence in the country. However, not long into his presidency, Kabila faced enormous pressure from the Congolese people who wanted their country rid of foreign troops. When Kabila ordered Rwandan troops out of the country, tensions developed between him and his former allies. Accusing the Congolese leader of permitting cross-border raids by Hutu militias from the DRC into Rwanda, the Rwandan government withdrew its support from him. Consequently, backed by Uganda, Rwanda switched allegiance to the rebel forces of the Rally for Congolese Democracy (RCD) opposed to the Congolese president. With Uganda and Rwanda now against Kabila, the president turned to and found new allies in Angola, Namibia, Zimbabwe, and Chad. The injection of more foreign forces into the DRC not only intensified the civil war but also regionalized it. The conflict had become "Africa's first world war."

The civil war also hosted a myriad of armed groups ranging from local criminal gangs to foreign militias. Kabila himself was aligned to one of the foreign armed groups, the Democratic Forces for the Liberation of Rwanda (FDLR), a DRC-based rebel organization that had been responsible for the 1994 Rwandan genocide. Another rebel movement that played a role in the war was UNITA, which had been fighting the Angolan government. The assassination of Kabila in January 2001 was an indication of the volatility of the political situation in the DRC.

A rather complex set of factors accounted for the involvement of the parties in the DRC conflict. The paramount motivation was the country's enormous mineral wealth. The war was essentially a bloody struggle for the control of DRC's diamonds, gold, and other precious resources by local armed groups and neighboring states' forces. Diamond mines were attacked at will and plundered for gains. In the final analysis, it was DRC resources that funded the war and turned it into a never-ending one.

Extreme violence and brutality characterized the war in the DRC, which prompted the International Rescue Committee (IRC), a humanitarian aid organization active in the country, to tag it as "the world's deadliest documented conflict since WW II."[70] The armed groups in the conflict committed unspeakable atrocities against the civilian population of eastern Congo, the main theatre of the war. Constant attacks on villages often left in their wake death and destruction. According to a 2007 survey conducted by the IRC, an estimated 5.4 million people had died in the conflict and its attendant humanitarian crisis since 1998.[71]

In particular, an act of terrorism prevalent in eastern Congo, and which reached epidemic proportions, was sexual violence against women. Rape of girls and women by marauding armed militias was so rampant that the DRC was frequently described as "the rape capital of the world." The plight of the women in this part of the Congo was, indeed, a pitiful one as mass rape escalated in the mid-2000s and became an instrument of war. Sexual violence as part of the daily lives of the women came with serious health implications. Women who suffered from beatings and brutal acts of abuse such as rape did not often have access to medical assistance and psychological support because of the collapsed health-care infrastructure of the country. Rape victims seldom found justice in the corrupt Congolese judicial system; and culturally, they were often ostracized in the society as rape was considered a social stigma. By 2009, thousands of women had been sexually assaulted with impunity in the eastern provinces.

The presence of UN peacekeeping forces in the DRC has had little effect on the conflict. Also, peace accords as attained in 1999 and 2002, for example, have not brought about an end to the bloody conflict. Tens of thousands of lives continue to be lost, not only to militias' deadly attacks on civilians, but also to hunger and malnutrition and a variety of preventable diseases made fatal by the war situation. Internal displacement of populations has also constituted a huge crisis as millions of people uprooted from their homes are forced to flee to the bush or deplorable refugee camps. The conflict has continued to be driven by armed groups' desire to control the resources of the DRC.

An otherwise potentially rich nation given its huge resources, the DRC has become one of the poorest nations of the world after years of internal political chaos, economic strangulation, foreign exploitation, and devastating conflicts. This retrogressive post-independence history has been aptly articulated by political scientist, Peter Schwab:

The Congo has been in a state of acute crisis for almost the entire period of its existence as an independent state. In more than 40 years of war, civil war, and rebellion, refugees have become life's norm, as death, murder, disease, hunger, and famine prowl the countryside. With the confluence of multifarious African states into the never-ending conflict, indigenous rebellion has been transformed into an African world war.[72]

Notes

1. Roger M. Williams, "Slaughter in Burundi," *World*, Nov. 21, 1972, 20.

2. "Somalia's Dangerous Waters," *BBC News Africa*, September 26, 2005, retrieved on September 15, 2009, from: http://news.bbc.co.uk/2/hi/africa/4283396.stm.

3. IGAD "Secretariat on Peace in the Sudan." Retrieved on September 23, 2009, from: http://www.reliefweb.int/rw/RWFiles2005.nsf/FilesByRWDoc UNIDFileName/EVIU-6AZBDB-sud-sud-09janPart%20II.pdf/$File/sud-sud-09 janPart%20II.pdf.

4. Cited in "Uganda conflict 'worse than Iraq,'" BBC News, November 10, 2003, retrieved on August 11, 2009, from: http://news.bbc.co.uk/2/hi/africa/3256929.stm.

5. Nicholas D. Kristof, "The Weapon of Rape," *New York Times*, June 15, 2008, retrieved on October 26, 2009, from: http://www.nytimes.com/2008/06/15/opinion/15kristof.html?_r=3&adxnnl=1&oref=slogin&adxnnlx=1256659459-F6FBVjfoY7HrFneFCsUyUA.

6. For ancient history of Ethiopia, see, for example, Paul B. Henze, *Layers of Time: A History of Ethiopia* (New York: Palgrave, 2000); and Richard Pankhurst, *The Ethiopian Borderlands: Essays in Regional History from Ancient Times to the End of the 18th century* (Lawrenceville, NJ: Red Sea Press, 1997). On Aksum, see Stuart Munro-Hay, *Aksum: An African Civilization* (Edinburgh: Edinburgh University Press, 1991).

7. History of modern Ethiopia is discussed in numerous works. See the following for instance: Bahru Zewde, *A History of Modern Ethiopia, 1855–1991* (Oxford, UK: James Currey, 2001); Teshale Tibebu, *The Making of Modern Ethiopia, 1896–1974* (Lawrenceville, NJ: Red Sea Press, 1995); and Sven Rubenson, *The Survival of Ethiopian Independence* (London: Heinemann, 1976).

8. For a study of Italian colonial history, see Patrizia Palumbo (ed.), *A Place in the Sun: Africa in Italian Colonial Culture from Post-Unification to the Present* (Berkeley: University of California Press, 2003), and Ruth Ben-Ghiat and Mia Fuller (eds.), *Italian Colonialism* (New York: Palgrave Macmillan, 2005).

9. Perspectives on Haile Selassie are provided in many works including Hans Wilhelm Lockot, *The Mission: The Life, Reign, and Character of Haile Selassie I* (New York: St. Martin's Press, 1989); Peter Schwab, *Haile Selassie I: Ethiopia's Lion of Judah* (Chicago: Nelson-Hall, 1979); and Harold Marcus, *Haile Selassie I: The Formative Years, 1892–1936* (Berkeley: University of California Press, 1987).

10. For more discourse on the Ethiopian revolution, see Donald Lewis Donham, *Marxist Modern: An Ethnographic History of the Ethiopian Revolution* (Berkeley: University of California Press, 1999); Teferra Haile-Selassie, *The Ethiopian Revolution, 1974–91: From a Monarchical Autocracy to a Military Oligarchy* (New York: Kegan Paul International, 1997); Andargachew Tiruneh, *The Ethiopian Revolution, 1974–1987: A Transformation from an Aristocratic to a Totalitarian Autocracy* (Cambridge, UK: Cambridge University Press, 1993); Christopher Clapham, *Transformation and Continuity in*

Revolutionary Ethiopia (Cambridge, UK: Cambridge University Press, 1988); John W. Harbeson, *The Ethiopian Transformation: The Quest for the Post-Imperial State* (Boulder, CO: Westview Press, 1988); Edmond Keller, *Revolutionary Ethiopia: From Empire to People's Republic* (Bloomington: Indiana University Press, 1988); Paul H. Brietzke, *Law, Development, and the Ethiopian Revolution* (London: Associated University Presses, 1982); Fred and Molyneux Halliday, *The Ethiopian Revolution* (London: New Left Books, 1981); and Marina and David Ottaway, *Ethiopia: Empire in Revolution* (New York: Africana Publishing Co., 1978).

11. For more on colonial Eritrea, see Tekeste Negash, *Italian Colonialism in Eritrea, 1882–1941: Policies, Praxis, and Impact* (Stockholm: Uppsala University, 1987).

12. For more on this movement, see David Pool, *From Guerrillas to Government: The Eritrean People's Liberation Front* (Oxford, UK: James Currey, 2001).

13. A good study of the war of independence is provided in Ruth Iyob, *The Eritrean Struggle for Independence: Domination, Resistance, Nationalism, 1941–1993* (Cambridge: Cambridge University Press, 1995).

14. See J. Abbink, "Briefing: The Eritrean-Ethiopian Border Dispute, *African Affairs*, Vol. 97, No. 389 (October 1998: 552).

15. See Xan Rice, "After 70,000 Deaths, Eritrea and Ethiopia Prepare for War Again," *The Times*, December 8, 2005, retrieved on September 4, 2009, from: http://www.timesonline.co.uk/tol/news/world/article754553.ece.

16. See Irwin Arieff, "Ethiopia-Eritrea impasse could lead to new war–UN," Reuters, January 24, 2007, retrieved on September 4, 2009, from: http://www.reuters.com/article/latestCrisis/idUSN24485835.

17. Somali irredentism is discussed in S. S. Samatar, "The Somali Dilemma: Nation in Search of a State," in A. I. Asiwaju (ed.), *Partitioned Africans* (Lagos, Nigeria: University of Lagos Press, 1984); S. Touval, *Somali Nationalism* (Cambridge, MA: Harvard University Press, 1963).

18. Discourses on the civil war are provided in Maria Bongartz, *The Civil War in Somalia: Its Genesis and Dynamics* (Uppsala, Sweden: Nordiska Afrikainstitutet, 1991).

19. On this subject, see the following, for instance, Abdullah A. Mohamoud, *State Collapse and Post-Colonial Development in* Africa (West Lafayette, IN: Purdue University Press, 2006); Maria H. Brons, *Society, Security, Sovereignty and the State in Somalia: From Statelessness to Statelessness?* (Utrecht, the Netherlands: International Books, 2001); Abdisalam M. Issa-Salwe, *The Collapse of the Somali State: The Impact of the Colonial Legacy* (London: Haan Associates, 1994).

20. For more on the nature of American intervention, see John L. Hirsch and Robert B. Oakley, *Somalia and Operation Restore Hope: Reflections on Peacekeeping and Peacemaking* (Washington, DC: United States Institute of Peace Press, 1995); John R. Bolton, "Wrong Turn in Somalia," *Foreign Affairs*, Vol. 73, No. 1 (January/February 1994: 56–66); and Walter Clarke and Jeffrey Herbst, "Somalia and the Future of Humanitarian Intervention," *Foreign Affairs*, Vol. 75, No. 2 (March/April 1996: 70–85).

21. The text of Bush's speech can be found in the *Washington Post*, December 5, 1992, A16.

22. Ibid.

23. For instance, the U.S. ambassador to Kenya, Smith Hempstone, cautioned the administration about involvement in the crisis. See "Think three times before you embrace the Somali Tarbaby," *U.S. News and World Report*, December 14, 1992, 30.

24. See, for such contention, Ted Galen Carpenter, "Setting a Dangerous Precedent in Somalia," *Cato Institute Foreign Policy Briefing*, No. 2, December 18, 1992, 7.

25. Apart from the 18 killed in this circumstance, the Department of Defense reported a total of 44 American casualties, and 175 injured or wounded. See Werner Biermann, (ed.), *Africa Crisis Response Initiative: The New U.S. Africa Policy*, (Piscataway, NJ: Transaction Publishers, 1999), 40.

26. Herbert M. Howe, *Ambiguous Order: Military Forces in African States* (Boulder, CO: Lynne Rienner, 2001), 247.

27. "Clinton Administration Policy on Reforming Multilateral Peace Operations (PDD 25)," Bureau of International Organizational Affairs, U.S. Department of State, February 22, 1996, retrieved on September 10, 2009, from: http://ftp.fas.org/irp/offdocs/pdd25.htm.

28. Ibid.

29. Some details of the attack are provided in "U.S. Warship near Boat Carrying Pirates," CNN.com/world, April 9, 2009, retrieved on September 15, 2009, from: http://www.cnn.com/2009/WORLD/africa/04/08/ship.hijacked/index.html?iref=newssearch.

30. A concise discourse on piracy in the Gulf of Aden and the Indian Ocean is provided in Lauren Ploch, et al., "Piracy off the Horn of Africa," *Congressional Research Service (CRS) Report for Congress*, April 24, 2009, 1–31, retrieved on September 15, 2009, from: http://www.fas.org/sgp/crs/row/R40528.pdf.

31. See the following: "IMB Reports Unprecedented Rise in Maritime Hijackings," January 16, 2009 (http://www.icc-cs.org/index.php?option=com_content&view=article&id=332:imb-reports-unprecedented-rise-in-maritime-hijackings&catid=60:news&Itemid=51); and "IMB Report: Maritime Piracy Doubled in First Half of 2009!" July 16, 2009 (http://www.maritimeterrorism.com/2009/07/16/imb-report-maritime-piracy-doubled-in-first-half-of-2009/). Both sources were retrieved on September 15, 2009.

32. Estimate provided by Ploch, "Piracy off the Horn of Africa," summary page.

33. Full text of the resolution is provided in: http://www.un.org/News/Press/docs/2008/sc9467.doc.htm, retrieved on September 17, 2009.

34. See Res. 1846, December 2008 at: http://www.un.org/News/Press/docs/2008/sc9514.doc.htm, retrieved on September 17, 2009.

35. For further discussion of this subject, see Douglas H. Johnson, *The Root Causes of Sudan's Civil Wars* (Oxford, UK: James Currey, 2003).

36. Cited in "Comprehensive Peace in Sudan Act of 2004," Public Law 108–497, 108th Congress, December 23, 2004, retrieved on September 23, 2009, from: http://www.gpo.gov/fdsys/pkg/STATUTE-118/pdf/STATUTE-118-Pg4012.pdf.

37. Save Darfur Coalition, "Unity Statement," retrieved on September 23, 2009, from: http://www.savedarfur.org/pages/unity_statement.

38. See ibid., for example.

39. See Glenn Kessler and Colum Lynch, "U.S. Calls Killings in Sudan Genocide," *Washington Post*, September 10, 2004, A01.

40. Manish Chand, "No Signs of Peace in Darfur, But Hope Lives," *Africa Quarterly*, August–October 2007, 59.

41. "The United Nations and Darfur," UN Dept. of Public Information, August 2009, 4. The Darfur conflict has attracted a lot of study. Some of the important works include Julie Flint & Alexander De Waal, *Darfur: A New History of a Long War* (London: Zed Books, 2008); Alex de Waal (ed.), *War in Darfur and the Search for Peace* (Cambridge, MA: Harvard University Press, 2007); Leora Kahn (ed.), *Darfur: Twenty Years of War and Genocide in Sudan* (Brooklyn, NY: PowerHouse Books, 2007); Don Cheadle and John Prendergast, *Not on Our Watch: The Mission to End Genocide in Darfur and Beyond* (New York: Hyperion, 2007); J. Millard Burr & Robert O. Collins, *Darfur: The Long Road to Disaster* (Princeton, NJ: Markus Wiener, 2006); and Joyce Apsel (ed.), *Darfur: Genocide Before Our Eyes* (New York: Institute for the Study of Genocide, 2005).

42. See Bernard Weinraub, "U.S. Jets Hit 'Terrorist Centers' in Libya; Reagan Warns of New Attacks if Needed," *New York Times*, April 15, 1986, 1.

43. Frank Gardner, "With Little Fanfare, America Opens a New Front on the War on Terror, *Independent* (London), February 20, 2003, 2.

44. Useful bibliography of terrorism in Africa is provided in Thomas P. Ofcansky, "Preliminary Terrorism Reading List for Sub-Saharan Africa," *African Research and Documentation*, Vol. 103 (2007: 9–31).

45. For a recent study of Museveni's regime, see Aili Mari Tripp, *Museveni's Uganda: Paradoxes of Power in a Hybrid Regime* (Boulder, CO: Lynne Rienner, 2010).

46. Scott Johnson, "Hard Target: The Hunt for Africa's Last Warlord," *Newsweek*, May 25, 2009, 61.

47. For studies on this movement, see Heike Behrend, *Alice Lakwena and Holy Spirits: War in Northern Uganda, 1985–97* (Columbus: Ohio University Press, 1999).

48. For a report of this operation, see "U.S. Aided a Failed Plan to Rout Ugandan Rebels," *New York Times*, February 7, 2009, A1.

49. For more analysis of the LRA war, see Tim Allen and Koen Vlassenroot (eds.), *The Lord's Resistance Army: War, Peace and Reconciliation in Northern Uganda* (London: London School of Economics and Political Science, 2008).

50. For more on the Rwandan genocide, see the following: Gerard Prunier, *The Rwanda Crisis: History of a Genocide* (New York: Columbia University

Press, 1995); Howard Adelman and Astri Suhrke (eds.), *The Path of a Genocide: The Rwanda Crisis from Uganda to Zaire* (New Brunswick, NJ: Transaction Publishers, 1999); and "Report of the Independent Inquiry into the Actions of the United Nations during the 1994 Genocide in Rwanda," December 15, 1999, http://www.ess.uwe.ac.uk/documents/RwandaReport1.htm.

51. UN Security Council Resolution 846 (1993), http://daccessdds.un.org/doc/UNDOC/GEN/N93/366/31/IMG/N9336631.pdf?OpenElement.

52. UN Security Council Resolution 872 (1993).

53. "Rwanda: Department of Defense Policy Options," Memo. for Ass. Sec. of Defense for International Security Affairs, April 11, 1994.

54. See Secretary-General, "Statement on Receiving the Report of the Independent Inquiry into the Actions of the United Nations during the 1994 Genocide in Rwanda," December 16, 1999, http://www.un.org/News/ossg/sgsm_rwanda.htm.

55. UN Security Council Resolution 912 (1994).

56. See "Talking Points for UNAMIR Withdrawal," Cable #94, State to USUN, April 15, 1994, http://www.gwu.edu/~nsarchiv/NSAEBB/NSAEBB53/rw041594.pdf.

57. Cable #127262, "Rwanda: Security Council Discussions," State to USUN, May 13, 1994, http://www.gwu.edu/~nsarchiv/NSAEBB/NSAEBB53/index.htm.

58. William Ferroggiaro, "The U.S. and the Genocide in Rwanda 1994: Information, Intelligence and the U.S. Response," March 24, 2004, http://www.gwu.edu/%7Ensarchiv/NSAEBB/NSAEBB117/index.htm.

59. See, for instance, Cable #127262, "Rwanda: Security Council Discussions," State to USUN, New York, May 13, 1994, http://www.gwu.edu/~nsarchiv/NSAEBB/NSAEBB53/rw051394.pdf.

60. "Rwanda: Department of Defense Policy Options."

61. This was widely reported by the media. See, for instance, BBC News, April 8, 1998, http://news.bbc.co.uk/1/hi/world/africa/74737.stm.

62. United Nations, International Criminal Tribunal for Rwanda, "General Information," retrieved on October 19, 2009, from: http://www.ictr.org/default.htm.

63. *Gacaca* has variously been evaluated. For perspectives on the system, see Phil Clark and Zachary D. Kaufman (eds.), *After Genocide: Transitional Justice, Post-Conflict Reconstruction and Reconciliation in Rwanda and Beyond* (New York: Columbia University Press, 2009); Jacques Fierens, "*Gacaca* Courts: Between Fantasy and Reality," *Journal of International Criminal Justice*, Vo. 3 (2005: 896–919); Peter E. Harrell, *Rwanda's Gamble: Gacaca and a New Model of Transitional Justice* (New York: Writers Club Press, 2003); Amnesty International, *Rwanda—Gacaca: A Question of Justice* (London: Amnesty International, International Secretariat, 2002); Rosilyne M. Borland, "The Gacaca Tribunals and Rwanda after Genocide: Effective Restorative Community Justice or Further Abuse of Human Rights?" retrieved on October 19, 2009, from: http://www1.sis.american.edu/students/sword/Current_Issue/essay1.pdf; Peter Uvin, "The *Gacaca* Tribunals in Rwanda," retrieved on

October 19, 2009, from: http://www.idea.int/publications/reconciliation/upload/reconciliation_chap07cs-rwanda.pdf; and Susanne Buckley-Zistel, "The *Gacaca* Tribunals in Rwanda: Community Justice?" (Frankfurt/Main and Berlin: Hessische Stiftung Friedens-und Konfliktforschung), retrieved on October 19, 2009, from: http://www.konfliktbearbeitung.net/downloads/file831.pdf.

64. William Butler and George Obiozor, "The Burundi Affair, 1972" (Geneva: International Commission of Jurists and the International League for the Rights of Man, 1972). On the conflict, see Rene Lemarchand, *Burundi: Ethnic Conflict and Genocide* (New York: Woodrow Wilson Center Press, 1996); Thomas Patrick Melady, *Burundi: The Tragic Years* (Maryknoll, NY: Orbis Books, 1974); Rene Lemarchand and David Martin, *Selective Genocide in Burundi* (London: The Minority Rights Group, 1974); and Norman Wingert, *No Place to Stop Killing* (Chicago: Moody Press, 1974).

65. "Rwanda: Department of Defense Policy Options."

66. See UN Security Council, "Secretary General to President of the Security Council," S/1995/1068, 1.

67. Ibid.

68. UN Security Council, *Report of the Secretary General on the Situation in Burundi*, February 15, 1996.

69. For a study of ethnic conflicts in Burundi, see Johnson Makoba and Elavie Ndura, "The Roots of Contemporary Ethnic Conflict and Violence in Burundi," in Santosh Saha (ed.), *Perspectives on Contemporary Ethnic Conflict: Primal Violence or the Politics of Conviction?* (Lanham, MD: Lexington Books, 2006); Ahmedou Ould-Abdallah, *Burundi on the Brink* (Washington, DC: U.S. Institute of Peace, 2000); Human Rights Watch, *Proxy Targets: Civilians in the War in Burundi* (New York: Human Rights Watch, 1998); René Lemarchand, *Burundi: Ethnocide as Discourse and Practice* (Washington, DC: Woodrow Wilson Institute, 1994); and David Reiss, *The Burundi Ethnic Massacres, 1988* (Lewiston: Edwin Mellen Press, 1992).

70. International Rescue Committee, "Mortality in the Democratic Republic of Congo: An Ongoing Crisis," 2007, retrieved on October 27, 2009, from: http://www.theirc.org/sites/default/files/migrated/resources/2007/2006-7_congomortalitysurvey.pdf.

71. Report is provided in ibid.

72. Peter Schwab, *Africa: A Continent Self-Destructs* (New York: St. Martin's Press, 2001), 59. For some of the extensive literature on the DRC war, see the following for example: Gérard Prunier, *From Genocide to Continental War: the 'Congolese' Conflict and the Crisis of Contemporary Africa* (London: Hurst, 2009); Rene Lemarchand, *The Dynamics of Violence in Central Africa* (Philadelphia: University of Pennsylvania Press, 2009); Michael Nest, François Grignon, and Emizet F. Kisangani, *The Democratic Republic of Congo: Economic Dimensions of War and Peace* (Boulder, CO: Lynne Rienner, 2006); John F. Clark (ed.), *The African Stakes of the Congo War* (Kampala, Uganda: Fountain Publishers, 2003); and Herbert Weiss, *War and Peace in the Democratic Republic of the Congo* (Uppsala, Sweden: Nordiska Afrikainstitutet, 2000).

Appendix: Independence Dates for African States

State	Independence Date	Colonizing Power
Liberia	July 26, 1847	None[1]
South Africa	May 31, 1910	Britain
Egypt	February 28, 1922	Britain
Ethiopia	May 5, 1941	Italy[2]
Libya	December 24, 1951	Britain
Sudan	January 1, 1956	Britain/Egypt
Morocco	March 2, 1956	France
Tunisia	March 20, 1956	France
Ghana	March 6, 1957	Britain
Guinea	October 2, 1958	France
Cameroon	January 1, 1960	France
Togo	April 27, 1960	France
Mali	June 20, 1960	France
Senegal	June 20, 1960	France
Madagascar	June 26, 1960	France
Democratic Republic of Congo	June 30, 1960	Belgium
Somalia	July 1, 1960	Britain
Benin	August 1, 1960	France
Niger	August 3, 1960	France
Burkina Faso	August 5, 1960	France
Côte d'Ivoire	August 7, 1960	France

(Continued)

State	Independence Date	Colonizing Power
Chad	August 11, 1960	France
Central African Republic	August 13, 1960	France
Congo (Brazzaville)	August 15, 1960	France
Gabon	August 17, 1960	France
Nigeria	October 1, 1960	Britain
Mauritania	November 28, 1960	France
Sierra Leone	April 27, 1961	Britain
Tanzania	December 9, 1961	Britain
Burundi	July 1, 1962	Belgium
Rwanda	July 1, 1962	Belgium
Algeria	July 3, 1962	France
Uganda	October 9, 1962	Britain
Kenya	December 12, 1963	Britain
Malawi	July 6, 1964	Britain
Zambia	October 24, 1964	Britain
Gambia	February 18, 1965	Britain
Botswana	September 30, 1966	Britain
Lesotho	October 4, 1966	Britain
Mauritius	March 12, 1968	Britain
Swaziland	September 6, 1968	Britain
Equatorial Guinea	October 12, 1968	Spain
Guinea-Bissau	September 10, 1974	Portugal
Mozambique	June 25, 1975	Portugal
Cape Verde	July 5, 1975	Portugal
Comoros	July 6, 1975	France
São Tomé and Principe	July 12, 1975	Portugal
Angola	November 11, 1975	Portugal
Western Sahara	February 28, 1976	Spain
Seychelles	June 29, 1976	Britain
Djibouti	June 27, 1977	France
Zimbabwe	April 18, 1980	Britain
Namibia	March 21, 1990	South Africa
Eritrea	May 24, 1993	Ethiopia

[1]Liberia was under the control of the American Colonization Society, which established the colony until independence.

[2]Although largely independent, Ethiopia was under Italian occupation for five years.

Selected Bibliography

Abbink, Jon, *Eritreo-Ethiopian Studies in Society and History: 1960–1995* (Leiden, The Netherlands: African Studies Centre, 1996).

——, Mirjam de Bruijn, and Klaas Van Walraven, eds., *Rethinking Resistance: Revolt and Violence in African History* (Boston: Brill, 2003).

——, and Ineke van Kessel, eds., *Vanguard or Vandals: Youth, Politics, and Conflict in Africa* (Boston: Brill, 2005).

Abdullah, Ibrahim, "Bush Path to Destruction: The Origin and Character of the Revolutionary United Front/Sierra Leone," *Journal of Modern African Studies*, Vol. 36, No. 2 (1998: 203–235).

Abegunrin, Olayiwola, *Africa in Global Politics in the Twenty-First Century: A Pan African Perspective* (New York: Palgrave Macmillan, 2009).

——, *Nigeria and the Struggle for the Liberation of Zimbabwe: A Study of Foreign Policy Decision Making of an Emerging Nation* (Stockholm, Sweden: Bethany Books, 1992).

Adebajo, Adekeye, *Liberia's Civil War: Nigeria, ECOMOG, and Regional Security in West Africa* (Boulder, CO: Lynne Rienner, 2002).

——, and Abdul Raufu Mustapha, eds., *Gulliver's Troubles: Nigeria's Foreign Policy after the Cold War* (Scottsville, South Africa: University of KwaZulu-Natal Press, 2008).

——, and Ismail Rashid, eds., *West Africa's Security Challenges: Building Peace in a Troubled Region* (Boulder, CO: Lynne Rienner, 2004).

Adelman, Howard, and Astri Suhrke, eds., *The Path of a Genocide: The Rwanda Crisis from Uganda to Zaire* (New Brunswick, NJ: Transaction Publishers, 1999).

Afoaku, Osita G., *Explaining the Failure of Democracy in the Democratic Republic of Congo: Autocracy and Dissent in an Ambivalent World* (Lewiston, NY: E. Mellen Press, 2005).

Afrah, Mohamoud M., *Mogadishu: A Hell on Earth* (Nairobi, Kenya: Copos Ltd., 1993).

Agbu, Osita, *West Africa's Trouble Spots and the Imperative for Peace-Building* (Dakar, Senegal: Council for Development of Social Science Research in Africa, 2006).

Akinwumi, Olayemi, *Crisis and Conflicts in Nigeria: A Political History since 1960* (Piscataway, NJ: Transaction Publishers, 2004).

Alao, Abiodun, *Brothers at War: Dissidence and Rebellion in Southern Africa* (London: British Academic Press, 1994).

―――――, *Natural Resources and Conflict in Africa: The Tragedy of Endowment* (Rochester, NY: Rochester Press, 2007).

―――――, *The Burden of Collective Goodwill: The International Involvement in the Liberian Civil War* (Aldershot, UK: Ashgate, 1998).

―――――, John Mackinlay, and Funmi Olonisakin, *Peacekeepers, Politicians, and Warlords: The Liberian Peace Process* (New York: United Nations University Press, 1999).

Ali, Taisier M., and Robert O. Matthews, eds., *Civil Wars in Africa: Roots and Resolution* (Montreal: McGill-Queen's University Press, 1999).

Allen, Tim, and Koen Vlassenroot, eds., *The Lord's Resistance Army: War, Peace and Reconciliation in Northern Uganda* (London: London School of Economics and Political Science, 2008).

Anglin, Douglas, *Conflict in Sub-Saharan Africa, 1997–1998* (Bellville, South Africa: Centre for Southern African Studies, 1997).

Aning, Emmanuel Kwesi, *The United States and Africa's New Security Order* (Accra: Ghana Center for Democratic Development, 2001).

Apsel, Joyce, ed., *Darfur: Genocide before Our Eyes* (New York: Institute for the Study of Genocide, 2005).

Arlinghaus, Bruce E., ed., *Arms for Africa: Military Assistance and Foreign Policy in the Developing World* (Lexington, MA: Lexington Books, 1983).

Assensoh, A. B., and Yvette M. Alex-Assensoh *African Military History and Politics: Coups and Ideological Incursions, 1900–Present* (New York: Palgrave, 2001).

Awolowo, Obafemi, *Path to Nigerian Freedom* (London: Faber and Faber, 1947).

Bakut, Tswah Bakut, and Sagarika Dutt, eds., *Africa at the Millennium: An Agenda for Mature Development* (New York: Palgrave, 2000).

Ball, Simon J., *The Cold War: An International History, 1947–1991* (New York: St. Martin's Press, 1998).

Baregu, Mwesiga, and Christopher Landsberg, ed., *From Cape to Congo: Southern Africa's Evolving Security Challenges* (Boulder, CO: Lynne Rienner, 2003).

Barkely, Russell L., ed., *AFRICOM: Security, Development, and Humanitarian Functions* (New York: Nova Science Publishers, 2009).

Beckman, Björn, "Peasants and Democratic Struggles in Nigeria, *Review of African Political Economy*, Vol. 15, No. 41 (Spring 1988: 30–44).

Behrend, Heike, *Alice Lakwena and Holy Spirits: War in Northern Uganda, 1985–97* (Columbus: Ohio University Press, 1999).

Bekoe, Dorina A., ed., *East Africa and the Horn: Confronting Challenges to Good Governance* (Boulder, CO: Lynne Rienner, 2006).

Berschinski, Robert G., *AFRICOM's Dilemma: The "Global War on Terrorism," "Capacity Building," Humanitarianism, and the Future of U.S. Security Policy in Africa* (Carlisle, PA: Strategic Studies Institute, U.S. Army War College, 2007).

Bøas, Morten, and Kevin C. Dunn, eds., *African Guerrillas: Raging against the Machine* (Boulder, CO: Lynne Rienner, 2007).

Bongartz, Maria, *The Civil War in Somalia: Its Genesis and Dynamics* (Uppsala, Sweden: Nordiska Afrikainstitutet, 1991).

Breslauer, George W., ed., *Soviet Policy in Africa* (Berkeley: University of California Press, 1992).

Brett, Rachel, and Irma Specht, *Young Soldiers: Why They Choose to Fight* (Boulder, CO: Lynne Rienner, 2004).

Brietzke, Paul H., *Law, Development, and the Ethiopian Revolution* (London: Associated University Presses, 1982).

Broch-Due, Vigdis, ed., *Violence and Belonging: The Quest for Identity in Post-Colonial Africa* (New York: Routledge, 2005).

Brons, Maria H., *Society, Security, Sovereignty and the State in Somalia: From Statelessness to Statelessness?* (Utrecht, The Netherlands: International Books, 2001).

Bruce, Arlinghaus, ed., *Arms for Africa: Military Assistance and Foreign Policy in the Developing World* (Lexington, MA: Lexington Books, 1983).

Bujra, Abdalla, *African Conflicts: Their Causes and Their Political and Social Environment* (Addis Ababa, Ethiopia: Development Policy Management Forum, 2002).

Burr, J. Millard, and Robert O. Collins, *Africa's Thirty Years War: Libya, Chad, and the Sudan, 1963–1993* (Boulder, CO: Westview Press, 1999).

———— and ————, *Darfur: The Long Road to Disaster* (Princeton, NJ: Markus Wiener, 2006).

Callaghy, Thomas M., *The State-Society Struggle: Zaire in Comparative Perspective* (New York: Columbia University Press, 1984).

Cervenka, Zdenek, *The Nigerian War, 1967–1970* (Ibadan: Onibonoje Press, 1972).

Chabal, Patrick, Ulf Engel, and Anna-Maria Gentili, eds., *Is Violence Inevitable in Africa?: Theories of Conflict and Approaches to Conflict Prevention* (Boston: Brill, 2005).

Chamberlain, Muriel E., *The Scramble for Africa* (London: Longman, 1999).

Chan, Stephen, and Moisés Venâncio, *War and Peace in Mozambique* (New York: St. Martin's Press, 1998).

Chau, Donovan C., *U.S. Counterterrorism in Sub-Saharan Africa: Understanding Costs, Cultures, and Conflicts* (Carlisle, PA: Strategic Studies Institute, 2008).

Cheadle, Don, and John Prendergast, *Not on Our Watch: The Mission to End Genocide in Darfur and Beyond* (New York: Hyperion, 2007).

Chingono, M. F., *Conspicuous Destruction: War, Famine and the Reform Process in Mozambique, 1975–1992* (New York: Human Rights Watch, 1992).

Chrétien, Jean-Pierre, *The Great Lakes of Africa: Two Thousand Years of History* (New York: Zone Books, 2003).

Cilliers, Jakkie, and Kathryn Sturman, eds., *Africa and Terrorism: Joining the Global Campaign* (Pretoria, South Africa: Institute for Security Studies, 2002).

Ciment, James, ed., *Angola and Mozambique: Postcolonial Wars in Southern Africa* (New York: Facts on File, 1997).

———, *Encyclopedia of Conflicts since World War II* (Armonk, NY: M. E. Sharpe, 2007).

Clapham, Christopher, ed., *African Guerrillas* (Bloomington: Indiana University Press, 1998).

———, *Transformation and Continuity in Revolutionary Ethiopia* (Cambridge, UK: Cambridge University Press, 1988).

Clark, John F., ed., *The African Stakes of the Congo War* (Kampala, Uganda: Fountain Publishers, 2003.

———., *The Failure of Democracy in the Republic of Congo* (Boulder, CO: Lynne Rienner, 2008).

Clark, Phil, and Zachary D. Kaufman, eds., *After Genocide: Transitional Justice, Post-Conflict Reconstruction and Reconciliation in Rwanda and Beyond* (New York: Columbia University Press, 2009).

Collier, Paul. *Wars, Guns, and Votes: Democracy in Dangerous Places* (New York: HarperCollins, 2009).

Commins, Stephen K., Michael F. Lofchie, and Rhys Payne, eds., *Africa's Agrarian Crisis: The Roots of Famine* (Boulder, CO: Lynne Rienner, 1986).

Copson, Raymond W., *The United States in Africa* (London: Zed Books, 2007).

Corfield, F. D., *Historical Survey of the Origins and Growth of Mau Mau* (London: Her Majesty's Stationery Office, 1960).

Cox, Dan G., John Falconer, and Brian Stackhouse, *Terrorism, Instability, and Democracy in Asia and Africa* (Boston: Northeastern University Press, 2009).

Crenshaw, Martha, ed., *Terrorism in Africa* (New York: Maxwell Macmillan International, 1994).

Crowder, Michael, ed., *West African Resistance: The Military Response to Colonial Occupation* (London: Hutchinson, 1978).

Crowe, Sybil E., *The Berlin West African Conference, 1884–1985* (New York: Longman, 1942).

David, Steven R., *Third World Coups D'état and International Security* (Baltimore: Johns Hopkins University Press, 1987).

Davidson, Basil, *The People's Cause: A History of Guerrillas in Africa* (London: Longman, 1981).

De Maio, Jennifer L., *Confronting Ethnic Conflict: The Role of Third Parties in Managing Africa's Civil Wars* (Lanham, MD: Lexington Books, 2009).

De Waal, Alex, ed., *Famine that Kills: Darfur, Sudan* (Oxford, UK: Oxford University Press, 2005).

———, *Islamism and Its Enemies in the Horn of Africa* (Bloomington: Indiana University Press, 2004).

————, *War in Darfur and the Search for Peace* (Cambridge, MA: Harvard University Press, 2007).

————, *Who Fights? Who Cares?: War and Humanitarian Action in Africa* (Trenton, NJ: Africa World Press, 2000).

Dokken, Karin, *African Security Politics Redefined* (New York: Palgrave Macmillan, 2008).

Donham, Donald Lewis, *Marxist Modern: An Ethnographic History of the Ethiopian Revolution* (Berkeley: University of California Press, 1999).

Doom, Ruddy, and Jan Gorus, eds., *Politics of Identity and Economics of Conflict in the Great Lakes Region* (Brussels: VUB University Press, 2000).

Edie, Carlene J. *Politics in Africa: A New Beginning?* (Belmont, CA: Wadsworth Thomson Learning, 2003).

Ekwe-Ekwe, Herbert, *The Biafra War: Nigeria and the Aftermath* (Lewiston, NY: Edwin Mellen Press, 1990).

Engleber, Pierre, *Africa: Unity, Sovereignty, and Sorrow* (Boulder, CO: Lynne Rienner, 2009).

Erlich, Haggai, *The Struggle over Eritrea, 1962–1978: War and Revolution in the Horn of Africa* (Stanford, CA: Hoover Institution Press, 1983).

Falola, Toyin, *Africa: The End of Colonial Rule: Nationalism and Decolonization, Volume 4* (Durham, NC: Carolina Academic Press, 2002).

————, *Violence in Nigeria: The Crisis of Religious Politics and Secular Ideologies* (Rochester, NY: University of Rochester Press, 1998).

————, and Okpeh Ochayi Okpeh, Jr., eds., *Population Movements, Conflicts, and Displacements in Nigeria* (Trenton, NJ: Africa World Press, 2008).

————, and Raphael Chijioke Njoku, (eds.), *War and Peace in Africa* (Durham, NC: Carolina Academic Press, 2009).

Fawole, Alade, and Charles Ukeje, eds., *The Crisis of the State and Regionalism in West Africa: Identity, Citizenship and Conflict* (Dakar, Senegal: Council for the Development of Social Science Research in Africa, 2005).

Ferguson, James, *Global Shadows: Africa in the Neoliberal World Order* (Durham, NC: Duke University Press, 2006).

Flint, Julie, and Alexander De Waal, *Darfur: A New History of a Long War* (London: Zed Books, 2008).

Förster, Stig, Wolfgang J. Mommsen, and Ronald Edward Robinson, *Bismarck, Europe, and Africa: The Berlin Africa Conference 1884–1885 and the Onset of Partition* (Oxford, UK: Oxford University Press, 1989).

Francis, David J., ed., *Civil Militia: Africa's Intractable Security Menace?* (Burlington, VT: Ashgate, 2005).

————, ed., *U.S. Strategy in Africa: AFRICOM, Terrorism, and Security Challenges* (New York: Routledge, 2010).

Franke, Benedikt, *Security Cooperation in Africa: A Reappraisal* (Boulder, CO: First Forum Press, 2009).

Frankel, Philip H., *An Ordinary Atrocity: Sharpeville and Its Massacre* (New Haven, CT: Yale University Press, 2001).

Fukui, Katsuyoshi, and John Markakis, eds., *Ethnicity & Conflict in the Horn of Africa* (Athens: Ohio University Press, 1994).

Furley, Oliver, and Roy May, ed., *Ending Africa's Wars: Progressing to Peace* (Burlington, VT: Ashgate, 2006).

Gberie, Lansana, *A Dirty War in West Africa: The RUF and the Destruction of Sierra Leone* (Bloomington: Indiana University Press, 2005).

Gebrewold, Belachew, *Anatomy of Violence: Understanding the Systems of Conflict and Violence in Africa* (Burlington, VT: Ashgate, 2009).

George, Edward, *The Cuban Intervention in Angola, 1965–1991: From Che Guevara to Cuito Cuanavale* (New York: Frank Cass, 2005).

Gifford, Prosser, and William Roger Louis, eds., *The Transfer of Power in Africa: Decolonization, 1940–1960* (New Haven, CT: Yale University Press, 1982).

Godfrey Okoth, P., and Bethwell A. Ogot, eds., *Conflict in Contemporary Africa* (Nairobi: Jomo Kenyatta Foundation, 2000).

Gordon, April A., and Donald L. Gordon, eds., *Understanding Contemporary Africa*, 4th ed. (Boulder, CO: Lynne Rienner, 2006).

Guimarães, Fernando Andresen, *The Origins of the Angolan Civil War: Foreign Intervention and Domestic Political Conflict* (New York: St. Martin's Press, 1998).

Gyimah-Boadi, E., ed., *Democratic Reform in Africa: The Quality of Progress* (Boulder, CO: Lynne Rienner, 2004).

Haile-Selassie, Teferra, *The Ethiopian Revolution, 1974–91: From a Monarchical Autocracy to a Military Oligarchy* (New York: Kegan Paul International, 1997).

Hall, Margaret, and Tom Young, *Confronting Leviathan: Mozambique since Independence* (Athens: Ohio University Press, 1997).

Hamilton, Carolyn, ed., *The Mfecane Aftermath: Reconstructive Debates in Southern African History* (Pietermaritzburg, South Africa: University of Natal Press, 1995).

Hanlon, Joseph, *Beggar Your Neighbours: Apartheid Power in Southern Africa* (London: James Currey, 1986).

Harbeson, John W., Donald Rothchild, and Naomi Chazan, eds., *Civil Society and the State in Africa* (Boulder, CO: Lynne Rienner, 1994).

Harrell, Peter E., *Rwanda's Gamble: Gacaca and a New Model of Transitional Justice* (New York: Writers Club Press, 2003).

Harvey, Robert, *The Fall of Apartheid: The Inside Story from Smuts to Mbeki* (New York: Palgrave Macmillan, 2001).

Hayes, Patricia, et al., eds., *Namibia under South African Rule: Mobility and Containment, 1915–46* (Athens: Ohio University Press, 1998).

Herbstein, Denis, and John Evenson, *The Devils Are among Us: The War for Namibia* (London: Zed Books, 1990).

Hirsch, John L., and Robert B. Oakley, *Somalia and Operation Restore Hope: Reflections on Peacekeeping and Peacemaking* (Washington, DC: United States Institute of Peace Press, 1995).

Honwana, Alcinda, *Child Soldiers in Africa* (Philadelphia: University of Pennsylvania Press, 2006).

Horne, Alistair, *Savage War of Peace: Algeria, 1954–1962* (New York: New York Review of Books, 2006).

Howe, Herbert M., *Ambiguous Order: Military Forces in African States* (Boulder, CO: Lynne Rienner, 2001).

Hunter, Allen, ed., *Rethinking the Cold War* (Philadelphia: Temple University Press, 1998).

Ilesanmi, S. O., *Religious Pluralism and the Nigerian State* (Athens: Ohio University Center for International Studies, 1997).

Imobighe, T. A., and A. N. T. Eguavoen, eds., *Terrorism and Counter-Terrorism: An African Perspective* (Ibadan, Nigeria: Heinemann Educational Books, 2006).

Issa-Salwe, Abdisalam M., *The Collapse of the Somali State: The Impact of the Colonial Legacy* (London: Haan Associates, 1994).

Ityavyar, Dennis, and Zacharys Gundu, *Stakeholders in Peace and Conflicts: A Case of Ethno-Religious Conflicts in Plateau & Kaduna, Nigeria* (Jos, Nigeria: International Centre for Gender & Social Research, 2004).

Iyob, Ruth, "The Ethiopian–Eritrean Conflict: Diasporic vs. Hegemonic States in the Horn of Africa, 1991–2000," *Journal of Modern African Studies*, Vol. 38, No. 4 (December 2000: 659–682).

———, and Gilbert M. Khadiagala, *Sudan: The Elusive Quest for Peace* (Boulder, CO: Lynne Rienner, 2006).

———, *The Eritrean Struggle for Independence: Domination, Resistance, Nationalism, 1941–1993* (Cambridge, UK: Cambridge University Press, 1995).

Jackson, Henry F., *From the Congo to Soweto: U.S. Foreign Policy toward Africa since 1960* (New York: Morrow, 1982).

Jalloh, Alusine, and Toyin Falola, eds., *The United States and West Africa: Interactions and Relations* (Rochester, NY: University of Rochester Press, 2008).

James, Wendy. *War and Survival in Sudan's Frontierlands: Voices from the Blue Nile* (Oxford, UK: Oxford University Press, 2007).

Job, Brian L., ed., *The Insecurity Dilemma: National Security of Third World States* (Boulder, CO: Lynne Rienner, 1992).

Johnson, Douglas H. *The Root Causes of Sudan's Civil Wars* (Bloomington: Indiana University Press, 2003).

Joseph, Richard, ed., *State, Conflict, and Democracy in Africa* (Boulder, CO: Lynne Rienner, 1999).

Kadende-Kaiser, Rose M., and Paul J. Kaiser, eds., *Phases of Conflict in Africa* (Willowdale, ON: de Sitter Publications, 2005).

Kahn, Leora, ed., *Darfur: Twenty Years of War and Genocide in Sudan* (Brooklyn, NY: PowerHouse Books, 2007).

Keen, David, *Conflict & Collusion in Sierra Leone* (New York: Palgrave, 2005).

Keller, Edmond J., and Donald Rothschild, eds., *Africa in the New International Order* (Boulder, CO: Lynne Rienner, 1996).

Kendie, Daniel, *The Five Dimensions of the Eritrean Conflict, 1941–2004: Deciphering the Geo-Political Puzzle* (Prairie View, TX: Signature Book, 2005).

Khadiagala, Gilbert M., ed., *Security Dynamics in Africa's Great Lakes Region* (Boulder, CO: Lynne Rienner, 2006).

———, and Terrence Lyons, *African Foreign Policies: Power and Process* (Boulder, CO: Lynne Rienner, 2001).

Kieh, George Klay, and Ida Rousseau Mukenge, eds., *Zones of Conflict in Africa: Theories and Cases* (Westport, CT: Praeger, 2002).

Kirk-Greene, A. H. M., *Crisis and Conflict: A Documentary Sourcebook, Vols. I & II* (London: Oxford University Press, 1971).

Korn, David A., *Ethiopia, the United States, and the Soviet Union* (Carbondale: Southern Illinois University Press, 1986).

Kriger, Norma J., *Zimbabwe's Guerrilla War: Peasant Voices* (Cambridge, UK: Cambridge University Press, 1992).

Kukah, Matthew Hassan, and Toyin Falola, *Religious Militancy and Self-Assertion: Islam and Politics in Nigeria* (Aldershot, UK: Ashgate, 1996).

Larémont, Ricardo René, ed., *Borders, Nationalism, and the African State* (Boulder, CO: Lynne Rienner, 2005).

———, *The Causes of War and the Consequences of Peacekeeping in Africa* (Portsmouth, NH: Heinemann, 2002).

Lefebvre, Jeffrey A., *Arms for the Horn: U.S. Security Policy in Ethiopia and Somalia 1953–1991* (Pittsburgh, PA: University of Pittsburgh Press, 1991).

Leffler, Melvyn, ed., *Origins of the Cold War: An International History* (New York: Routledge, 1994).

Legassick, Martin, *Armed Struggle and Democracy: The Case of South Africa* (Uppsala, Sweden: Nordiska Afrikainstitutet, 2002).

Lemarchand, Rene, *Burundi: Ethnic Conflict and Genocide* (New York: Woodrow Wilson Center Press, 1996).

———, *Burundi: Ethnocide as Discourse and Practice* (Washington, DC: Woodrow Wilson Institute, 1994).

———, and David Martin, *Selective Genocide in Burundi* (London: The Minority Rights Group, 1974).

Levitt, Jeremy, *The Evolution of Deadly Conflict in Liberia: From 'Paternaltarianism' to State Collapse* (Durham, NC: Carolina Academic Press, 2005).

Lewis, Peter M., *Growing Apart: Oil, Politics, and Economic Change in Indonesia and Nigeria* (Ann Arbor, MI: University of Michigan Press, 2007).

Lind, Jeremy, and Kathryn Sturman, eds., *Scarcity and Surfeit: The Ecology of Africa's Conflicts* (Pretoria, South Africa: Institute for Security Studies, 2002).

Lofchie, Michael F., ed., *The State of the Nations: Constraints on Development in Independent Africa* (Berkeley: University of California Press, 1971).

Macharia, Kinuthia, and Muigai Kanyua, *The Social Context of the Mau Mau Movement in Kenya (1952–1960)* (Lanham, MD: University Press of America, 2006).

MacKinnon, Aran S., *The Making of South Africa: Culture and Politics* (Upper Saddle River, NJ: Pearson Prentice Hall, 2003).

Maddox, Gregory, ed., *Conquest and Resistance to Colonialism in Africa* (New York: Garland, 1993).

Magyar, Karl P., and Earl Conteh-Morgan, *Peacekeeping in Africa: ECOMOG in Liberia* (New York: St. Martin's Press, 1998).

Maier, Karl, *This House Has Fallen: Midnight in Nigeria* (New York: Public Affairs, 2000).

Maloba, Wunyabari O., *Mau Mau and Kenya: An Analysis of a Peasant Revolt* (Bloomington: Indiana University Press, 1993).

Mazrui, Ali, *UNESCO General History of Africa, VIII: Africa since 1935* (Paris: UNESCO, 1999).

McCormack, Jo, *Collective Memory: France and the Algerian War (1954–1962)* (Lanham, MD: Lexington Books, 2007).

Mekenkamp, Monique, Paul van Tongeren, and Hans van de Veen, eds., *Searching for Peace in Africa: An Overview of Conflict Prevention and Management Activities* (Utrecht, The Netherlands: European Platform for Conflict Prevention and Transformation, 1999).

Melady, Thomas Patrick, *Burundi: The Tragic Years* (Maryknoll, NY: Orbis Books, 1974).

Mentan, Tatah, *Dilemmas of Weak States: Africa and Transnational Terrorism in the Twenty-First Century* (Burlington, VT: Ashgate, 2004).

Miles, William F. S., ed., *Political Islam in West Africa: State-Society Relations Transformed* (Boulder, CO: Lynne Rienner, 2007).

Minter, William, *Apartheid's Contras: An Inquiry into the Roots of War in Angola and Mozambique* (London: Zed, 1994).

Mngxitama, Andile, Amanda Alexander, and Nigel C. Gibson, eds., *Biko Lives: Contesting the Legacies of Steve Biko* (New York: Palgrave, 2008).

Mohamoud, Abdullah A., *State Collapse and Post-Colonial Development in Africa* (West Lafayette, IN: Purdue University Press, 2006).

Mukisa, Richard S., "Toward a Peaceful Resolution of Africa's Colonial Boundaries," *Africa Today*, Vol. 44, No. 1 (January–March 1997).

Mukwaya, Aaron K. Kabweru, ed., *Uganda Riding the Political Tiger: Security and the Wars in the Greater Lakes Region* (Kampala, Uganda: Makerere University Printery, 2004).

Mullins, Christopher W., and Dawn L. Rothe, *Blood, Power, and Bedlam: Violations of International Criminal Law in Post-Colonial Africa* (New York: Peter Lang, 2008).

Mutua, Makau, *Kenya's Quest for Democracy: Taming Leviathan* (Boulder, CO: Lynne Rienner, 2008).

Nation, Craig R., and Mark V. Kauppi, *The Soviet Impact in Africa* (Lexington, MA: Lexington Books, 1984).

Ndulo, Muna, ed., *Democratic Reform in Africa: Its Impact on Governance & Poverty Alleviation* (Athens: Ohio University Press, 2006).

Nest, Michael, François Grignon, and Emizet F. Kisangani, *The Democratic Republic of Congo: Economic Dimensions of War and Peace* (Boulder, CO: Lynne Rienner, 2006).

Nhema, Alfred, and Paul Tiyambe Zeleza, eds., *The Roots of African Conflicts: The Causes & Costs* (Athens: Ohio University Press, 2008).

Nnoli, Okwudiba, ed., *Ethnic Conflicts in Africa* (Dakar, Senegal: Codesria, 1998).

Noer, Thomas J., *Cold War and Black Liberation: The United States and White Rule in Africa, 1948–1968* (Columbia, MO: University of Missouri Press, 1985).

Obasanjo, Olusegun, *My Command: An Account of the Nigerian Civil War, 1967–1970* (Ibadan, Nigeria: Heinemann, 1980).

Okafor, F. U., ed., *New Strategies for Curbing Ethnic and Religious Conflicts in Nigeria* (Enugu, Nigeria: Fourth Dimension, 1997).

Okafor, Obiora Chinedu, *Re-defining Legitimate Statehood: International Law and State Fragmentation in Africa* (Boston: M. Nijhoff Publishers, 2000).

Okechie-Offoha, Marcellina U., and Matthew N. O. Sadiku, eds., *Ethnic and Cultural Diversity in Nigeria* (Trenton, NJ: Africa World Press, 1995).

Okocha, Emmanuel, *Blood on the Niger: The Untold Story of the Nigerian Civil War* (Port Harcourt, Nigeria: Sunray Publishers, 1994).

Olonisakin, Funmi, *Peacekeeping in Sierra Leone: The Story of UNAMSIL* (Boulder, CO: Lynne Rienner, 2008).

Omeje, Kenneth, *High Stakes and Stakeholders: Oil Conflict and Security in Nigeria* (Aldershot, UK: Ashgate, 2006).

O'Meara, Dan, *Forty Lost Years: The Apartheid State and the Politics of the National Party, 1948–94* (Johannesburg: Ravan, 1996).

Onwumechili, Chuka, *African Democratization and Military Coups* (Westport, CT: Praeger, 1998).

Ould-Abdallah, Ahmedou, *Burundi on the Brink* (Washington, DC: U.S. Institute of Peace, 2000).

Oyebade, Adebayo, ed., *Culture and Customs of Angola* (Westport, CT: Greenwood, 2006).

———, *The Foundations of Nigeria: Essays in Honor of Toyin Falola* (Trenton, NJ: Africa World Press, 2003).

———, "Radical Nationalism and Wars of Liberation," in Toyin Falola (ed.), *Africa Vol. 4: The End of Colonial Rule: Nationalism and Decolonization* (Durham, NC: Carolina Academic Press, 2002).

———, "Reluctant Democracy: The State, the Opposition, and the Crisis of Political Transition," in Adebayo Oyebade, (ed.), *The Transformation of Nigeria: Essays in Honor of Toyin Falola* (Trenton, NJ: Africa World Press, 2002).

———, "The Role of the Organization of African Unity in the Civil War," in Toyin Falola (ed.), *Nigeria in the Twentieth Century* (Durham, NC: Carolina Academic Press, 2002).

———, ed., *The Transformation of Nigeria: Essays in Honor of Toyin Falola* (Trenton, NJ: Africa World Press, 2002).

———, and Abiodun Alao, eds., *Africa after the Cold War: The Changing Perspectives on Security* (Trenton, NJ: Africa World Press, 1998).

Paden, John N., *Faith and Politics in Nigeria: Nigeria as a Pivotal State in the Muslim World* (Washington, DC: U.S. Institute of Peace, 2008).

Patman, Robert G., *The Soviet Union in the Horn of Africa: The Diplomacy of Intervention and Disengagement* (Cambridge, UK: Cambridge University Press, 1990).

Peel, Michael. *A Swamp Full of Dollars: Pipelines and Paramilitaries of Nigeria's Oil Frontier* (London: I. B. Tauris, 2009).

Perry, Warren R., *Landscape Transformations and the Archaeology of Impact: Social Disruption and State Formation in Southern Africa* (New York: Kluwer Academic/Plenum, 1999).

Pharoah, Robyn, ed., *Generation at Risk?: HIV/AIDS, Vulnerable Children, and Security in Southern Africa* (Pretoria, South Africa: Institute for Security Studies, 2004).

Polk, William R., *Violent Politics: A History of Insurgency, Terrorism and Guerrilla War, From the American Revolution to Iraq* (New York: Harper, 2007).

Pool, David, *From Guerrillas to Government: The Eritrean People's Liberation Front* (Athens: Ohio University Press, 2001).

Prendergast, John, *Angola's Deadly War: Dealing with Savimbi's Hell on Earth* (Washington, DC: United States Institute of Peace, 1999).

Presley, Cora Ann, *Kikuyu Women, the Mau Mau Rebellion, and Social Change in Kenya* (Boulder, CO: Westview Press, 1992).

Prunier, Gérard, *Darfur: The Ambiguous Genocide* (Ithaca, NY: Cornell University Press, 2007).

——————, *The Rwanda Crisis: History of a Genocide* (New York: Columbia University Press, 1995).

Pumphrey, Carolyn, and Rye Schwartz-Barcott, eds., *Armed Conflict in Africa* (Lanham, MD: Scarecrow Press, 2003).

Reiss, David, *The Burundi Ethnic Massacres, 1988* (Lewiston, NY: Edwin Mellen Press, 1992).

Reno, S. W., *Corruption and State Politics in Sierra Leone* (Cambridge, UK: University Press, 1995).

Reno, William, *Warlord Politics and African States* (Boulder, CO: Lynne Rienner, 1998).

Richards, Paul, *Fighting for the Rain Forest: War, Youth and Resources in Sierra Leone* (Portsmouth, NH: Heinemann, 1996).

Rodman, Peter W. *More Precious than Peace: The Cold War and the Struggle for the Third World* (New York: Charles Scribner's Sons, 1994).

Rotberg, Robert I., ed. *Crafting the New Nigeria: Confronting the Challenges* (Boulder, CO: Lynne Rienner, 2004).

Rothchild, Donald, and Naomi Chazan, eds., *The Precarious Balance: State and Society in Africa* (Boulder, CO: Westview Press, 1988).

Saha, Santosh, ed., *Perspectives on Contemporary Ethnic Conflict: Primal Violence or the Politics of Conviction?* (Lanham, MD: Lexington Books, 2006).

Saro-Wiwa, Ken, *Genocide in Nigeria: The Ogoni Tragedy* (Port Harcourt, Nigeria: Saros International Publishers, 1992).

Schwab, Peter, *Africa: A Continent Self-Destructs* (New York: St. Martin's Press, 2001).

Segell, Glen, *Stability and Intervention in Sub-Sahara Africa* (London: G. Segell, 1998).

Seib, Philip, ed., *Africom: The American Military and Public Diplomacy in Africa* (Los Angeles: Figueroa Press, 2008).

Selassie, Bereket Habte, *Conflict and Intervention in the Horn of Africa* (New York: Monthly Review Press, 1980).

Sesay, Amadu, et al., eds., *Ethnic Militias and the Future of Democracy in Nigeria* (Ile-Ife, Nigeria: Obafemi Awolowo University Press, 2003).

Shekhawat, Seema, and Debidatta Aurobinda Mahapatra, *Afro-Asian Conflicts: Changing Contours, Costs and Consequences* (New Delhi: New Century, 2008).

Shepard, Todd, *The Invention of Decolonization: The Algerian War and the Remaking of France* (Ithaca, NY: Cornell University Press, 2006).

Sikainga, Ahmad A., and Ousseina Alidou, *Postconflict Reconstruction in Africa* (Trenton, NJ: Africa World Press, 2006).

Soyinka, Wole. *You Must Set Forth at Dawn* (New York: Random House, 2006).

Stremlau, John J., *The International Politics of the Nigerian Civil War, 1967–1970* (Princeton: NJ: Princeton University Press, 1977).

Suttner, Raymond, *The ANC Underground in South Africa, 1950–1976* (Boulder, CO: First Forum Press, 2009).

Tarimo, Aquiline, and Paulin Manwelo, *African Peacemaking and Governance* (Nairobi, Kenya: Acton Publishers, 2008).

Thornton, John K., *Warfare in Atlantic Africa 1500–1800* (New York: Routledge, 1999).

Tiruneh, Andargachew, *The Ethiopian Revolution, 1974–1987: A Transformation from an Aristocratic to a Totalitarian Autocracy* (Cambridge, UK: Cambridge University Press, 1993).

Tripp, Aili Mari, *Museveni's Uganda: Paradoxes of Power in a Hybrid Regime* (Boulder, CO: Lynne Rienner, 2010).

Vaughan, Olufemi, *Nigerian Chiefs: Traditional Power in Modern Politics, 1890s–1990s,"* (Rochester, NY: University of Rochester Press, 2000).

Vines, Alex, *Renamo: From Terrorism to Democracy in Mozambique* (London: James Currey, 1996).

———, *Renamo: Terrorism in Mozambique* (Bloomington: Indiana University Press, 1991).

Vogt, M. A., ed., *The Liberian Crisis and ECOMOG* (Lagos, Nigeria: Gabumo Publishing Co., 1992).

———, and L. S. Aminu, eds., *Peacekeeping as a Security Strategy in Africa: Chad and Liberia as Case Studies* (Enugu, Nigeria: Fourth Dimension Publishers, 1996).

Vogt, Margaret A., ed., *The Liberian Crisis and ECOMOG: A Bold Attempt at Regional Peace Keeping* (Lagos, Nigeria: Gabumo Publishing Co., 1992).

Waterhouse, Rachel, *Mozambique: Rising from the Ashes* (Oxford, UK: OXFAM, 1996).

Weiss, Herbert, *War and Peace in the Democratic Republic of the Congo* (Uppsala, Sweden: Nordiska Afrikaninstitutet, 2000).

Weiss, Taya, *Local Catalysts, Global Reactions: Cycles of Conflict in the Mano River Basin* (Pretoria, South Africa: Institute for Security Studies, 2005).

West, Deborah L., *Combating Terrorism in the Horn of Africa and Yemen* (Cambridge, MA: World Peace Foundation, 2005).

Westley, David M., *The Mfecane: An Annotated Bibliography* (Madison: African Studies Program, University of Wisconsin-Madison, 1999).

Wingert, Norman, *No Place to Stop Killing* (Chicago: Moody Press, 1974).

Woodward, Peter, *US Foreign Policy and the Horn of Africa* (Burlington, VT: Ashgate, 2006).

Wright, Stephen, and Julius Emeka Okolo, eds., *West African Regional Cooperation and Development* (Boulder, CO: Westview Press, 1990).

Zack-Williams, Tunde, Diane Frost, and Alex Thomson, eds., *Africa in Crisis: New Challenges and Possibilities* (Sterling, VA: Pluto Press, 2002).

Zartman, I. William (ed.), *Collapsed States: The Disintegration and Restoration of Legitimate Authority*, (Boulder, CO: Lynne Rienner, 1995).

————, *Ripe for Resolution: Conflict and Intervention in Africa* (New York: Oxford University Press, 1989).

Non-print Sources

Africa Center for Strategic Studies http://africacenter.org/

Africa Confidential http://www.africa-confidential.com/news

African Court on Human and Peoples' Rights (AFCHPR) http://www.african-court.org/en/

African Union http://www.africa-union.org/root/au/index/index.htm

All Africa.com http://allafrica.com/

AMANI Forum: The Great Lakes Parliamentary Forum of Peace http://www.amaniforum.org/

CIA: The World Factbook https://www.cia.gov/library/publications/the-world-factbook/

Economic Community of West African States (ECOWAS) http://www.ecowas.int/

Human Rights Watch: Africa http://www.hrw.org/en/africa

Stockholm International Peace Research Institute http://www.sipri.org/databases

U.S. Africa Command http://www.africom.mil/

U.S. Agency for International Development (USAID) http://www.usaid.gov/

U.S. Department of State: Bureau of African Affairs http://www.state.gov/p/af/

United States Institute of Peace (USIP) http://www.usip.org/

Index

About the Authors

TOYIN FALOLA is the Frances Higginbotham Nalle Centennial Professor in History and a Distinguished Teaching Professor at the University of Texas at Austin. He serves as series editor of both the University of Rochester's Studies in African History and the Diaspora, and the Greenwood Press series on Culture and Customs of Africa. His numerous books on African history include *Key Events in African History: A Reference Guide* (Greenwood, 2008).

ADEBAYO O. OYEBADE is Professor of History at Tennessee State University, Nashville. He has written extensively on African history and his books include *Culture and Customs of Angola* (Greenwood, 2007). He is a recipient of many scholarly awards including the Fulbright. He serves on the editorial board of a number of scholarly journals.